Reasoning Olympiad

Class 7

Reasoning Olympiad

Highly useful for all school students participating
in Various Olympiads & Competitions

Series Editor Keshav Mohan

Author Amogh Goel

Class 7

arihant

ARIHANT PRAKASHAN, MEERUT

ARIHANT PRAKASHAN, MEERUT

All Rights Reserved

卐 **Administrative & Production Offices**

Corporate Office 'Ramchhaya' 4577/15, Agarwal Road, Darya Ganj New Delhi -110002
Tele: 011- 47630600, 43518550; Fax: 011- 23280316

Head Office Kalindi, TP Nagar, Meerut (UP) - 250002
Tele: 0121-2401479, 2512970, 4004199; Fax: 0121-2401648

All disputes subject to Meerut (UP) jurisdiction only.

卐 **Sales & Support Offices**

Agra, Ahmedabad, Bengaluru, Bhubaneswar, Bareilly, Chennai, Delhi, Guwahati, Haldwani, Hyderabad, Jaipur, Jalandhar, Jhansi, Kolkata, Kota, Lucknow, Meerut, Nagpur & Pune

卐 **ISBN**   978-93-5203-391-1

卐 **Price**   ₹90

Typeset by Arihant DTP Unit at Meerut
Printed & Bound by Arihant Publications (I) Ltd. (Press Unit)

Production Team

Publishing Manager	Mahendra Singh Rawat	*Page Layouting*	Krishna Kumar Saini
Project Head	Mona Yadav	*DTP Operator*	Shravan Pandey & Ravindar Rawat
Project Coordinator	Akanksha Jain	*Cover Designer*	Syed Darin Zaidi
Proof Reader	Sachin Kumar Prajapati, Gora Sharma	*Inner Designer*	Deepak Kumar

For further information about the products from Arihant
log on to www.arihantbooks.com or email to info@arihantbooks.com

Preface

Reasoning Olympiad Series for Class 6th-10th is a series of books, which will challenge the young inquisitive minds by the non-routine and exciting Reasoning or Logic based problems.

The main purpose of this series is to make the students ready for competitive exams, as Reasoning is an integral section of almost all competitive examinations. All the questions given in this series are objective in nature so, they will provide students a feel of competitive examinations as school/board exams are of qualifying nature, but not competitive, which mainly have Objective Questions.

- **Need of Olympiad Series**

  This series helps students, who are willing to sharpen their problem solving skills through logical thinking. Unlike typical assessment books, which emphasise on drilling practice, the focus of this series is on practising problem solving techniques.

- **Development of Logical Approach**

  The thought provoking questions given in this series will help students to attain a deeper understanding of the concepts and through, which students will be able to imbibe reasoning/Logical/Analytical skills in themselves.

- **Complement Your School Studies**

  This series complements the additional preparation needs of students for regular school/board exams. As most of the schools conduct aptitude test on a regular basis. Along with, it will also address all the requirements of the students, who are approaching National/State level competitions or Olympiads.

We shall welcome criticism from the students, teachers, educators and parents. We shall also like to hear from all of you about errors and short comings, which may have remained in this edition and the suggestions for their improvement the next edition.

Editor & Author

Contents

Verbal Reasoning

7

Playing with Words

A word is a combination of letters. In 'Playing with Words', we use alphabets to play with words. In this word game, we make new words with the help of given word, complete the words by inserting the missing letters into it etc.

In playing with words, questions are based on following three types

   (i) Making one word from two   (ii) Word formation   (iii) Letter insertion

Making One Word from Two

In making one word from two the two words are joined to form a new word.

In this type of questions, two groups are given, each group consists of three words.

Students are required to find two words, one from each group which when joined together form a new word. The word from left group always comes first and the word from right group always comes second to form a new word.

For example, Consider the following two groups of words and find two words, one from each group, that together make a new, meaningful word.

1	2	3		A	B	C
CAT	DRAW	BLUE		BACK	TAKE	TRUE

(a) 1C   (b) 2A   (c) 2B   (d) 3A

Here, the words DRAW and BACK when joined together make a new word i.e. DRAWBACK. So, the correct answer is 2A.

Hence, option (b) is correct.

In making one word from two, following types of questions are generally asked

EXAMPLE 1 Find the two words, one from each group, that together make a new, meaningful word.

1	2	3		A	B	C
COPY	ALL	CAN		EVER	CAT	COAT

   (a) 2B   (b) 1B   (c) 2A   (d) 3C

Think • First of all, take first word of the left hand side group and try to make a meaningful word by joining this word with each and every word, one-by-one, of right hand side group.

   • Repeat above step by taking second and third words of first group, one by one, until you get your answer.

Sol. The words are COPY and CAT, because when joined together, in that order, these two words make a new word 'COPYCAT'. So, the correct answer is 1B.

Hence, option (b) is correct.

Word Formation

Word formation is the creation of a new word. In this type of questions, two words are given. Students are required to make two new words by taking a letter from the first word, in such a way that a valid word remains meaningful, and placing it into the letters of the second word to form a completely new word.

For example, Consider the following two words and choose a letter that can be moved from the word on the left to the word on the right, making the new words.

| HAIR | EAR |

(a) H   (b) A   (c) I   (d) R

Here, if we move letter 'H' from the word on the left to the word on the right, the word on the left will become AIR and the word on the right will become HEAR. Therefore, the correct answer is 'H'.

Hence, option (a) is correct.

In word formation, following types of questions are generally asked

EXAMPLE 1 Identify the letter to be moved from the first word in the second word given below to make meaningful words.

| TRAIN | HEN |

(a) R   (b) A   (c) T   (d) N

Think • First of all, read the first word carefully and identify a letter that when removed, leaves a new meaningful word.
      • Now, place that letter in second word at a proper place to make a new meaningful word.

Sol. 'T' moves from the first word 'TRAIN' to leave the new word 'RAIN' and is placed into the second word to make another new word 'THEN'. Hence, option (c) is correct.

Letter Insertion

In letter insertion, words are formed by inserting the missing letter(s). The last letter of the first word and the first letter of the second word in each set is left blank. Students are required to find the one letter that completes the first word and begins the second word of both sets of brackets.

For example, Find the letter that will complete the words given below.

FI ⟨?⟩ IP, BI ⟨?⟩ UB

(a) G   (b) T   (c) S   (d) D

Here, we can see that, there are four words i.e.FI ?, ? IP, BI ? and ? UB

To make the words meaningful, we need to identify the missing letter. Here, the letter 'T' will complete all the four words as FIT, TIP, BIT and TUB.

Hence, option (b) is correct.

In letter insertion, following types of questions are generally asked

EXAMPLE 1 Insert letter to complete the words in the figure given below.

(a) E   (b) D
(c) K   (d) U

Think Look at the figure carefully and identify the letter that will complete the words.

Sol. Letter 'U' will complete all the two words as shown in adjacent figure.
The two words are ELUDE and SCURF.
Hence, option (d) is correct.

Practice
Centre

Direction (Q. Nos. 1-10) In the following questions, find the two words, one from each group that together make a new, meaningful word. The word from the first group always comes first.

1.

A	B	C
NEWS	TALL	IN

1	2	3
PAPER	ROCK	GOT

a A2   b A1   c B2   d C3

2.

1	2	3
DARK	EYE	LIE

X	Y	Z
TIN	OR	BALL

a 3X   b 1Y   c 2X   d 2Z

3.

1	2	3
HIS	SNOW	BED

P	Q	R
ROOM	IS	BOY

a 1P   b 3R   c 3P   d 2R

4.

L	M	N
AIR	NEVER	SHE

1	2	3
TO	CHAIR	PLANE

a L3   b M1   c N1   d L2

5.

1	2	3
UP	CLASS	HE

X	Y	Z
BAR	NO	ROOM

a 1Z   b 2Z   c 3X   d 2X

6.

A	B	C
CUT	DOOR	MISS

1	2	3
LIFE	BELL	HER

a A1   b C1   c C2   d B2

7.

1	2	3
BAD	VERY	GOOD

P	Q	R
COW	NIGHT	IS

a 3Q   b 1P
c 3P   d 3R

8.

L	M	N
IN	HIGH	SAD

1	2	3
OVER	ON	TO

a L2   b M3
c L3   d N1

9.

1	2	3
KEY	FISH	ICE

P	Q	R
TIME	BOARD	IN

a 2P   b 1Q
c 3R   d 1P

10.

A	B	C
MY	NET	HIS

1	2	3
DOG	BOOK	SELF

a A3   b B2   c A1   d A2

Direction (Q.Nos. 11-20) In each of the following questions, you are given two words. Choose one letter that can be moved from the word on the left to the word on the right, making two new words. You cannot rearrange any letters, but the letter that you move can fit anywhere in the second word.

11. WHEAT   MAT

a E   b A   c H   d T

12. SAND   EVER

a A   b N   c S   d D

13. READ   ROD

a E   b R   c A   d D

14. PAGE   LAN

a A   b P   c E   d G

15. NEWS   STEP

a S   b N   c E   d W

16. COAT   HELL

a T   b C   c O   d A

17. BLANK   AND

a L   b A   c K   d N

18. TIRE   ASH

a R   b I   c T   d E

19. MAN   TIE

a M   b A   c N   d T

20. WET   EAR

a W   b E   c A   d T

21. AREA⬚INGS, RISE⬚HOUT
   a T   **b** U   **c** S   **d** W

22. REWAR⬚OWRY, TREA⬚EBAR
   a D   **b** M
   c A   **d** C

23. BRONZ⬚NOUGH, HURDL⬚MPLOY
   a L   **b** G
   c B   **d** E

24. CHANNE⬚ESSONS, QUARRE⬚EARNER
   a D   **b** L   **c** C   **d** A

25. CAR⬚ASE DIC⬚VEN
   a B   **b** A   **c** E   **d** G

26. PANI⬚AVIL, CIVI⬚ABLE
   a P   **b** M   **c** T   **d** C

27. CRO⬚IND, FLE⬚ORM
   a T   **b** A   **c** W   **d** G

28. DEM⬚PEN, RED⬚VAL
   a O   **b** N   **c** S   **d** L

29. ABAC⬚NOBS, QUIC⬚NEEL
   a L   **b** N   **c** K   **d** P

30.

31.

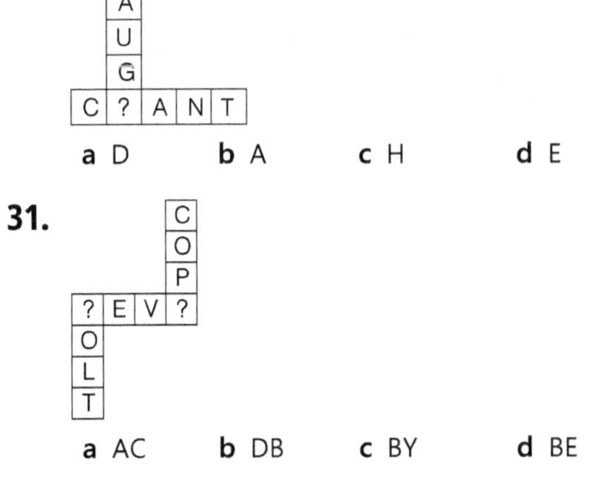

   a D   **b** A   **c** H   **d** E

   a AC   **b** DB   **c** BY   **d** BE

32.

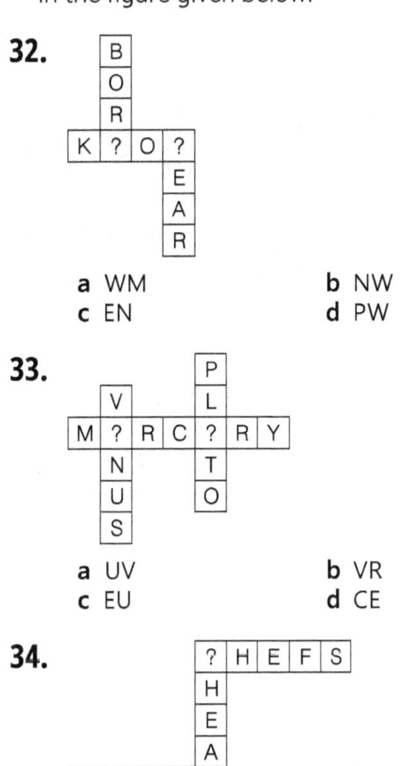

   a WM   **b** NW
   c EN   **d** PW

33.

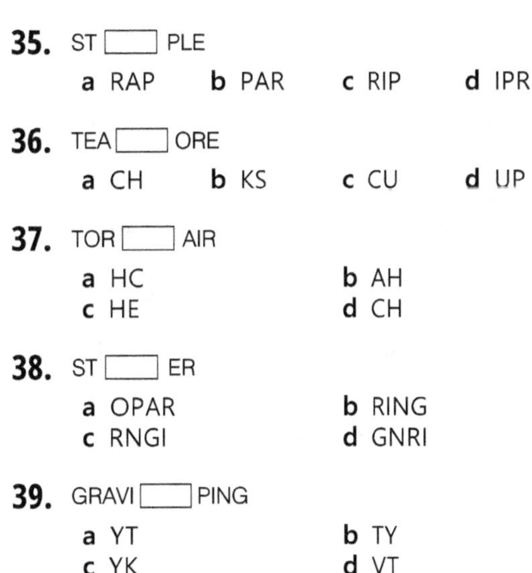

   a UV   **b** VR
   c EU   **d** CE

34.

   a VT   **b** CT
   c CB   **d** GH

35. ST⬚PLE
   a RAP   **b** PAR   **c** RIP   **d** IPR

36. TEA⬚ORE
   a CH   **b** KS   **c** CU   **d** UP

37. TOR⬚AIR
   a HC   **b** AH
   c HE   **d** CH

38. ST⬚ER
   a OPAR   **b** RING
   c RNGI   **d** GNRI

39. GRAVI⬚PING
   a YT   **b** TY
   c YK   **d** VT

Chapter 2

Using Letters for Numbers

In this chapter, we use letters for numbers. Here, students are required to find the missing value that will balance the given equation. To balance/solve the equation, we need to follow the correct sequence of mathematical operations using 'BODMAS' rule.

Do first		B	Brackets	( ), [ ], { }
		O	Power Of	$\sqrt{\ }$, ( )^2
		D	Division	/, $\div$
		M	Multiplication	$\times$
		A	Addition	$+$
Do last		S	Subtraction	$-$

For example, If $C = 3$, $D = 14$, $O = 8$ and $L = 2$, then $D - C \times L = ?$

(a) C (b) O (c) D (d) L

Here, putting the values of the letters in the given equation, we get

$$D - C \times L$$
$$= 14 - 3 \times 2 = 14 - 6 = 8$$

Here, we can see that, the value '8' represents the letter 'O' (as given in question).

So, the equation will be $D - C \times L = O$

Hence, option (b) is correct.

In using letters for numbers, following types of questions are generally asked

EXAMPLE 1 If, letters take place of numbers, such as $A = 1$, $B = 2$, $C = 3$, $D = 4$, ..., $Z = 26$, then find the value of the following word by adding the letters together.

FEED

(a) 30 (b) 20 (c) 10 (d) 15

Think · Here, the letter's positional values in English alphabets in forward order is given.

· Add all the positional values of the given letter.

Sol. On putting the values of the letters, we get

$$\begin{array}{cccc} F & E & E & D \\ \downarrow & \downarrow & \downarrow & \downarrow \\ 6 & 5 & 5 & 4 \end{array}$$

Now, $6 + 5 + 5 + 4 = 20$

So, the value of the given word FEED is 20.

Hence, option (b) is correct.

Practice
Centre

Direction (Q. Nos. 1-5) In the following questions, letters stand for numbers. Find the missing letter to complete the given equations.

1. If $P = 4$, $C = 12$, $I = 3$ and $H = 13$, then
$C \div I \times P - H = ?$
 a P   **b** I   **c** H   **d** K

2. If $F = 7$, $W = 6$, $O = 12$, and $R = 4$, then
$F - W + R + F = ?$
 a F   **b** W   **c** O   **d** R

3. If $V = 7$, $X = 4$, $W = 6$, and $Y = 3$, then
$W \times W \div X - Y = ?$
 a X   **b** V   **c** Y   **d** W

4. If $F = 9$, $X = 18$, $G = 4$ and $K = 2$, then
$X \div F + G - K = ?$
 a X   **b** F   **c** G   **d** K

5. If $R = 81$, $S = 9$, $T = 10$ and $U = 20$, then
$R \div S + U \div T = ?$
 a R   **b** S   **c** U   **d** T

Direction (Q. Nos. 6-8) In the following questions, letters take place of numbers such as $A = 1$, $B = 2$, $C = 3$, $D = 4$, ..., $Z = 26$, then find the value of the following words by adding the letters together.

6. B E A D
 a 12   **b** 15   **c** 8   **d** 10

7. S E E K
 a 15   **b** 28   **c** 40   **d** 31

8. T E L L
 a 50   **b** 48   **c** 49   **d** 42

Direction (Q. Nos. 9-11) In the following questions, letters take place of numbers such as $A = 1$, $B = 2$, $C = 3$, $D = 4$, ..., $Z = 26$. Answer the following equations in numbers.

9. $O \div C - B + T = ?$
 a 18   **b** 15   **c** 20   **d** 23

10. $Y \div E \times J - O = ?$
 a 25   **b** 20   **c** 35   **d** 30

11. $N \div G \times B + P - J = ?$
 a 10   **b** 15   **c** 12   **d** 11

Direction (Q. Nos. 12-15) In the following questions, letters take place of numbers in reverse order such as $A = 26$, $B = 25$, $C = 24$, $D = 23$, $E = 22$, ..., $Z = 1$. Find the missing letter of the given equation on the basis of the above numbers.

12. $R \times R + R = Q \times Q - [?]$
 a E   **b** Q   **c** T   **d** P

13. $V \times X + Q = P + O + [?]$
 a O   **b** S   **c** Y   **d** H

14. $Y + X + [?] = S$
 a K   **b** H   **c** E   **d** X

15. $Y \times (N + Y) = Q + [?] + L$
 a J   **b** V   **c** O   **d** F

Direction (Q. Nos. 16-20) Find the missing letter.

16. If $N = 14$, $V = 2$, $K = 7$, $I = 4$, then $\dfrac{N \times V}{K} = [?]$
 a I   **b** K   **c** N   **d** V

17. If $Z = 26$, $S = 20$, $X = 13$, $Y = 2$, $W = 48$, $T = 6$ and $H = 50$, then
$X \div Z \times S + H - T \times Y = [?]$
 a T   **b** S   **c** W   **d** X

18. If $P = 4$, $S = 5$, $W = 12$, $N = 20$ and $T = 10$ then $T \div S \times W - P = [?]$
 a P   **b** S   **c** N   **d** W

19. If $P = 9$, $Q = 15$, $R = 4$ and $S = 16$ then $S - P + Q = [?]$
 a P   **b** Q   **c** R   **d** S

20. If $A = 1$, $B = 3$, $C = 14$, $D = 20$, and $E = 21$, then $A \times D - B - C = [?]$
 a A   **b** B   **c** C   **d** D

Chapter 3

Similar Pairs

In 'Similar Pairs', a pair of words/numbers/letters have a particular relationship and similar relationship is followed by another pair of words/numbers/letters. This is also known as 'Analogy' or 'Matching pairs'.

For example, Train is related to Railway track, in the same way as Ship is related to

(a) Road   (b) Building   (c) Water   (d) Iron

Here, as train runs on railway track, similarly ship sails on water.

So, water will complete the second pair.

Hence, option (c) is correct.

In similar pairs, questions are based on the following three types

(i) Similarity of numbers   (ii) Similarity of letters   (iii) Similarity of words

Similarity of Numbers

Similarity of numbers means that the numbers in one pair possess a certain relation which is also possessed by the numbers in the other pair.

In similarity of numbers, following types of questions are generally asked

EXAMPLE 1 35 is related to 4, in the same way as 93 is related to

(a) 5   (b) 6   (c) 8   (d) 9

Think • First of all, look at the first pair of numbers and try to find out the relation between first and second numbers.

• After observation we find that, the second number is half of the addition of digits of the first number.

Sol. As, $35 = 3 + 5 = 8$ and $8 \div 2 = 4$

Similarly, $93 = 9 + 3 = 12$ and $12 \div 2 = 6$

So, 93 is related to 6.

Hence, option (b) is correct.

Similarity of Letters

Similarity of letters means that the letters (letters' groups) in one pair possess certain relation which is also possessed by the letters (letters' groups) in the other pair.

Following letters' position table in English alphabetical series will help the students to solve some special type of questions

Forward	1	2	3	4	5	6	7	8	9	10	11	12	13	14	15	16	17	18	19	20	21	22	23	24	25	26
Alphabet	A	B	C	D	E	F	G	H	I	J	K	L	M	N	O	P	Q	R	S	T	U	V	W	X	Y	Z
Backward	26	25	24	23	22	21	20	19	18	17	16	15	14	13	12	11	10	9	8	7	6	5	4	3	2	1

In similarity of letters, following types of questions are generally asked

EXAMPLE 1 Complete the second pair in the same way as first pair.

KT is to JS, as PZ is to

    (a) QA   (b) OY   (c) QY   (d) OT

Think • First of all, look at the first pair of letters and try to find out the relation between the first group of letters and second group of letters.

• After careful observation we find that, each letter of the second group is 1 position behind to its corresponding letter in first group.

Sol. As, 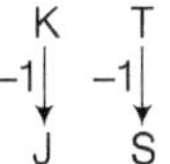 Similarly, 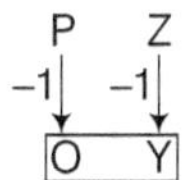

So, OY will complete the second pair.

Hence, option (b) is correct.

EXAMPLE 2 LMNO is related to OMNL, in the same way ABCD is related to

    (a) EFGH   (b) DBCA   (c) DCBA   (d) HGFE

Think After careful observation, we see that the position of the first and last letters are interchanged.

Sol. As, 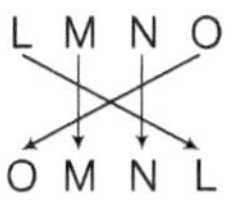 Similarly, 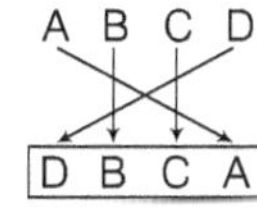

So, DBCA is related to ABCD, in the same way as LMNO is related to OMNL.

Hence, option (b) is correct.

Similarity of Words

Similarity of words means that the words in one pair possess some relation, which is also possessed by the words in the other pair.

In similarity of words, following types of questions are generally asked

EXAMPLE 1 'Fan' is related to 'Blades', in the same way as 'Wheel' is related to

    (a) Cars   (b) Spokes   (c) Round   (d) Moves

Think • First of all, consider the first pair of words and try to find the relation between these two words.

• After observing carefully we find that, second one is the part of first one.

Sol. As, blades are the parts of the fan, in the same way spokes are the parts of wheel.

Hence, option (b) is correct.

EXAMPLE 2 Choose the pair/group of words that show the same relationship, which is most similar to that of the given pair/group of words.

Rectangle : Pentagon :: ? : ?

    (a) Triangle : Rectangle   (b) Diagonal : Perimeter

    (c) Side : Angle   (d) Circle : Square

Think After observing carefully, we see that the second geometrical figures has sides one more than the first.

Sol. In the given pair, the second geometrical figure is having one side more than the first. Similarly, triangle and rectangle is the correct pair as, rectangle has one side more than the triangle.

Hence, option (a) is correct.

Practice Centre

Similarity of Numbers

✏️ **Direction** (Q. Nos. 1-10) Which number completes the second pair in the same way as the first pair?

1. 6 is to 36, as 9 is to
- **a** 25
- **b** 49
- **c** 64
- **d** 81

2. 53 is to 2, as 74 is to
- **a** 2
- **b** 3
- **c** 8
- **d** 10

3. 65 is to 30, as 88 is to
- **a** 64
- **b** 16
- **c** 26
- **d** 54

4. 81 is to 9, as 64 is to
- **a** 10
- **b** 2
- **c** 24
- **d** 6

5. 982 is to 289, as 761 is to
- **a** 716
- **b** 161
- **c** 617
- **d** 167

6. 1215 is to 2151, as 1113 is to
- **a** 3111
- **b** 1131
- **c** 1313
- **d** 3131

7. 48 : 16 :: 72 : ?
- **a** 14
- **b** 24
- **c** 34
- **d** 42

8. 850 : 40 :: 782 : ?
- **a** 17
- **b** 23
- **c** 58
- **d** 61

9. 6 : 216 :: 5 : ?
- **a** 125
- **b** 343
- **c** 64
- **d** 428

10. 64 : 10 :: 81 : ?
- **a** 15
- **b** 12
- **c** 12
- **d** 11

Similarity of Letters

✏️ **Direction** (Q. Nos. 11-16) Choose the letters' group that complete the second pair in the same way as the first pair.

11. 

- **a** TV
- **b** RS
- **c** AB
- **d** TU

12. ASB : DSC :: OFP : ?
- **a** RFQ
- **b** QST
- **c** XTU
- **d** MNP

13. aCeG : bDfH :: iKmO : ?
- **a** qStU
- **b** jLnP
- **c** kMnO
- **d** None of these

14. CDE : GHI :: LMN : ?
- **a** PQR
- **b** UVW
- **c** ZAB
- **d** JKE

15. ANT is to TNA , as BAT is to ?
- **a** BTA
- **b** TAB
- **c** ABT
- **d** None of these

16. HORSE is to HQRUE , as TIGER is to ?
- **a** TKGFR
- **b** TKGGR
- **c** TJGFR
- **d** REGIS

17. SIMILAR is related to MISIRAL, in the same way JUMBLED is related to
- **a** DELBMUJ
- **b** MBJULED
- **c** MUJBDEL
- **d** MJUBDLE

18. TOM is related to RMK, in the same way as HUT is related to
- **a** FSR
- **b** IVW
- **c** GTS
- **d** JSV

19. PACE is related to QCFI, in the same way as OATH is related to

  a RCWU   **b** PBUI
  c NBVG   **d** PCWL

20. DFHJ is related to GCKG, in the same way as MOQS is related to

  a NPRU   **b** PLTP
  c PRTV   **d** JRTP

21. NATION is related to ANITNO, in the same way as HUNGRY is related to

  a NUHXRG   **b** YRGNUIT
  c UHGNYR   **d** GRYHUN

Similarity of Words

22. TREE is related to ROOT, in the same way as SMOKE is related to

  a Wood   **b** Fire
  c Heat   **d** Cigarette

23. GOOD is related to BAD, in the same way as ROOF is related to

  a Wall   **b** Window
  c Pillar   **d** Floor

24. OVAL is related to CIRCLE, in the same way as RECTANGLE is related to

  a Square   **b** Diagonal
  c Triangle   **d** None of these

25. EYE is related to SEE, in the same way as EAR is related to

  a Ring   **b** Sound
  c Hear   **d** Smell

26. OXYGEN is related to INHALE, in the same way as CARBON DIOXIDE is related to

  a Longs   **b** Heart
  c Exhale   **d** Exitinguish

27. Guilt is related to past, in the same way as hope is related to

  a Today   **b** Present
  c Future   **d** Hopeless

Direction (Q. Nos. 28-34) Choose the pair/group of words that shows the relationship which is most similar to that of the given pair/group of words.

28. SUMMER : RAINING :: ? : ?

  a Monday : Sunday   **b** Summer : Winter
  c December : January   **d** None of these

29. WATER : SWIM :: ? : ?

  a Ground : Play   **b** Plant : Implement
  c Flood : Damage   **d** Knot : Tie

30. JACKAL : DOG :: ? : ?

  a Crow : Bat
  b Orange : Lemon
  c Tiger : Wolf
  d Ant : Antepol

31. STRAWS : NEST :: ? : ?

  a Water : Stream
  b Wood : Paper
  c Animals : Zoo
  d Threads : Cloth

32. CRICKET : OUTDOOR GAME :: ? : ?

  a Squash : Outdoor game
  b Badminton : Indoor game
  c Chess : Outdoor game
  d Lawn tennis : Indoor game

33. BOOK : PUBLISHER :: ? : ?

  a Film : Director
  b Car : Driver
  c Court : Judge
  d Pant : Shirt

34. HOT : OVEN :: ? : ?

  a Ink : Pen   **b** Ice : Cold
  c Cold : Refrigerator   **d** Door : Bell

Direction (Q. Nos. 35-39) Which word completes the second pair in the same way as first pair.

35. Bread : Yeast : : Curd : ?

  a Fungi   **b** Milk
  c Virus   **d** Bacteria

36. Push : Pull :: Throw : ?

  a Jump   **b** Pick
  c Collect   **d** Game

37. Man : Trousers :: Woman : ?

  a Clothing   **b** Skirt
  c Hat   **d** Blanket

38. Truthfulness : Court :: Cleanliness : ?

  a Virtue   **b** Restaurant
  c Bath   **d** Pig

39. Arrival : Departure :: ? : Death

  a Life   **b** Person
  c Birth   **d** Train

Chapter 4

What Comes Next?

'What Comes Next' means finding the next term based on the given arrangement of letters, numbers or both. 'What Comes Next' is also known as 'Series'.

For example, Find the next term in the following series.

$$15, 18, 22, 27, 33, ?$$

(a) 35 (b) 40 (c) 39 (d) 42

Here, in the given series the number to be added to obtain the next number is increasing by 1 in each successive step as shown below

$$15 \xrightarrow{+3} 18 \xrightarrow{+4} 22 \xrightarrow{+5} 27 \xrightarrow{+6} 33 \xrightarrow{+7} \boxed{40}$$

So, '40' will come next.

Hence, option (b) is correct.

In what comes next, questions are based on three types

(i) Number series (ii) Letter series (iii) Alpha-numeric series

Number Series

In number series, numbers are arranged in a specific pattern by following certain mathematical rules based on addition, subtraction, division, multiplication or combination of these, square roots, cube roots etc.

In number series, following types of questions are generally asked

EXAMPLE 1 Find the next term for the given series.

$$3 \quad 6 \quad 7 \quad 14 \quad 15 \quad ?$$

(a) 20 (b) 30 (c) 12 (d) 16

Think • First of all, look at the series and try to find out the relation between each of the succeeding number and preceding number.

• After observing carefully we find that, numbers are multiplied by 2 and added by 1, alternatively.

Sol. The numbers are arranged in the following pattern

$$3 \quad 6 \quad 7 \quad 14 \quad 15 \quad \textcircled{30}$$

$$\underset{\times 2}{\llcorner} \quad \underset{+1}{\llcorner} \quad \underset{\times 2}{\llcorner} \quad \underset{+1}{\llcorner} \quad \underset{\times 2}{\llcorner}$$

Therefore, the next number will be 30.

Hence, option (b) is correct.

EXAMPLE 2 Find the number which does not belong to the given series.

| 1, | 2, | 4, | 8, | 20, | 32 |

(a) 4   (b) 8   (c) 20   (d) 32

Think • First of all, look at the series and try to find out the common pattern, which is followed by most of the terms.
• After observing, we find that in first four terms the successive term is double to the previous term.

Sol. The numbers are arranged in the following pattern

$$1 \xrightarrow{\times 2} 2 \xrightarrow{\times 2} 4 \xrightarrow{\times 2} 8 \xrightarrow{\times 2} \boxed{20}^{16} \xrightarrow{\times 2} 32$$

Here, 16 should come in place of 20. So, 20 does not belong to the series.

Hence, option (c) is correct.

Letter Series

In letter series, letters of the English alphabet are arranged in a specific pattern based on the position of letters in English alphabetical order.

In letter series, following types of questions are generally asked

EXAMPLE 1 Find the missing term in the given series.

| EP | FO | ? | HM | IL |

(a) NG   (b) GN   (c) PQ   (d) NO

Think • After observing we find that, there are two series in the given letter series.
• In first letter series, each successive letter is 1 place ahead to its previous letter (in English alphabetical order) and in second letter series, each successive letter is 1 place behind to its previous letter (in English alphabetical order).

Sol. The series can be represented as

$$E \xrightarrow{+1} F \xrightarrow{+1} \boxed{G} \xrightarrow{+1} H \xrightarrow{+1} I$$
$$P \xrightarrow{-1} O \xrightarrow{-1} \boxed{N} \xrightarrow{-1} M \xrightarrow{-1} L$$

So, 'GN' is the missing term.

Hence, option (b) is correct.

Alpha-Numeric Series

In alpha-numeric series, letters and numbers together are arranged in a specific pattern.

In alpha-numeric series, following types of questions are generally asked

EXAMPLE 1 Find the next term for the given series.

P2   Q3   R4   ?

(a) S5   (b) T5   (c) U5   (d) V5

Think • First of all, look at the series and try to find out the relation among letters and numbers, separately.
• After observing, we find that each successive letter is 1 place ahead to its previous letter (in English alphabetical order) and each successive number is also 1 more than to its previous number.

Sol. The series can be represented as

$$P \xrightarrow{+1} Q \xrightarrow{+1} R \xrightarrow{+1} \boxed{S}$$
$$2 \xrightarrow{+1} 3 \xrightarrow{+1} 4 \xrightarrow{+1} \boxed{5}$$

Therefore, the next term will be S5.

Hence, option (a) is correct.

Practice
Centre

Number Series

1. 45 44 42 39 35 ?

   a 27   **b** 30   **c** 18   **d** 19

2. 1 9 25 49 ?

   a 64   **b** 36   **c** 81   **d** 16

3. 234 236 239 243 248 ?

   a 249   **b** 252   **c** 253   **d** 254

4. ? 3006 3009 3012

   a 3001   **b** 3002   **c** 3003   **d** 3004

5. 5 6 4 7 3 8 2 9 ? ?

   a 10, 1   **b** 10, 2   **c** 1, 10   **d** 1, 11

6. 11 13 17 19 23 ?

   a 24   **b** 27   **c** 28   **d** 29

7. 32 16 8 4 ?

   a 3   **b** 2   **c** 1   **d** 4

8. (66-12) (75-12) (84-12) (?)

   a (92-12)   **b** (88-14)

   c (93-12)   **d** (78-14)

9. 8 13 18 24 28 33

   a 13   **b** 18   **c** 24   **d** 33

10. 52 53 55 56 59

   a 53   **b** 55

   c 59   **d** 52

11.

8	27	64	126	216

   a 8   **b** 164

   c 27   **d** 126

12.

96	48	24	13	6

   a 48   **b** 24

   c 13   **d** 6

13.

3	9	26	81	243

   a 3   **b** 26

   c 81   **d** 9

14.

12/21	13/19	14/17	15/15	16/12	17/11

   a 16/12   **b** 13/11   **c** 15/15   **d** 17/12

15. Find the missing figure at the place of question mark.

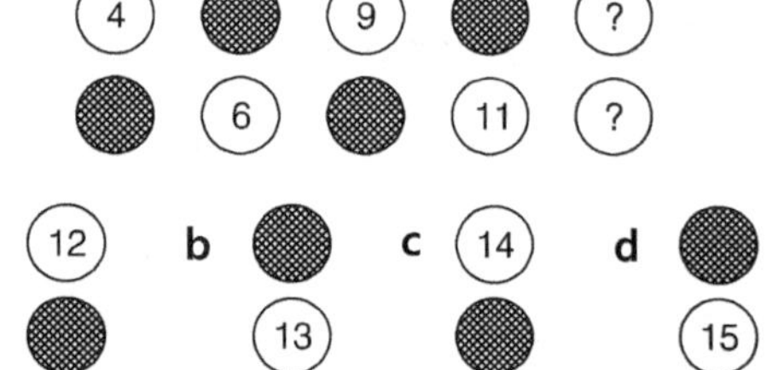

   a 12   **b** ●   **c** 14   **d** ●

   ●   13   ●   15

Letter Series

16. U W Y A ?

   a X

   b Z

   c B

   d C

17. (MN) (LO) (KP) (JQ) (?)

- **a** RI
- **b** HS
- **c** IR
- **d** SH

18. (ABZ) (CDY) (EFX) (GHW) (?)

- **a** RJV
- **b** IJV
- **c** JIV
- **d** KJI

19. (YZ) (XY) (WX) (VW) (?)

- **a** UT
- **b** UW
- **c** UV
- **d** US

20.

EG	?	KM	NP	QS

- **a** HJ
- **b** FH
- **c** IJ
- **d** HI

21.

JK	MN	PQ	?	VW	YZ

- **a** RS
- **b** TU
- **c** SU
- **d** ST

22. (J) (L) (N) (O) (R)

- **a** L
- **b** O
- **c** N
- **d** J

23. (Nn) (Oo) (PP) (Qq) (Rr)

- **a** Nn
- **b** Oo
- **c** PP
- **d** Rr

24. (Hh) (Ii) (JJ) (Kk) (Ll)

- **a** Ii
- **b** Kk
- **c** Hh
- **d** JJ

25. (Hh) (Di) (Ak) (Yn) (Xs)

- **a** Di
- **b** Ak
- **c** Yn
- **d** Xs

26. (TUV) (XYZ) (BCD) (EFG) (JKL)

- **a** XYZ
- **b** EFG
- **c** JKL
- **d** BCD

Alpha-Numeric Series

27. (E6) (F8) (G10) (H12) (?)

- **a** I13
- **b** I14
- **c** J13
- **d** K14

28.

L	N	P	R	?
4	9	16	25	?

- **a** T / 36
- **b** Q / 36
- **c** U / 36
- **d** O / 36

29.

| EF/24 | ?/? | IJ/20 | KL/18 | MN/16 |

- **a** GH / 23
- **b** CD / 21
- **c** AB / 24
- **d** GH / 22

30.

| P/1 | O/3 | N/9 | ?/? | L/81 |

- **a** M / 27
- **b** K / 26
- **c** M / 25
- **d** K / 28

31.

A	C	E	G	?
3	9	6	12	?

- **a** K / 11
- **b** I / 10
- **c** I / 9
- **d** K / 19

32.

A	F	?	P
1	2	?	4

- **a** B / 2
- **b** D / 4
- **c** E / 2
- **d** K / 3

33.

A	B	D	D	E
3	4	5	6	7
8	10	11	14	16

- **a** D / 6 / 14
- **b** D / 5 / 11
- **c** A / 3 / 8
- **d** B / 4 / 10

34. (PQR1) (STU3) (VWX5) (ZAB6) (BCD9)

- **a** ZAB6
- **b** BCD9
- **c** STU3
- **d** PQR1

Chapter 5

Odd One Out

'Odd One Out' means finding an odd term from a given set which is based on arrangement of letters, words or numbers. In such types of problems, some items are given. All these items except one are similar in some manner. A student is required to find that item.

'Odd One Out' is also known as 'Classification'.

For example, Consider the following set of words and choose a word which does not belong to the group.

(a) Guitar   (b) Tabla   (c) Violin   (d) Sitar

Here, except tabla all others are stringed instruments.

So, tabla does not belong to the group.

Hence, option (b) is correct.

In odd one out, questions are based on four types

   (i) Word classification   (ii) Number classification

  (iii) Letter classification   (iv) Mixed classification

Word Classification

In word classification, a set of words is classified on the basis of some common properties such as names, places, uses etc.

In word classification, following types of questions are generally asked

EXAMPLE 1 Find the word which is different from others.

    (a) Ears   (b) Fingers   (c) Hands   (d) Legs

Think • Observe all the words carefully and try to find out the common property or characteristic which is possessed by most of the words.
• After observing we find that, the words follow count property.

Sol. Except fingers, all other parts of body are in pairs. So, fingers is different from others.
Hence, option (b) is correct.

EXAMPLE 2 Find the word which does not belong to the group.

    (a) Plant   (b) Branch   (c) Root   (d) Leaf

Think After observing we see that, three words are the part of fourth one.

Sol. Branch, root and leaf are the parts of a plant. Therefore, plant does not belong to the group.
Hence, option (a) is correct.

Number Classification

In number classification, a set of numbers is classified on the basis of common properties such as even numbers, odd numbers, prime numbers etc.

In number classification, following types of questions are generally asked

EXAMPLE 1 Find the odd one out.   (a) (10)   (b) (22)   (c) (18)   (d) (5)

Think • First of all, look at the set of numbers and try to find out the common property, which is possessed by all the numbers except one.

• After careful observation we find that, numbers possess even number property.

Sol. Except 5, all others are even numbers, while 5 is an odd number. So, 5 is odd one out.

Hence, option (d) is correct.

Letter Classification

In letter classification, a set of letters is classified on the basis of some common properties such as position of letters in English alphabetical order (either forward or backward order).

The following table shows the position of letters in forward and backward order in English alphabetical order

Forward	1	2	3	4	5	6	7	8	9	10	11	12	13	14	15	16	17	18	19	20	21	22	23	24	25	26
Alphabet	A	B	C	D	E	F	G	H	I	J	K	L	M	N	O	P	Q	R	S	T	U	V	W	X	Y	Z
Backward	26	25	24	23	22	21	20	19	18	17	16	15	14	13	12	11	10	9	8	7	6	5	4	3	2	1

In letter classification, following types of questions are generally asked

EXAMPLE 1 Find the odd one which does not belong to the group.

    (a) HI   (b) JK   (c) OQ   (d) RS

Think After observing we see that, most of the groups contain consecutive letters.

Sol. The relation between the letters is shown as   H I J, K O, Q R S with +1, +1, +2, +1

Here, we see that letters HI, JK and RS follow a similar relationship, but letters OQ do not follow the similar relationship. So, OQ does not belong to the group.

Hence, option (c) is correct.

Mixed Classification

In mixed classification, a set of combination of letters and numbers are arranged in a specific pattern in which all the combinations except one have common properties. The combination having the different properties is the odd term.

In mixed classification, following types of questions are generally asked

EXAMPLE 1 Find the odd one out.   (a) 13M   (b) 15O   (c) 17Q   (d) 18S

Think • Analyse each group and try to find out the relation between number and alphabet.

• After observing we see that, the alphabets and numbers have letters' place values relation.

Sol. Here, 13 M, 15O and 17Q have common properties i.e. each number written on the left side is the alphabetical order of the letter written on the right side, but the term 18S does not follow this pattern. We know that, the position of S is 19 in alphabetical order. So, 18S is odd one out.

Hence, option (d) is correct.

Practice Centre

Word Classification

Direction (Q.Nos. 1-5) Find the word which is different from others.

1. a Cube b Sphere c Cylinder d Square

2. a Universe b Mars c Star d Moon

3. a Tiger b Fox c Lion d Leopard

4. a Odour b Smell c Fragrance d Foul

5. a City b Town c Home d Village

Number Classification

Direction (Q.Nos. 6-17) Find the one which does not belong to the group.

6. a 32 b 49 c 36 d 25

7. a 6 b 12 c 25 d 18

8. a 73 b 81 c 64 d 55

9. a 21, 3 b 35, 8 c 52, 7 d 92, 11

10. a 24-12 b 26-13 c 32-15 d 28-14

11. a 78 b 112 c 121 d 124

12. a 1 b 22 c 3333 d 4444

13. a 8 b 25 c 27 d 64

14. a 81 b 61 c 41 d 31

15. a 36-12 b 39-13 c 45-15 d 50-16

16. a $\dfrac{42}{3}$ b $\dfrac{27}{3}$ c $\dfrac{75}{3}$ d $\dfrac{57}{3}$

17. a $\dfrac{36}{2}$ b $\dfrac{48}{3}$ c $\dfrac{56}{4}$ d $\dfrac{85}{5}$

Letter Classification

Direction (Q.Nos. 18-28) Find the letter/group of letters which is different from the others.

18. a A b C c F d G

19. a E b I c H d O

20. a aBc b eFg c lmn d pQr

21. a ML b TS c AB d JI

22. a ABD b EFH c JKM d PQR

23. a ADE b BEG c EAF d FBI

24. a CA b GE c MK d JI

25. a EGI b JKL c OQS d TVX

26. a WD b VE c UF d SG

27. a ACDF b EGHJ c IKLM d NPQR

28. a ABC b ACD c BCF d CDG

Mixed Classification

Direction (Q. Nos.29-35) Find the odd one out.

29. a 4E1 b 3J6 c 6H2 d 5L7

30. a N14 b P16 c 20U d W23

31. a 1F5 b 2I8 c 9M4 d 7O8

32. a 26X2 b 24V2 c 20Q2 d 22T2

33. a 8E3 b 10C6 c 20O5 d 18J8

34. a B D 4 2 b A Z 10 20 c K M 13 11 d P R 18 16

35. a 10 L J 11 b 14 O N 15 c 3 E C 5 d 7 H G 8

Chapter 6

Coding Decoding

Coding means to convert the plain text into some codes to hide the actual meaning of the text and decoding means to convert the codes into meaningful text to understand the message.

For example, In a certain code language, if 'MAN' is coded as 'OCP', then how will 'RAT' be written in that code language?

(a) SBU   (b) TBU   (c) TCV   (d) SCV

Here, each letter of the word is moved 2 steps forward of its position in the English alphabet to get the corresponding letters of the coded word OCP.

As,   Basic Word $\longrightarrow$ M A N $+2\downarrow +2\downarrow +2\downarrow$ Coded Word $\longrightarrow$ O C P

Similarly,   Basic Word $\longrightarrow$ R A T $+2\downarrow +2\downarrow +2\downarrow$ Coded Word $\longrightarrow$ T C V

So, RAT would be coded as TCV.

Hence, option (c) is correct.

In coding, questions are based on four types

    (i) Letter coding   (ii) Number coding

    (iii) Symbol coding   (iv) Miscellaneous coding

Letter Coding

In letter coding, the actual alphabets are replaced by certain other alphabets according to a specific rule. Letters are used in forward or backward or in both the orders for making some code language.

Following table shows the position of letters in forward and backward order in English alphabetical order

Forward	1	2	3	4	5	6	7	8	9	10	11	12	13	14	15	16	17	18	19	20	21	22	23	24	25	26
Alphabet	A	B	C	D	E	F	G	H	I	J	K	L	M	N	O	P	Q	R	S	T	U	V	W	X	Y	Z
Backward	26	25	24	23	22	21	20	19	18	17	16	15	14	13	12	11	10	9	8	7	6	5	4	3	2	1

In letter coding, following types of questions are generally asked

EXAMPLE 1 In a certain code, 'DONKEY' is written as 'YEKNOD'. How is 'HORSE' written in that code?

    (a) HESRO   (b) IPSTF   (c) HPSTE   (d) ESROH

Think • First of all, consider the given word and its code and try to find out the rule that is used to generate the code.

      • After analysing we find that, the letters of the original word are written in reverse order to obtain the code.

Sol. As, DONKEY $\xrightarrow[\text{order}]{\text{Reverse}}$ YEKNOD Similarly, HORSE $\xrightarrow[\text{order}]{\text{Reverse}}$ ESROH

So, HORSE would be coded as ESROH.

Hence, option (d) is correct.

Number Coding

In number coding, either numerical code values are assigned to a word or alphabetical code letters are assigned to the numbers.

In number coding, following types of questions are generally asked

EXAMPLE 1 If '256' is the code for 'BOY' and '3517' is the code for 'HOUR', then 7126 is the code for

(a) RUBY (b) BOUR (c) ROUB (d) BORY

Think
- First of all, try to find out the pattern that is used to code a letter as number.
- After analysing we see that, each number is coded as a particular letter.

Sol. Given numbers are coded as $2 \longrightarrow B, 5 \longrightarrow O, 6 \longrightarrow Y, 3 \longrightarrow H, 1 \longrightarrow U, 7 \longrightarrow R$

Here, 7 is coded as R, 1 is coded as U, 2 is coded as B and 6 is coded as Y. Thus, the code for 7126 is RUBY.

Hence, option (a) is correct.

Symbol Coding

In symbol coding, either symbolic code values are assigned to a word or alphabetical code letters are assigned to the symbols.

In symbol coding, following types of questions are generally asked

EXAMPLE 1 In a certain language, 'BEE' is coded as $ ★★ and 'ANT' is coded as ÷ @ #, how is 'BAT' written in that code ?

(a) $★★ (b) $÷# (c) #★@ (d) #@÷

Think After observing we see that, each letter is assigned a particular symbol as a code.

Sol. As given, the letters are coded as $B \longrightarrow $, E \longrightarrow ★, A \longrightarrow ÷, N \longrightarrow @, T \longrightarrow #$

Here, B is coded as $, A is coded as ÷ and T is coded as #. So, the code for BAT is $ ÷ #.

Hence, option (b) is correct.

Miscellaneous Coding

In miscellaneous coding, we have to deal with problems based on substitution coding, mixed letter coding and mixed number.

In miscellaneous coding, following types of questions are generally asked

EXAMPLE 1 If 'white' is called 'blue', 'blue' is called 'red', 'red' is called 'yellow', 'yellow' is called 'green', 'green' is called 'black', 'black' is called 'violet' and 'violet' is called 'orange', then what would be the colour of human blood ?

(a) Red (b) Green (c) Yellow (d) Violet

Think
- First of all, read the last line of the question to obtain the information i.e. colour of human blood.
- After this, we have to correlate this information with the given coding.

Sol. We know that, the colour of human blood is 'red', but here 'red' is called 'yellow'. So, the colour of human blood will be 'yellow'.

Hence, option (c) is correct.

Practice
Centre

1. If in a certain code, 'MONDAY' is written as 'NPOEBZ', then how will 'FRIDAY' be written in that code?

   a YADIRF **b** GSJEBZ **c** IRFYAD **d** FSJEBY

2. If in a certain code, 'ELEPHANT' is written as 'CJCNFYLR', then how will 'BIRTHDAY' be written in that code?

   a YADHTRIB   **b** TRIBYADH
   c ZGPRFBYW   **d** AHQSGCZX

3. If in a certain code, 'CRICKET' is written as 'IRCCTEK', then how will 'BROTHER' be written in that code?

   a REHTORB   **b** BREHTOR
   c CSPUIFS   **d** ORBTREH

4. If in a certain code, 'JANUARY' is written as 'YRAUNAJ', then how will 'OCTOBER' be written in that code?

   a OREBOTC   **b** REBOTCO
   c PDUPCFS   **d** TCOOREB

5. If in a certain code, 'DOCTOR' is written as 'URWFRG', then how will 'JUNGLE' be written in that code?

   a KVOHMF   **b** HOJQXM
   c MXQJOH   **d** NUJELG

6. If in a certain code, 'HEN' is written as 'IDO', then how will 'FAN' be written in that code?

   a FNA   **b** NAF   **c** EZM   **d** GZO

7. If in a certain code, 'HEN' is written as 'MEN' and 'CAT' is written as 'HAT', then how will 'RAN' be written in that code?

   a TAN   **b** VAN   **c** LAN   **d** WAN

8. If 'DUBAI' is coded as 'GWECL', then what is the code of 'CHINA' in the same language?

   a DIJOB   **b** ANIHC
   c FJLPD   **d** BGHMZ

9. If 'SEARCH' can be coded as 'RCXNXB', then how would you code 'PREACH'?

   a HCAERP   **b** QSFBDI
   c QTGCEJ   **d** OPBWXB

10. In a certain code, 'QUANTUM' is written as 'nAWmkAb'. How will 'AUNT' be coded?

   a WAmk   **b** bkmW
   c kmWA   **d** nAkb

11. In a certain code, 'DELHI' is written as 68341 and 'CALCUTTA' is written as 75379225, how is 'CALICUT' be written in that code?

   a 2971357 **b** 5713729 **c** 7531792 **d** 6713452

12. In a certain code, 'LINGER' is written as 123456 and 'FORCE' is written as 78695, then how is 'FIERCE' be written in that code?

   a 127569 **b** 725695 **c** 345677 **d** 526789

13. If in a certain code, 'PALE' is written as 2134, 'EARTH' is written as 41590, how is 'PEARL' be written in that code?

   a 29530 **b** 24153 **c** 25413 **d** 25430

14. If in a certain code, 'ENGLAND' is written as 1234526 and 'FRANCE' is written as 785291 and how is 'GREECE' be written in that code?

   a 381171 **b** 381191 **c** 832252 **d** 835545

15. In a certain code, a number 13479 is written as BRGKM and 5268 is written as ENQO. How is 396824 written in that code?

   a RMQOKL **b** RMQBNG **c** RGNOQM **d** RMQONG

16. In a certain code, a number 15789 is written as XTZAL and 2346 is written as NPSU. How is 23549 written in that code?

   a NPTUL **b** PNTSL **c** NPTSL **d** NBTSL

17. The number in each question below is to be codified in the following code:

Digit code	7	2	1	5	3	9	8	6	4
Letter code	W	L	M	S	I	N	D	J	B

How is 879341 be written in coded form?

a DWNIBS **b** DWNBIM **c** DWNIBM **d** NDWBIM

18. If E = 5 and GIVE = 43, then THINK = ?

a 60 **b** 62 **c** 70 **d** 72

19. If W = 4, T = 7 and TEN = 42, then SWEET = ?

a 63 **b** 65 **c** 67 **d** 69

20. In, a certain language, A is coded as 2, B is coded as 3, C is coded as 4, ... then 'HEAD' is coded as

a 8514 **b** 7423
c 9625 **d** 5269

21. In a certain language, 'GIVE' is coded as '@ ⋆ $ #' and 'BAT' is coded as '+ > <', then how is 'BITE' written in that code?

a @⋆<$ **b** +⋆<# **c** @⋆>$ **d** +⋆>#

22. In a certain language, 'CANDLE' is coded as '+ > < ⋆ $ @' and 'NEST' is coded as '< @ ? −', then how is 'LAND' written in that code?

a +$>⋆ **b** ⋆−?@ **c** $><⋆ **d** @?−⋆

23. In a certain language, '− ⋆ @ ? + >' is the code for 'STEADY' and '$? + @' is the code for MADE, then ⋆ @ ? $ is the code for

a TEAM **b** MAET **c** MATE **d** AMTE

24. In a certain language, '# @ ? ÷ > < +' is the code for 'DESTINY,' then '÷ @ ? ÷ is' the code for

a ESTD **b** STES **c** DEST **d** TEST

25. In a certain code, 'NOTICE' is written as '5 $ @ 6 # ?' and 'SCENT' is written as '7 # ? 5 @', how is 'COIN' written in that code?

a #$65 **b** 56$# **c** 5@?# **d** @?#$

26. In a certain code, 'COMPUTER' is written as '8 + ⋆ 9 ÷ # 2 >', then 'PETER' may be coded as

a 9 2 # 2 > **b** > 2 # 2 9
c 8 2 # 9 2 **d** ÷ # 2 > 9

27. If 'orange' is called 'butter', 'butter' is called 'soap', 'soap' is called 'ink', 'ink' is called 'honey' and 'honey' is called 'pink', which of the following is used for washing clothes?

a Honey **b** Ink **c** Soap **d** Butter

28. If 'black' is called 'green', 'green' is called 'blue', 'blue' is called 'orange', 'orange' is called 'yellow' and 'yellow' is called 'red' and 'red' is called 'black', then which is the colour of clear sky?

a Blue **b** Yellow **c** Orange **d** Black

29. If 'rain' is called 'water', 'water' is called 'air', 'air' is called 'cloud', 'cloud' is called 'sky' , 'sky' is called 'sea' and 'sea' is called 'road', where do the aeroplanes fly?

a Road **b** Water **c** Cloud **d** Sea

30. If 'eye' is called 'hand', 'hand' is called 'mouth', 'mouth' is called 'ear', 'ear' is called 'nose' and 'nose' is called 'tongue', with which of the following would a person hear?

a Nose **b** Ear **c** Mouth **d** Eye

31. In a certain code language, 'ne me be' means 'nice big house', 'be le ke' means 'house is good' and 'pe le me' means 'big is high'. Which word stands for 'house' in that code language?

a le **b** me **c** be **d** ke

32. In a certain code language, 'sky is blue' means 'lib nib kib', 'blue colour' means 'kib tib' and 'colour is fun' means 'tib nib rib'. Which of the following means colour in that code language?

a rib **b** nib
c tib **d** kib

33. In a certain code language, '851' means 'good sweet fruit', '783' means 'good red rose' and '341' means 'rose and fruit'. Which of the following digits stands for 'fruit' in that language?

a 8 **b** 1
c 3 **d** 4

Chapter 7

Mathematical Reasoning

In 'Mathematical Reasoning,' problems are based on numbers and mathematical operations.

In this topic, we will discuss two types of problems

   (i) Mathematical operations   (ii) Number puzzle

Mathematical Operations

In mathematical operations, mathematical symbols are interchanged with other symbols.

Students are required to substitute the symbols to solve the equation. These questions are based on BODMAS rule, which is discussed below

(B) BRACKETS ( ) [ ] { } (O) ORDER OF (D) DIVIDE / ÷ (M) MULTIPLY / × (A) ADDITION / + (S) SUBTRACTION / –

Do first ⎯⎯⎯⎯⎯⎯⎯⎯⎯⎯⎯⎯⎯⎯⎯⎯⎯⎯⎯⎯⎯⎯⎯⎯⎯⎯→ Do last

For example, If '★' means '+' and '#' means '–', then find the value of 25★5#4.

(a) 25   (b) 26   (c) 24   (d) 30

Here, we will substitute the symbols as shown 25 ★5 # 4
$$\underset{+\qquad -}{\downarrow\quad\downarrow}$$

Now, $25 + 5 - 4 = 30 - 4 = 26$ [using BODMAS rule]

Therefore, the value of the given expression is 26.

Hence, option (b) is correct.

In mathematical operations, following types of questions are generally asked

EXAMPLE 1 If P denotes +, Q denotes –, R denotes × and S denotes ÷, then find the value of 24 S 6 R 2 P 4 Q 5, when simplified.

   (a) ④   (b) ⑤   (c) ⑦   (d) ⑨

Think • After observing we see that, each letter used in expression is assigned a specific mathematical operation.

• Use these operations in place of letters in the given expression to solve it.

Sol. By using correct symbols, we have

Given expression $= 24 \div 6 \times 2 + 4 - 5 = 4 \times 2 + 4 - 5 = 8 + 4 - 5 = 12 - 5 = 7$

So, the value of given expression is 7.

Hence, option (c) is correct.

EXAMPLE 2 If '+' denotes 'greater than', '★' denotes 'equal to', ϕ denotes 'not less than', '$' denotes 'not equal to', '<' denotes 'less than' and '>' denotes 'not greater than', then choose the correct statement for the statement $a + b < c$.

(a) $\boxed{a \star b < c}$ (b) $\boxed{c > b \phi a}$ (c) $\boxed{b \phi a + c}$ (d) $\boxed{a \phi b > c}$

Think • After reading given information carefully we find that, each symbol is assigned a particular operation.
 • Use these operations in place of symbols in the given equation as well as in options to get the correct answer.

Sol. Here, using the usual notations, we have, Given statement $a + b < c \Rightarrow a > b < c$

(a) $a \star b < c \Rightarrow a = b < c \neq a > b < c$, so it is false.
(b) $c > b \phi a \Rightarrow c \not> b \not< a \Rightarrow a \leq b \geq c \neq a > b < c$, so it is false.
(c) $b \phi a + c \Rightarrow b \not< a > c \Rightarrow b \geq a > c \neq a > b < c$, so it is false.
(d) $a \phi b > c \Rightarrow a \not< b \not> c \Rightarrow a \geq b \leq c = a > b < c$, so it is true.

Hence, option (d) is correct.

Number Puzzle

In number puzzle, a figure or a combination of figures having numbers or letters arranged according to a specific pattern is given and students are required to find out the missing number or letter.

For example, Find out the missing number in following figure.

3	?
5	7

(a) (11) (b) (12) (c) (15) (d) (16)

Here, we see that the consecutive prime numbers are given in the box in anti-clockwise direction starting from 3. So, 11 will replace the question mark as

3	11
5	7

Hence, option (a) is correct.

In number puzzle, following types of questions are generally asked

EXAMPLE 1 Find the number which replaces the question mark?

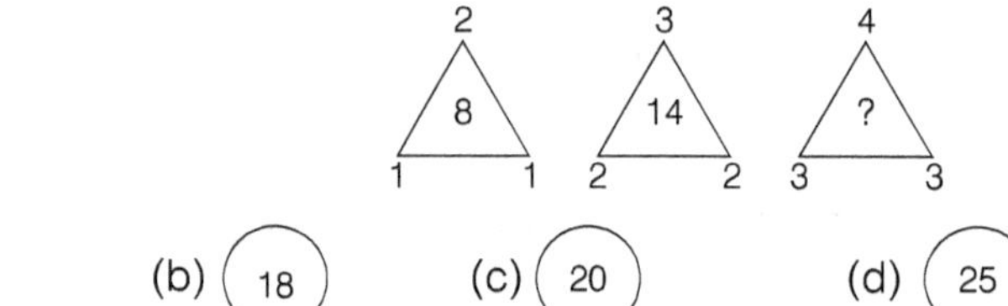

(a) (16) (b) (18) (c) (20) (d) (25)

Think • Look at the each figure, separately and try to find out the pattern which is used to obtain the number written in centre.
 • After observing we find that, the addition of numbers written at the corners is multiplied by 2 to get the central value.

Sol. In I figure, $1 + 1 + 2 = 4$, $4 \times 2 = 8$
In II figure, $2 + 2 + 3 = 7$, $7 \times 2 = 14$
Similarly, in III figure, $3 + 3 + 4 = 10$, $10 \times 2 = 20$
So, 20 will replace the question mark.
Hence, option (c) is correct.

Practice
Centre

Direction (Q. Nos. 1-4) Identify the rule that has been used to fill in the entries of the given square/rectangle and then determine which one of the four given options will replace the question mark?

1.

5	6	1
?	4	8
7	2	3

a 0   **b** 1
c 2   **d** 3

2.

8	10	90
6	9	63
4	?	40

a 5   **b** 6
c 7   **d** 8

3.

P	K	F
N	I	D
L	G	?

a B   **b** A
c H   **d** D

4.

1	5	25	125
3	12	?	192
7	14	28	56

a 24   **b** 26
c 48   **d** 45

Direction (Q. Nos. 5-6) Which term replaces the question mark in the given questions?

5.

41	53
73	?

a 51   **b** 57
c 93   **d** 67

6.

828	?
680	756

a 167   **b** 953
c 984   **d** 503

Direction (Q. Nos. 7-22) Find the number which replaces the question mark.

7.

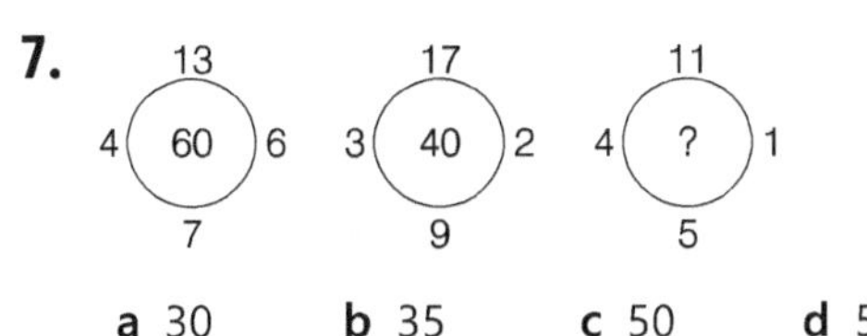

a 30   **b** 35   **c** 50   **d** 55

8.

a 12   **b** 13
c 14   **d** 15

9.

a 68   **b** 78
c 62   **d** 72

10.

a 49   **b** 17
c 48   **d** 18

11.

	62			52			62	
18	60	18	18	40	26	23	?	19
	2			20			24	

a 32   **b** 44   **c** 34   **d** 78

12.

a 47   **b** 45
c 37   **d** 35

13.

4	$\frac{2}{5}$	$\frac{18}{5}$
7	$\frac{5}{3}$	$\frac{16}{3}$
3	?	$\frac{25}{9}$

a $\frac{29}{9}$ **b** $\frac{6}{9}$
c $\frac{20}{9}$ **d** $\frac{2}{9}$

14.

a 340   **b** 277
c 145   **d** 225

15.

a 12   **b** 14   **c** 13   **d** 17

16.

a 16   **b** 32   **c** 61   **d** 14

17. 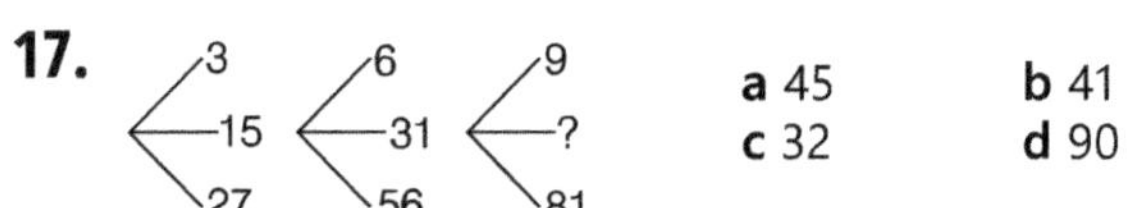

			a 45	**b** 41
			c 32	**d** 90

18. 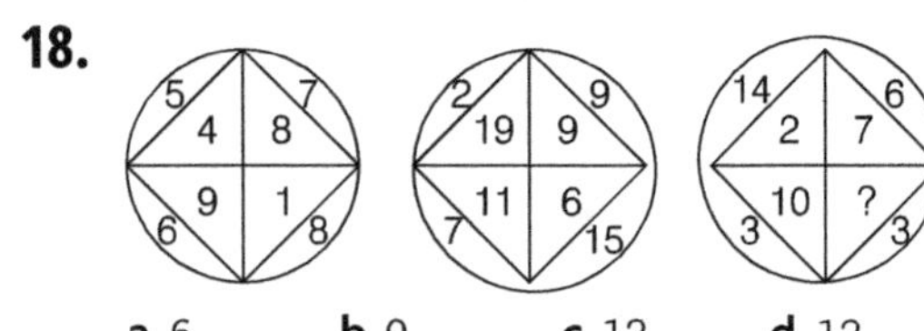

a 6   **b** 9   **c** 13   **d** 12

19. 

a 38	**b** 36
c 12	**d** 8

20. 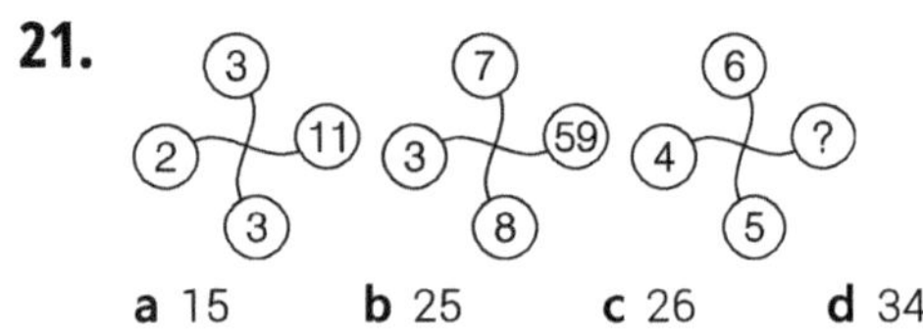

a 6	**b** 4
c 2	**d** 1

21. 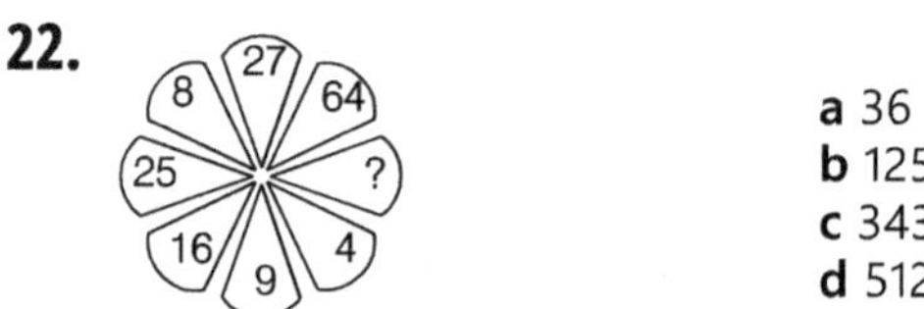

a 15   **b** 25   **c** 26   **d** 34

22.

a 36
b 125
c 343
d 512

23. If '+' denotes '−', '−' denotes '×', '÷' denotes '+' and '×' denotes '÷', then find the number which replaces the question mark?
$15 - 3 + 10 \times 5 \div 5 = ?$
a 5   **b** 22   **c** 48   **d** 52

24. If P means ÷, T means +, M means − and D means ×, then what will be the value of the expression 65 P 5 D 3 T 27 M 16 T 2?
a 52   **b** 54   **c** 60   **d** 62

25. If Δ means 'equal to', £ means 'not equal to', + means 'greater than', − means 'less than', × means 'not greater than' and ÷ means 'not less than', then choose the correct statement for the statement $a - b - c$.
a a−b+c   **b** c×b+a
c a£b£c   **d** c+b +a

26. If ϕ means 'equal to', $ means 'not equal to', + means 'greater than', − means 'less than', × means 'not greater than' and ÷ means 'not

less than', then choose the correct statement for the statement $a + b - c$.
a b−c−a **b** c−b+ a **c** c+ b − a **d** c×b÷a

27. Which two signs are to be interchange to make the below equation true?
$4 \times 2 + 6 \div 2 - 12 = 2$
a + and − **b** × and + **c** ÷ and × **d** ÷ and −

28. Which one of the following interchange in signs and numbers would make the equation $27 - 18 + 15 = 30$ true?
a 27 and 15, − and + **b** 27 and 18, − and +
c 15 and 18, − and + **d** None of these

29. If the digits '6' and '4', signs '+' and '×' are interchanged, then which one of the four equations would be correct?
a $6 + 4 \times 2 = 26$ **b** $6 + 4 \times 2 = 0$
c $4 \times 2 + 6 = 8$ **d** $4 + 6 \times 2 = 12$

30. If $7 \bigstar 2 = 81$ and $9 \bigstar 5 = 196$, then what is the value of $8 \bigstar 8 = ?$
a 128   **b** 256   **c** 64   **d** None of these

31. If $45 \ominus 25 = 97$ and $84 \ominus 32 = 125$, then $97 \ominus 34 = ?$
a 131   **b** 63   **c** 167   **d** 21

32. If $27 \times 37 \times 42 = 42 \times 27 \times 37$ and $65 \times 96 \times 23 = 23 \times 65 \times 96$, then $56 \times 84 \times 75 = ?$
a $56 \times 75 \times 84$ **b** $56 \times 84 \times 56$
c $75 \times 84 \times 56$ **d** $75 \times 56 \times 84$

33. If $72 \times 43 \times 13 = 974$ and $24 \times 43 \times 12 = 673$, then $52 \times 23 \times 21 = ?$
a 357   **b** 753
c 537   **d** 573

34. If # means 'greater than', ★ means 'less than' and $ means 'equal to' and if x # y and y$z, then
a x ★ z   **b** y ★ x
c z # x   **d** Both (a) and (b)

35. If '→' stands for 'addition', '←' stands for 'subtraction', '↑' stands for 'division', '↓' stands for 'multiplication' and '★' stands for 'equal to', then which of the following options is correct?
a 2↓5 ←6 →2★6   **b** 5 →7 ←3↑2★4
c 3↓6★2 →3 ←6★5   **d** 7 → 42↑6★5

Chapter 8

Puzzle Test

A 'Puzzle' is a problem in which the information is given in a jumbled form and to obtain the required information from given problem/information is known as 'Puzzle Test'.

For example, Four friends are sitting in a row facing North. B is sitting at the extreme left corner. A is sitting second to the right of B, D is sitting between B and A. Then, find the position of C.

(a) Extreme right corner (b) Between D and B
(c) Left of B (d) Cannot be determined

Here, B is sitting at the extreme left corner and this can be represented as

B _ _ _

Now, A is sitting second to the right of B.

So, B _ A _

Now, D is sitting between B and A.

B D A _

At the remaining position, C will sit as shown below

<u>B</u> <u>D</u> <u>A</u> <u>C</u>

It is clear from the above arrangement that, C is sitting at the extreme right corner.

Hence, option (a) is correct.

In puzzle test, following types of questions are generally asked

EXAMPLE 1 Four girls Reena, Madhu, Preeti and Sonam are standing in a single line. Madhu and Reena are standing to the left of Preeti and there are two girls standing between Madhu and Sonam. Who is standing at the extreme right position?

(a) Preeti (b) Sonam (c) Reena (d) Madhu

Think • First of all, read the information carefully.
• Now, draw a linear arrangement diagram and place the persons according to the information given in the question.

Sol. Mark the positions of four girls from left to right as 1, 2, 3 and 4.

Preeti cannot be either at position 1 or 2 because there are two girls standing to the left of Preeti. She also cannot be at position 4, because there will be no way left to accommodate two girls between Madhu and Sonam. So, Preeti stands at position 3. The only possible case is

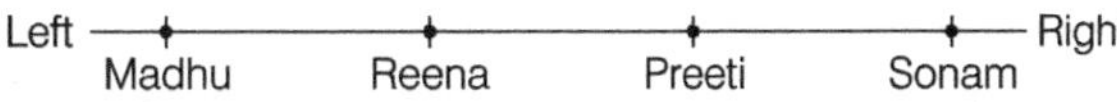

From the above arrangement it is clear that, Sonam is standing at the extreme right position.

Hence, option (b) is correct.

EXAMPLE 2 Six persons are sitting in a circle facing the centre of the circle. Prem is sitting between Bina and Naresh. Asha is sitting between Chitra and Pankaj. Chitra is to the immediate left of Bina. Who is to the immediate right of Bina?

    (a) Prem   (b) Pankaj   (c) Naresh   (d) Chitra

Sol. On the basis of given information, we can determine the positions of persons sitting in a circle facing the centre.

Here, Prem is between Bina and Naresh.

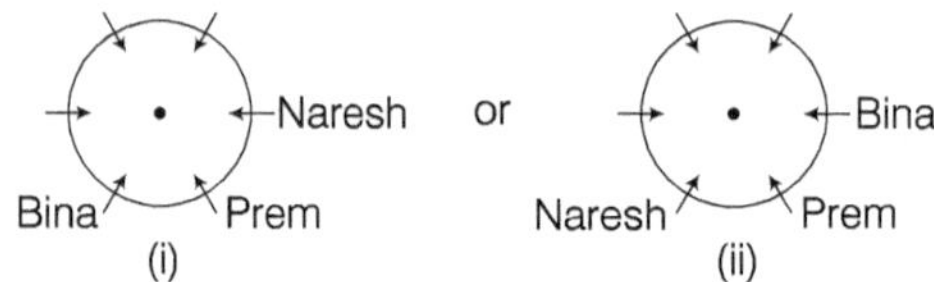

Now, Asha is between Chitra and Pankaj and Chitra is to the immediate left of Bina. So ,it is clear that Bina is sitting to the left of Prem. Thus, the correct arrangement is (i).

Now,

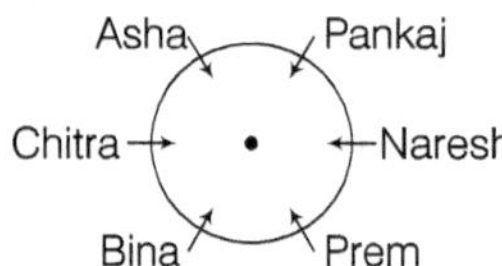

So, we can determine that Prem is sitting to the immediate right of Bina.

Hence, option (a) is correct.

Direction (Ex. No. 3) Study the following information carefully and answer the given questions. There is a group of five students A, B, C, D and E.

- B and E are good in Dramatics and Computer Science.
- A and B are good in Computer Science and Physics.
- A, D and C are good in Physics and History.
- C and A are good in Physics and Mathematics.
- D and E are good in History and Dramatics.

(i) Who is good in Physics, History and Dramatics?

    (a) A   (b) B   (c) D   (d) E

(ii) Who is good in Physics, History and Mathematics, but not in Computer Science.

    (a) A   (b) B   (c) C   (d) E

Solution (Ex. No. 3) On the basis of given information, we can draw the following table

Students	Dramatic	Computer Science	Physics	History	Mathematics
A	✗	✓	✓	✓	✓
B	✓	✓	✓	✗	✗
C	✗	✗	✓	✓	✓
D	✓	✗	✓	✓	✗
E	✓	✓	✗	✓	✗

(i) From the table, it is clear that, D is good in Physics, History and Dramatics.
Hence, option (c) is correct.

(ii) From the table, it is clear that C is good in Physics, History and Mathematics, but not in Computer Science.
Hence, option (c) is correct.

Practice Centre

1. There are five different houses A, B, C, D and E in a row. A is to the right of B and E is to the left of C and right of A. B is to the right of D. Which of the houses is in the middle?

   a  C   b  D   c  E   d  A

2. Five girls are sitting in a row. Veena is sitting next to Preeti but not Tina. Kavita is sitting next to Renu who is sitting on the extreme left and Tina is not sitting next to Kavita. Who are sitting adjacent to Veena?

a	Kavita and Preeti	b	Renu and Preeti
c	Preeti	d	Preeti and Tina

3. Raj, Gauri, Liya, Pihu and Ajay all go into a shop.

   - Only Gauri buys a Pizza.
   - Pihu, Liya and Raj buy a Pepsi each.
   - Everyone except Pihu buys a Milk shake each.
   - Pihu is the only one who buys pastry.
   - Nobody except Ajay and Liya chooses a sandwich.
   - Each of the girls buy a packet of Lays.

   Which child buys the most number of items?

   a  Pihu   b  Gauri   c  Liya   d  Ajay

 Direction (Q. Nos. 4-5) Read the following information and answer the questions that follow.
P, Q and R are three cities and each of them is famous for atleast one thing. P and R are not hill station. P and Q are not historical places. City R has no industries. P and Q are not alike in industries.

4. Which city is neither a historical city nor an industrial city?

a	P	b	R
c	Q	d	None of these

5. Which one of the city is industrial city?

a	Q	b	P
c	R	d	None of these

Direction (Q. Nos. 6-7) Read the following information and answer the questions that follow.

Mr. L, Mr. M, Mr. P and Mr. D are four teachers of a school. Mr L can teach English as well as Maths but not Hindi. Mr. M can teach English only. Mr. P can teach English as well as Hindi but not Maths. Mr. D can teach Maths only.

6. How many teachers can teach two subjects?

   a 2   b 1   c 4   d 3

7. For which subject there is only one teacher?

a	Maths	b	English
c	Hindi	d	None of these

Direction (Q. Nos. 8-10) Read the following information carefully to answer the question given below.

A group of seven singers, facing the audience, are standing in a line on the stage. D is to the immediate right of C. F is standing beside G. B is to the left of F. E is to the left of A. C and B have one person between them. A and D have one person between them.

8. Who is on the extreme right?

   a D   b F   c G   d E

9. Who is standing at the centre in a line on the stage?

   a C   b D   c B   d A

10. If we start counting from the left end. On which number is C?

   a 3rd   b 2nd   c 1st   d 5th

Direction (Q. Nos. 11-13) Read the information carefully to answer the questions that follow.

P, Q, R, S, T, V and W are sitting in a line facing the East. R is immediate right of S. Q is at one of the extreme ends and has T as his neighbour. W is between T and V. S is sitting third from the South end.

11. Who is sitting to the right of T ?

    a (P)   b (R)   c (W)   d (V)

12. Which of the following pairs of people are sitting at the extreme ends?

    a (P and Q)   b (R and T)   c (R and Q)   d (V and Q)

13. Name the person who should change place with R such that he gets the third place from the North end.

    a (T)   b (V)   c (W)   d (S)

Direction (Q. Nos. 14-16) Study the following information carefully and answer the given questions.
Eight friends A, B, C, D, E, F, G and H are sitting in a circle facing the centre. A, who is sitting immediately between G and C, is just opposite to F.

- E, who is sitting immediately between H and C is second to the right of A and second to the left of F.
- D is sitting second to the left of G.

14. Who is sitting between D and G?

    a A   b B   c F   d E

15. Who is sitting directly opposite to G?

    a E   b F   c H   d A

16. Who are the three friends sitting immediately to the right of B?

    a DFH   b GAC
    c AEC   d None of these

Direction (Q. Nos. 17-18) Study the following information carefully and answer the question that follow.

There are seven books one each on English, Hindi, Maths, Computer, History, Biology and Chemistry, lying on a table one above the other.

- Maths is on the top of all the books.
- History is immediately below Computer which is immediately below Maths.
- Biology is immediately above Chemistry but not in the middle.
- Hindi is immediately below Chemistry.

17. Biology is between which of the following books?

    a | History and Computer | b | Chemistry and Hindi |
    c | English and Chemistry | d | Chemistry and Maths |

18. If Maths and History, Computer and English and Biology and Hindi interchange their positions, then which book will be between Maths and Hindi?

    a | History | b | Computer |
    c | Chemistry | d | English |

Direction (Q. Nos. 19-22) Read the following information carefully and answer the questions given below.

P, Q, R, S, T, U and W are seven students in a class. They are sitting on three benches I, II and III in such a way that there are atleast two of them on each bench and there is atleast one girls on each bench. R, a girl student, does not sit with P, T and S. U, a boy student, sits with only Q. P sits with his best friend in bench I. W sits on bench III. T is brother of R.

19. On which bench do three students sit?

    a (I)   b (II)   c (III)   d (I) or (II)

20. How many boy students are there?

    a (2)   b (3)   c (4)   d (3 or 4)

21. Who sits with U?

    a (P)   b (Q)   c (R)   d (T)

22. Which of the following is a group of boys?

    a (QRS)   b (TWR)   c (TUW)   d (PWU)

Chapter 9

Direction Sense Test

'Direction Sense Test' is designed to test student's ability to determine the direction or movement of person or distance. The easiest way of solving he problems is to draw a diagram as you read the information given in the problem. The student should also be aware of directions.

- There are four main directions namely East (E), West (W), North (N) and South (S) as shown below

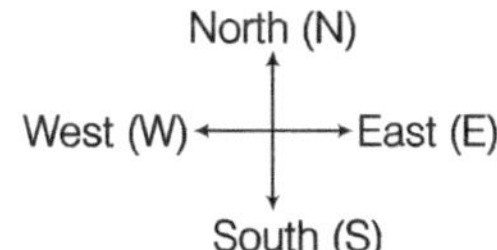

The word 'NEWS' stands for the information of all four directions.

- The other four subdirections (cardinal directions) are namely North-East (N-E), North-West (N-W), South-East (S-E) and South-West (S-W) as shown below

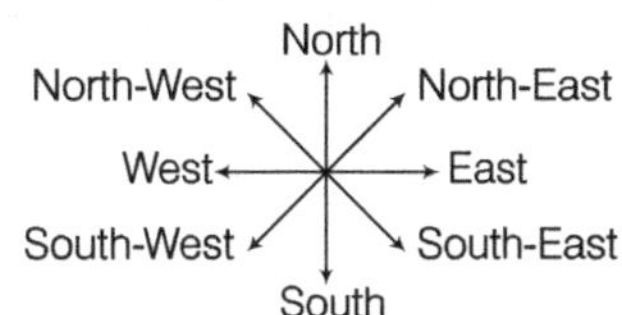

Standard direction graph

Clockwise and Anti-clockwise Direction

There are two cyclic directions namely clockwise direction (CW) and anti-clockwise direction (ACW). The direction of moving a clock's hand is called clockwise direction while its opposite direction is called anti-clockwise direction as shown in adjacent figure.

For example, Rahul is facing East, he turns 45° in the anti-clockwise direction. Which direction is he facing now?

(a) North   (b) North-East   (c) South   (d) South-East

Here, we know that the angle between two consecutive major and subdirections is always 45° .

So, Rahul is facing North-East as shown in adjacent figure.

Hence, option (b) is correct.

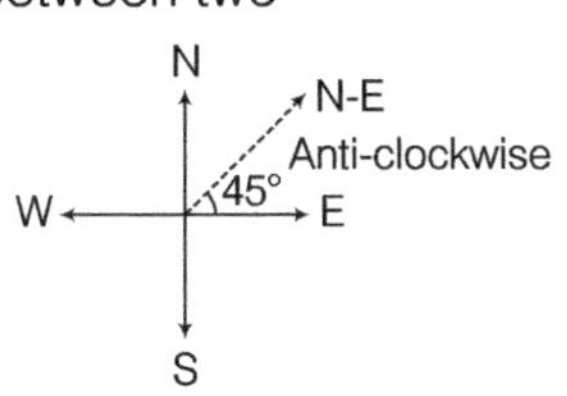

Important Points

- Angle between two consecutive major directions is always 90°.

- Angle between two consecutive subdirections is always 90°.

- Angle between two consecutive major and subdirections is always 45°.

- At the time of Sunrise, if a man stands facing East, his shadow will be towards West.

- At the time of Sunset the shadow of an object is always in the East.

- If a man stands facing the North, at the time of Sunrise his shadow will be towards his left and at the time of Sunset it will be towards his right.

- At 12 : 00 noon, the rays of the Sun are vertically downward, hence there will be no shadow.

In direction sense test, questions are based on following two types

    (i) Direction identification   (ii) Distance calculation

Direction Identification

In these types of questions, the path travelled by a person is given and students are required to find out the final direction.

In direction identification, following types of questions are generally asked

EXAMPLE 1 Rahul starts from his house facing towards East and moves 5 m, then turns right and moves 4 m. Again, he turns right and moves 5 m. Towards which direction is he facing now?

    (a) West   (b) South   (c) North   (d) East

Think • First of all, read the question and find out the initial direction of the person/object.

       • After observing we find that, initially Rahul is facing towards East, now we will draw a direction graph by following step-by-step information.

Sol. Rahul is facing towards East and moves 5 m.   Now, he takes right turn and moves 4 m.

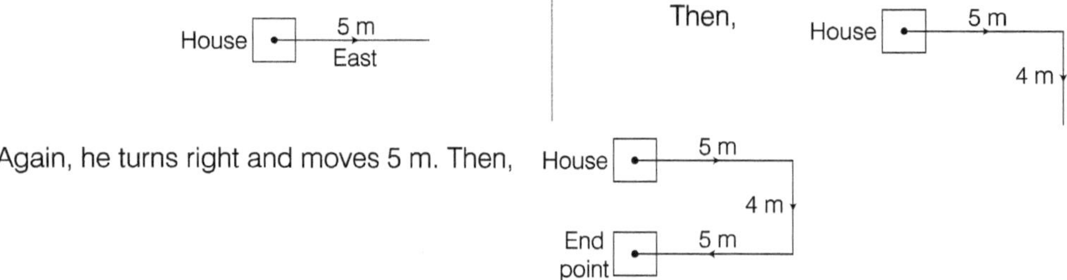

Again, he turns right and moves 5 m. Then,

Now, comparing the above drawn direction graph with standard direction graph we see that, Rahul is facing toward the 'West' direction.

Hence, option (a) is correct.

Distance Calculation

In these types of questions, total distance travelled by a person from his starting point to end point is calculated.

In distance calculation, following types of questions are generally asked

EXAMPLE 1 Manu starts from point P towards West. After covering 10 km, he turns to his right and covers 20 km, then again he turns to his left and covers 30 km. Find the total distance covered by Manu.

    (a) 30 km   (b) 40 km   (c) 50 km   (d) 60 km

Think It is clear that Manu starts towards West direction.

Sol. Manu starts from P and covers 10 km in West direction.

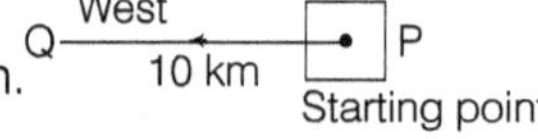

Now, he turns to his right and covers 20 km.   He again, turns to his left and travels 30 km.

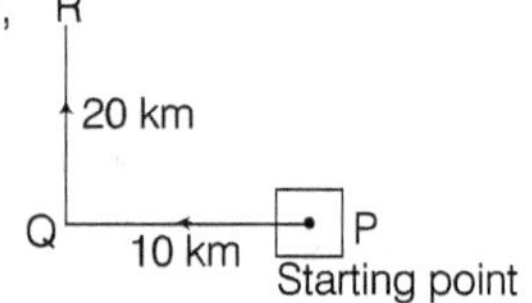 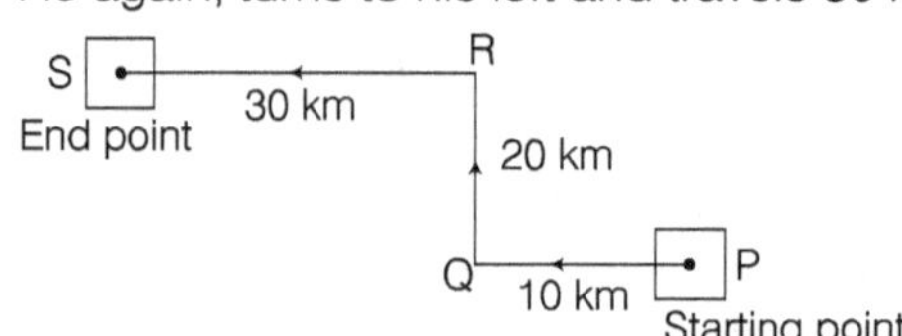

Now, total distance covered by Manu = PQ + QR + RS = 10 + 20 + 30 = 60 km

Hence, option (d) is correct.

 **Practice Centre**

Direction (Q. Nos. 1-4) Find the directions which replaces question mark (?) in the following questions.

1. 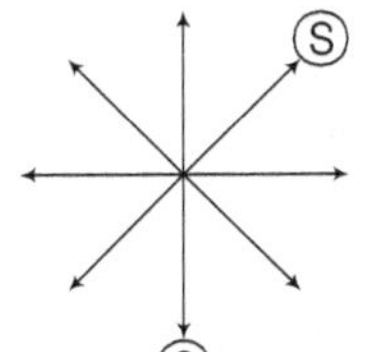

a N   b NW
c SW   d W

2. 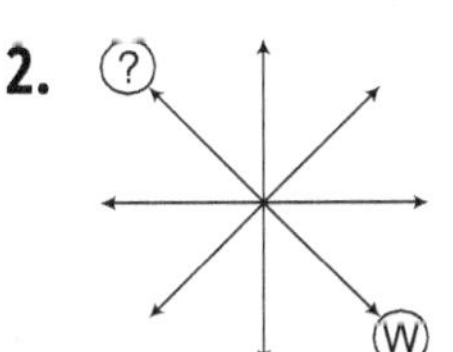

a S   b SE
c E   d NE

3. 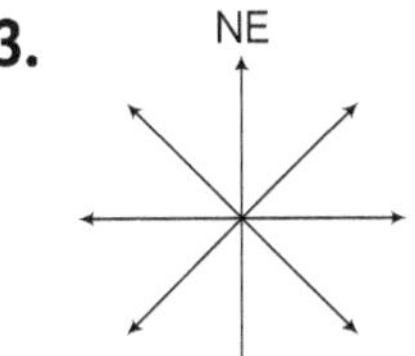

a SW   b SE
c W   d E

4. 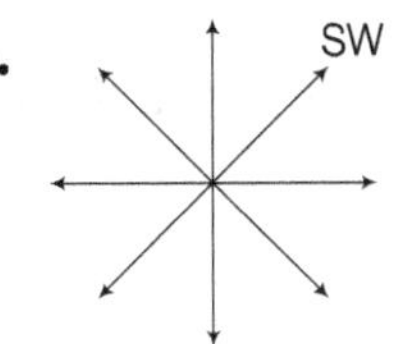

a NE   b S
c W   d N

Direction (Q. Nos. 5-6) In the following diagrams, if CW indicates clockwise and ACW indicates anti-clockwise and arrow indicates the direction of movement. Then, fill the appropriate directions in the circle.

5. 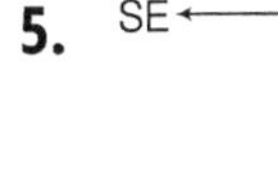

a NW   b NE
c SW   d N

6. 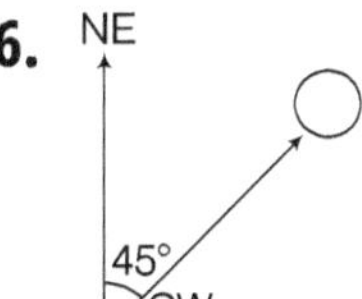

a S   b N
c E   d W

7. Manish starts towards South direction. Which of the following orders of directions will lead him to East direction?
a Left, Left, Left
b Right, Right, Right
c Left, Right, Right
d Right, Left, Right

8. A rat runs 30 m towards East, turns right and runs 20 m. He turns right and runs 8 m. He again turns left and runs 6 m and then turns left and runs 15 m. Finally he turns left and runs 7 m. Now, in which direction is the rat facing?
a North
b North-East
c East
d West

9. Village Chimur is 20 km to the North of village Rewa. Village Rahate is 16 km to the East of Village Rewa. Village Angne is 10 km to the West of Chimur. If Rahul starts from village Rahate and goes to village Angne, in which direction is he from his starting point?
a North
b North-West
c South
d South-East

10. A man walks 30 m towards South. Then, turning to his right he walks 30 m. Then, turning to his left he walks 20 m. Again turning to his left he walks 30 m. How far is he from his starting position?
a 30 m   b 50 m
c 20 m   d 60 m

11. Kajal is facing towards North and turns through 45° anti-clockwise, then 135° clockwise and again 90° clockwise. In which direction is she facing now?

  a East   **b** West

  c South   **d** North

12. Sorabh is facing towards West and turns through 90° clockwise, again 45° clockwise and then turns through 180° anti-clockwise. In which direction is he facing now?

  a North-West

  b South-West

  c North-East

  d South

13. If 'South-West' is called 'West', 'North-West' is called 'North', 'South-East' is called 'South', and so on, what will 'East' be called?

  a North

  b South-East

  c North-East

  d East

14. Gaurav is facing North-West. He turns 90° in the clockwise direction, then 180° in the anti-clockwise direction and then another 90° in the same direction. Which direction is he facing now?

  a South-East   **b** South

  c West   **d** South-West

15. A ship is sailing towards South-East. The captain ordered to turn the ship by angle of 135° in anti-clockwise direction and then 225° in clockwise direction. In which direction is it sailing now?

  a North-West   **b** South

  c South-West   **d** East

16. Sandeep was facing the 'DOMINOS' at the beginning. He turned anti-clockwise to face South-East. What angle did he turn through?

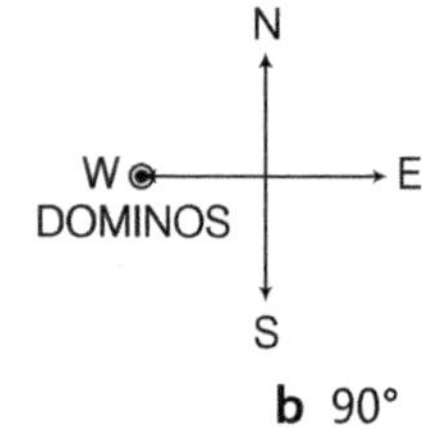

  a 45°   **b** 90°

  c 135°   **d** 80°

17. Starting from a point 'A', Harsh walked 20 m towards South. He turned to his left and walked 15 m. He then turned to his left and walked 25 m. He again turned to his right and walked 10 m. Find the total distance covered by Harsh.

  a 25 m   **b** 45 m

  c 60 m   **d** 70 m

18. Meenu walks 6 km to the East and then turns to the South and walks 5 km. Again she turns to the East and walks 6 km. Next, she turns Northwards and walks 10 km. How far is she now from her starting point?

  a 5 km   **b** 12 km

  c 13 km   **d** 17 km

19. Kuldeep puts his timepiece on the table in such a way that at 6 : 00 pm, hour hand points to North. In which direction the minute hand will point at 9 : 15 pm?

  a West   **b** South-East

  c North   **d** South

20. Vijay walks 10 km towards North from there, he walks 6 km towards South. Then, he walks 3 km towards East. How far and in which direction is he with reference to his starting point?

  a 5 km, West

  b 5 km, North-East

  c 7 km, East

  d 7 km, West

21. Abhishek, Tarun, Rohit and Sahil are friends. They play carrom board. Partner faces in opposite directions. Abhishek and Tarun become partners. Sahil faces South, if Abhishek faces towards East, then who faces towards North?

  a Tarun   **b** Rohit

  c Sahil   **d** Data inadequate

22. A lady leaves her office. She first walks 40 m in South-West direction then 40 m in South-East direction. Next she walks 40 m in North-East direction. Finally, she turns towards her office. In which direction is she moving now?

  a South-West

  b North-East

  c South-East

  d North-West

Chapter 10

Venn Diagram

A 'Venn Diagram' is a pictorial representation which is used to show relation between two or more objects or group of objects. The respective objects may or may not have common properties amongst them. To draw a Venn diagram, we generally use circles, triangles, squares and rectangles.

For example, Consider the three terms–hospital, doctor and patient. Which one of the given two Venn diagrams represents the relation among these three?

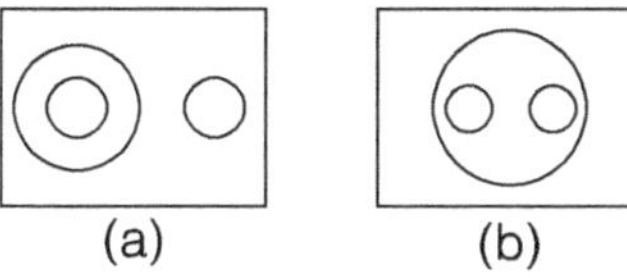

(a)   (b)

As we know that, both doctor and patient are different from each other but both of them are related to hospital. This can be represented in the figure below

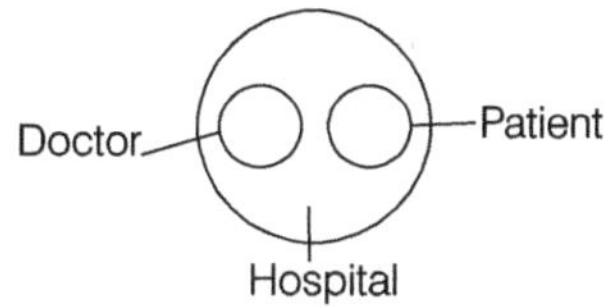

Hence, option (b) represents the correct relationship among hospital, doctor and patient.

In Venn diagram, following types of questions are generally asked

EXAMPLE 1 Study the diagram and identify the group of students who likes all the three items.

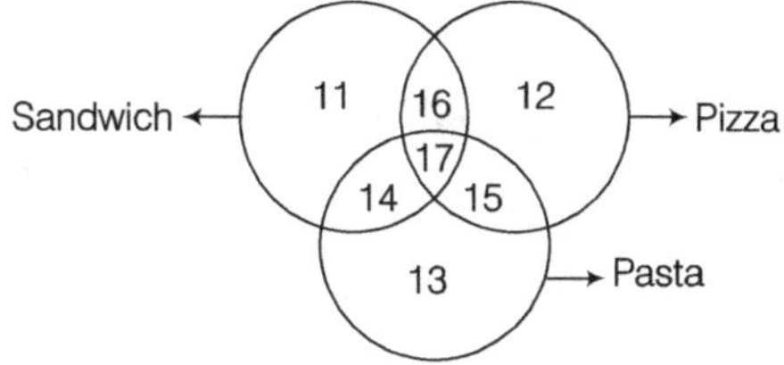

    (a) 17   (b) 16   (c) 14   (d) 15

Think After analysing we see that, all the three circles are labeled and there are some numbers written in the circles, with in the common region of two and three circles.

Sol. The group of students who likes all the three items is represented by the number 17, which is common to all the three circles.

Hence, option (a) is correct.

Practice Centre

Direction (Q. Nos. 1-4) Which of the following diagrams indicates the best relation amongst the given items?

1. Vegetable, fruit, brinjal

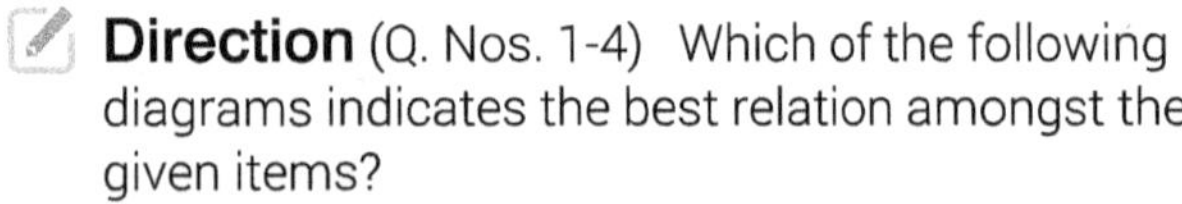

2. Door, window, house

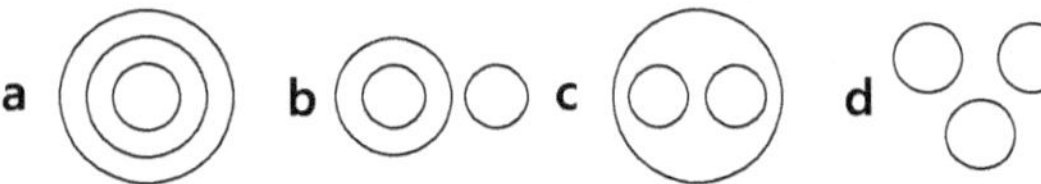

3. Honest, intelligent, poor

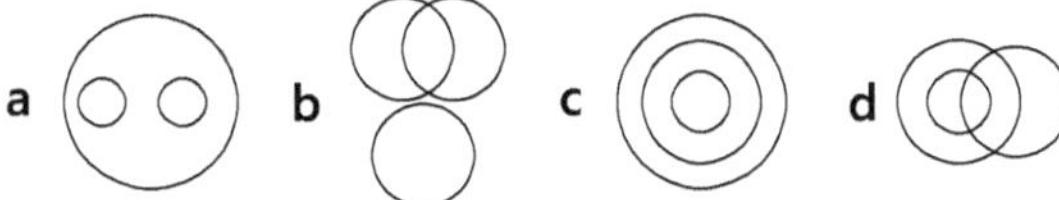

4. Keyboard, monitor, mouse

Direction (Q. Nos. 5-8) The four Venn diagrams (a), (b), (c) and (d) are given below. Elements in each of the following questions can be represented by any one of the Venn diagram.
Choose the correct Venn diagram from the options.

5. Chapter, book, topic   6. Picture, TV, radio

7. Cup, plate, spoon   8. Copy, stationery, car

Direction (Q. Nos. 9-10) Study the following figure and then answer the questions given below.

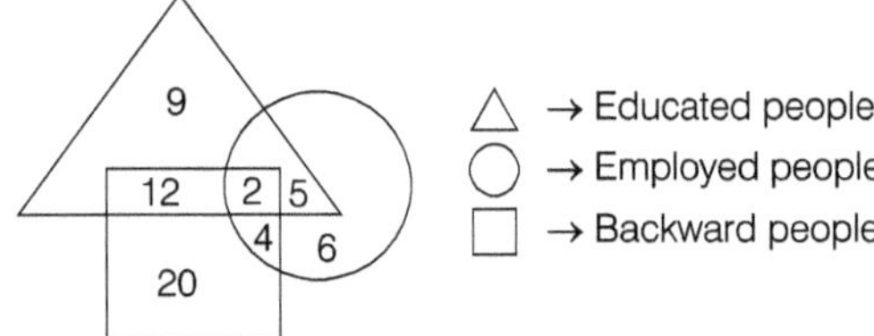

9. How many educated people are employed?
    a 5   b 7   c 11   d 6

10. How many people are educated who are neither employed nor backward?
    a 9   b 7   c 20   d 5

11. What is represented by the number '2' in the following figure?

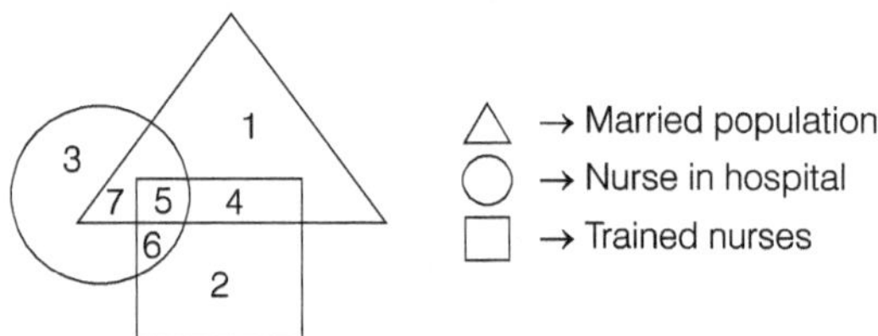

   a Married nurses in the hospital
   b Trained nurses who are neither married nor in hospital
   c Unmarried trained nurses
   d Married trained nurses

12. Which of the following Venn diagrams correctly describes the relationship amongst clothes, flowers, bright things?

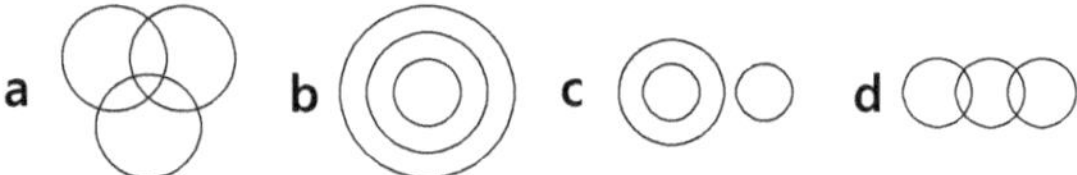

13. Study the diagram and identify the people who speak all the three languages.

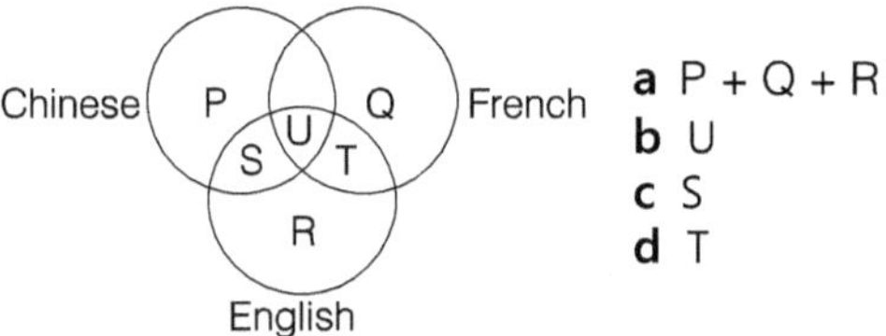

   a P + Q + R
   b U
   c S
   d T

14. Study the diagram and identify the student who likes ice-cream and cake, but not dosa?

   a E   b F   c D   d B

Chapter 11

Blood Relations

'Blood Relations' involve analysis of information showing relationship among members of a family. In these questions, a chain of relationship is given in the form of information and on the basis of this information relation between any two members of the chain is asked. Students are supposed to be familiar with the knowledge of different relationships in a family.

For example, If Ridhan is the son of my father's wife. Then, how is he related to me?

(a) Brother   (b) Uncle   (c) Nephew   (d) Cousin

Here, the wife of my father is my mother and the son of my mother is my brother.

So, Ridhan is my brother.

Hence, option (a) is correct.

Some important relations are provided below

1.	Mother's or Father's son	Brother	9.	Daughter's husband	Son-in-law
2.	Mother's or father's daughter	Sister	10.	Husband's or wife's father	Father-in-law
3.	Uncle's or Aunt's son or daughter	Cousin	11.	Husband's or wife's mother	Mother-in-law
4.	Mother's or Father's brother	Uncle	12.	Husband's or wife's brother	Brother-in-law
5.	Mother's or Father's sister	Aunt	13.	Husband's or wife's sister	Sister-in-law
6.	Mother's or Father's father	Grandfather	14.	Sister's Husband	Brother-in-law
7.	Mother's or Father's mother	Grandmother	15.	Brother's or sister's son	Nephew
8.	Son's wife	Daughter-in-law	16.	Brother's or sister's daughter	Niece

Maternal relations Relations on mother's side are called 'maternal'.

Paternal relations Relations on father's side are called 'paternal'.

Note *In blood relations, 'M' symbol is used to denote a male and 'F' symbol is used to denote a female.*

In blood relations, following types of questions are generally asked

EXAMPLE 1 Introducing Asha to guests, Banny said, "Her father is the only son of my father". How is Asha related to Banny?

(a) Niece   (b) Daughter   (c) Sister   (d) Mother

Think First of all, read the given information carefully and connect the relations with each other by following step-by-step procedure.

Sol. The only son of Banny's father is the Banny himself. This means that Banny is the father of Asha. So, Asha is the daughter of Banny.

Hence, option (b) is correct.

EXAMPLE 2 A is brother of Q, B is father of A, S is wife of B. What is S of Q?

    (a) Grandmother (b) Mother   (c) Uncle   (d) Aunt

Think Draw a relation diagram by following each statement.

Sol. Here, A is brother of Q, then

    B is father of A, then

    S is wife of B, then

It is clearly shown that, S is mother of Q.

Hence, option (b) is correct.

EXAMPLE 3 Read the following information and answer the questions that follow.

- P Q, R, S, T and U are six members of a family.
- One couple has parents and their children in the family.
- P is the son of R and T is the daughter of P.
- S is the daughter of U who is the mother of T.

(i) How many female members are there in the family?

    (a) 2   (b) 5   (c) 3   (d) 4

(ii) Which of the following pairs is the parents of the children?

    (a) Q and R   (b) P and U   (c) R and U   (d) Q and U

(iii) Who are the male members in the family?

    (a) P and R   (b) P, Q and S   (c) R and U   (d) Cannot be determined

Think • Analyse the given information and draw a relation diagram.

      • After drawing the relation diagram, read each and every question and answer it after observing the drawn diagram.

Sol. On the basis of given information, the relation diagram of a family can be drawn as shown below

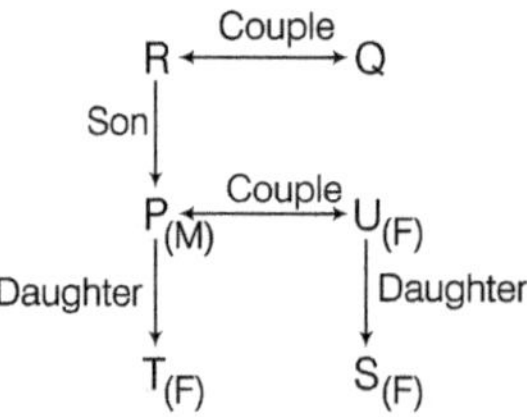

(i) From the above diagram, it is clearly shown that there are 4 females in the family is U, T, S and either R or Q.

Hence, option (d) is correct.

(ii) P and U are the parents of the children.

Hence, option (b) is correct.

(iii) Here, from the above diagram, we can see that P is a male but we cannot determined the gender of R and Q.

Hence, option (d) is correct.

Practice
Centre

1. Showing the lady in the park, Vineet said, "She is the daughter of my grandfather's only son". How is Vineet related to that lady?
   - **a** Cousin
   - **b** Brother
   - **c** Father
   - **d** Uncle

2. Introducing a man, a women said, "His wife is the only daughter of my father". How is that man related to the woman?
   - **a** Brother
   - **b** Father-in-law
   - **c** Husband
   - **d** None of these

3. Introducing a man, a woman said, "He is the only son of my mother's mother". How is the woman related to that man?
   - **a** Niece
   - **b** Mother
   - **c** Aunt
   - **d** Cousin

4. Pointing to a man in the park, Naman said, "His son is my son's uncle." How is the man related to Naman?
   - **a** Brother
   - **b** Grandfather
   - **c** Uncle
   - **d** Father

5. Introducing a man, Neeraj said, "His wife is the only daughter of my wife". How is Neeraj related to that man?
   - **a** Father-in-law
   - **b** Son
   - **c** Grandfather
   - **d** Brother

6. P is the mother of Q, but Q is not the daughter of P. What is q to P?
   - **a** Son
   - **b** Daughter
   - **c** Father
   - **d** None of these

7. Mr. Shyam's wife Sonam has two children Sahil and Shalu. Mitesh is the brother of Shyam. How is Mitesh related to Shalu?
   - **a** Father
   - **b** Mother
   - **c** Daughter
   - **d** Uncle

8. L and M are two children of O. Who is the father of L? To answer this question which of the following statements is/are necessary?
   - I. N is the brother of L and the son of P.
   - II. R is the mother of M.
   - **a** Only I
   - **b** Only II
   - **c** Either I or II
   - **d** Both I and II

9. A is the brother of B.C is the brother of A. To establish a relationship between B and C, which of the following information is required?
   - I. Gender of C
   - II. Gender of B
   - **a** Only I
   - **b** Only II
   - **c** Both I and II
   - **d** Neither I nor II

10. A is son of B, C is wife of A, E is daughter of C. How is E is related to B?
    - **a** Granddaughter
    - **b** Grandson
    - **c** Son
    - **d** Daughter

11. A is grandson of B, C and D are sons of B, A is son of C, how is A related to D?
    - **a** Niece
    - **b** Father
    - **c** Aunt
    - **d** Nephew

12. P is brother of Q, R is daughter of P, S is son of Q, how are R and S related?
    - **a** Cousins
    - **b** Brothers
    - **c** Sisters
    - **d** Not related

13. Introducing Reena, Sachin said, "Her Father is my mother's only son". How is Reena related to Sachin?
    - **a** Son
    - **b** Daughter
    - **c** Mother
    - **d** Father

14. P and Q are two brothers. L is M's brother, but M is the mother of P. What is L to Q?

   a Mother   **b** Uncle
   c Father   **d** Sister-in-law

15. A is the brother of B. C is the sister of A. What is C to B?

   a Sister   **b** Daughter
   c Mother   **d** Uncle

16. A husband and his wife have 4 married sons, one unmarried son and 3 unmarried daughters. How many members are there is the family?

   a 12   **b** 18
   c 9   **d** 14

17. A photograph shows Mr. A, Mr. B, Mrs. L and Mrs. N, Mrs. L and Mrs. N are sisters. Mrs. L is wife of Mr. A and Mrs. N is wife of Mr. B. What is Mr. A of Mr. B?

   a Father-in-law
   b Sister-in-law
   c Brother-in-law
   d Daughter-in-law

18. In Mr. Sharma's family, there are one grandfather, one grandmother, two fathers, two mothers, one father-in-law, one mother-in-law, four children, three grandchildren, one brother, two sisters, two sons, two daughters and one daughter-in-law. How many members are there in Mr. Shrama's family?

   a 17   **b** 23
   c 25   **d** 7

Direction (Q. Nos. 19-22) Study the following information carefully and answer the questions given below.

- Five persons are sitting around dinning table K, L, M, N and O.
- K is the mother of M, who is the wife of O.
- N is the brother of K.
- L is the husband of K.

19. How is L related to O?

   a Father-in-law
   b Mother-in-law
   c Father
   d Brother-in-law

20. How is K related to O?

   a Sister
   b Mother
   c Mother-in-law
   d Brother-in-law

21. How is N related to L?

   a Son
   b Brother-in-law
   c Uncle
   d Cousin

22. How is M related to L?

   a Aunt   **b** Niece
   c Mother   **d** Daughter

Direction (Q. Nos. 23-24) Study the following information carefully and answer the questions given below.

- There is a family of six persons A, B, C, D, E and F.
- There are two married couples.
- D is grandmother of A and mother of B.
- C is wife of B and mother of F.
- F is the granddaughter of E.

23. How is C related to A?

   a Mother
   b Daughter
   c Cousin
   d Grandmother

24. How many female members are there in the family?

   a 2
   b 3
   c 3 or 4
   d None of the above

Non-Verbal Reasoning

7

Chapter 12

Similar Pairs

In 'Similar Pairs', the figures or shapes of a pair are related to each other according to a certain pattern or characteristics. The figures or shapes in other pair are related to each other in the similar way as first pair.

'Similar Pairs' are also known as 'Analogy' and the pairs are called 'Analogous Pairs'.

For example, Consider the following figures and complete the second pair in the same way as first pair.

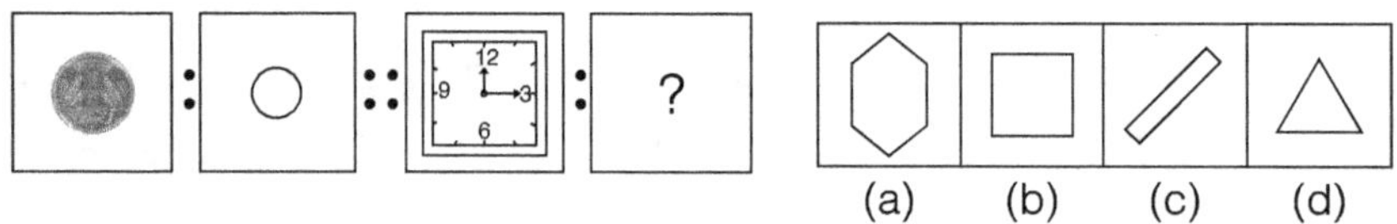

Here, as the shape of the coin is circular, Similarly, the shape of the given clock is square. So, option figure (b) will complete the second pair.

Hence, option (b) is correct.

In similar pairs, following types of questions are generally asked

EXAMPLE 1 Which figure will complete the second pair in the same way as first pair?

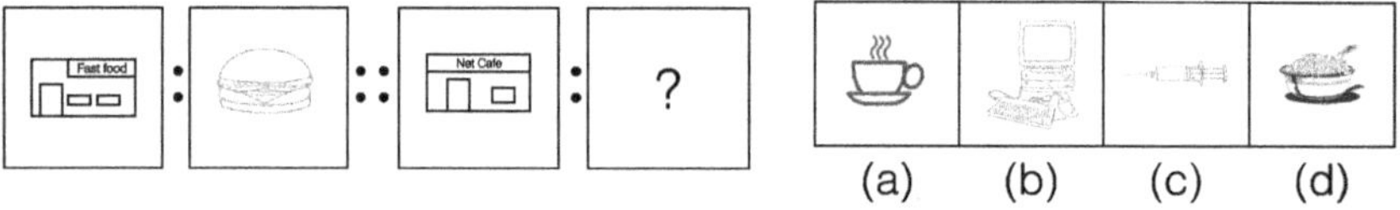

(**Think**) • First of all look at the first pair of figures and try to find out the relation between both the figures.
• After observing we see that, object in second figure can be obtained from the place given in first figure.

Sol. As, burger is related to fast food corner. Similarly, computer system is related to net cafe.
So, option figure (b) will complete the second pair.
Hence, option (b) is correct.

EXAMPLE 2 Find the correct figure which replaces the question mark.

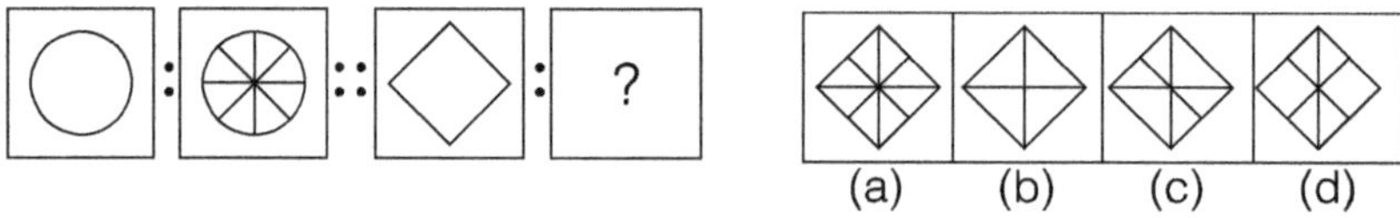

(**Think**) After observing we see that, first figure is divided into eight equal parts to obtain the second figure.

Sol. In first pair, the circle is divided into eight equal parts to obtain the second figure. Similarly, in the second pair the square will be divided into eight equal parts to obtain the second figure.
So, option figure (a) will complete the second pair.
Hence, option (a) is correct.

Practice
Centre

Direction (Q. Nos. 1-24) Which figure/pattern will complete the second pair in the same way as first pair?

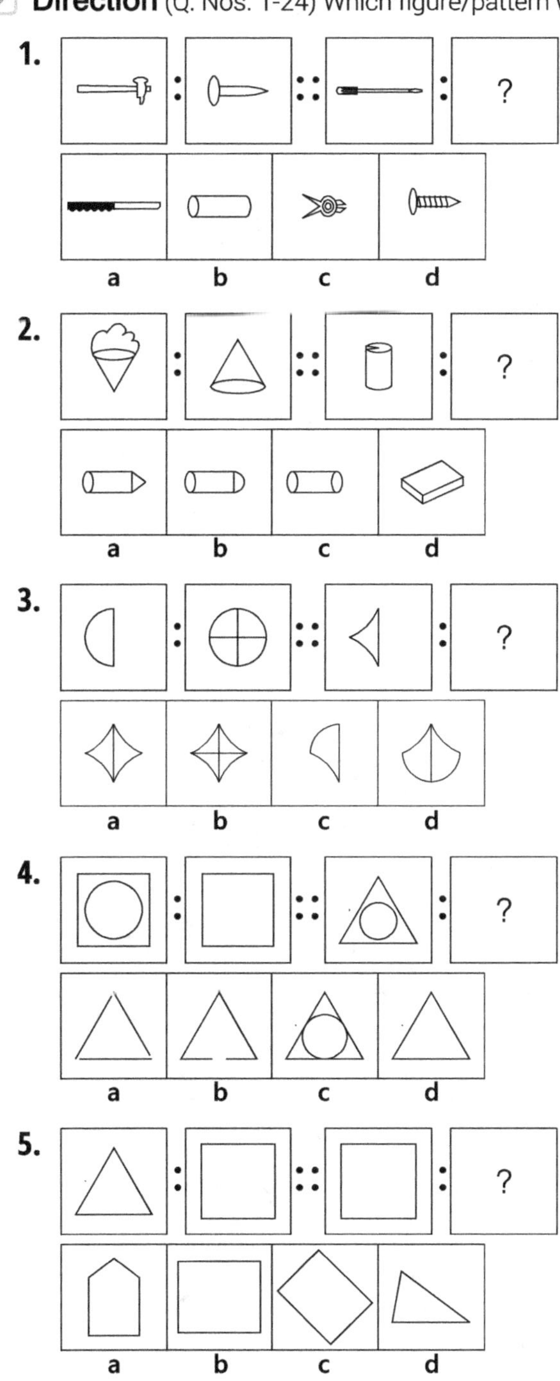

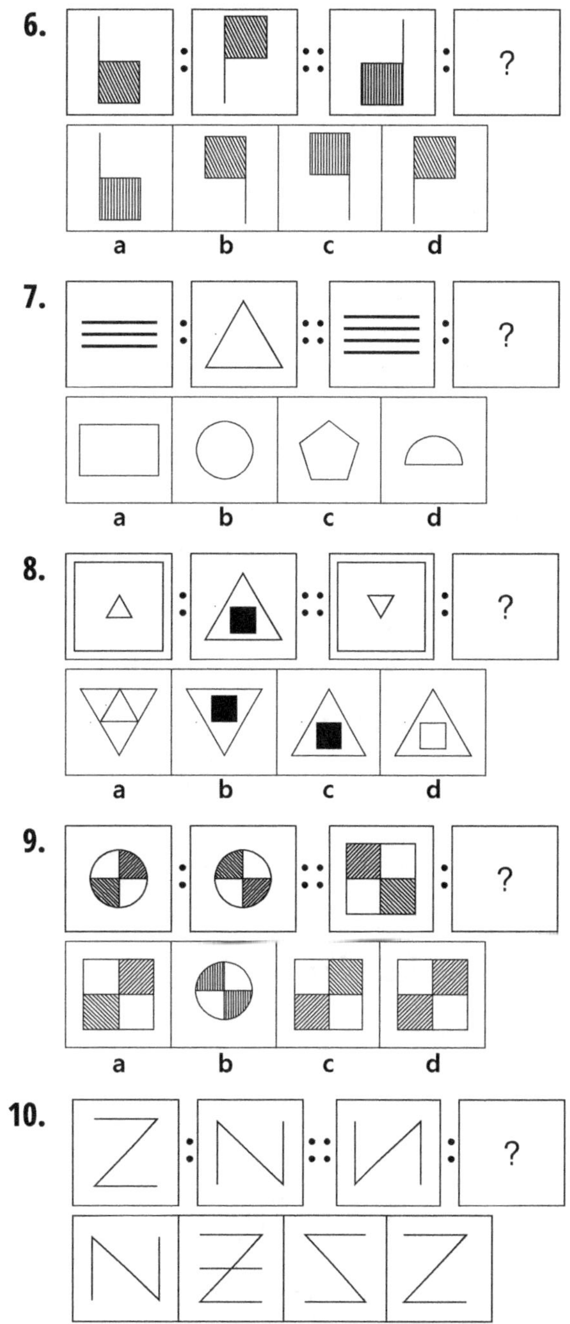

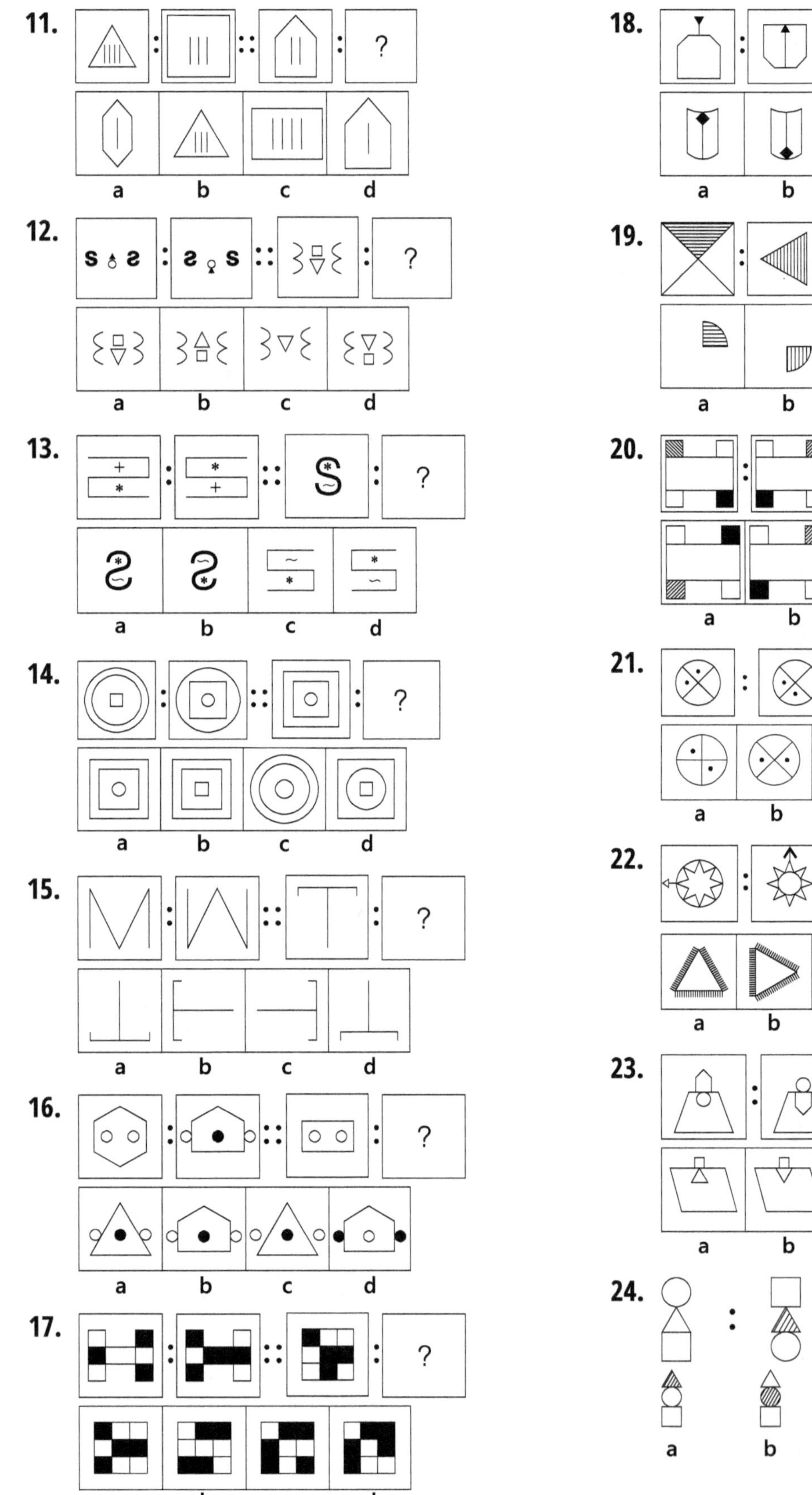

Chapter 13

What Comes Next?

In 'What Comes Next?', a set of figures or shapes is given. These figures or shapes follow a certain pattern. The students are required to identify the pattern and find out the next or missing figure or shape of the given set.

'What Comes Next?' is also known as 'Series'.

For example, Consider the following figures and find out the missing figure for this set.

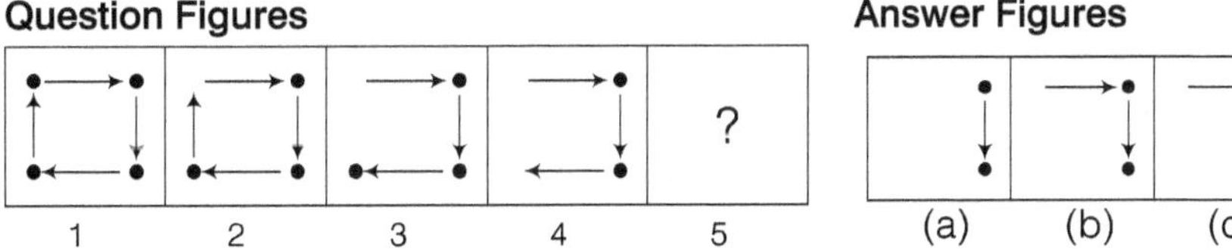

After careful observation we see that, in each successive step, an element is removed in anti-clockwise direction starting from the top left corner.

So, in fifth figure, the arrow placed at bottom centre will be removed.

Thus, will be the fifth figure of the above set of figures.

Hence, option (b) is correct.

In what comes next, following types of questions are generally asked

EXAMPLE 1 What comes next in the series given below?

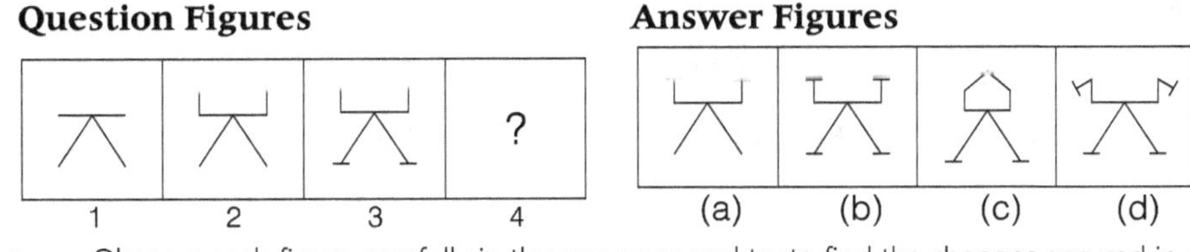

Think • Observe each figure carefully in the sequence and try to find the changes occured in each successive step.

• After observing we find that, in each successive figure, lines are added in a particular manner.

Sol. Here, each time two lines are added at top and bottom, respectively as shown below

Therefore, in fourth figure, the lines will be added at the top as shown in adjacent figure

So, option figure (b) will come next.

Hence, option (b) is correct.

EXAMPLE 2 Find the missing term of the series given below.

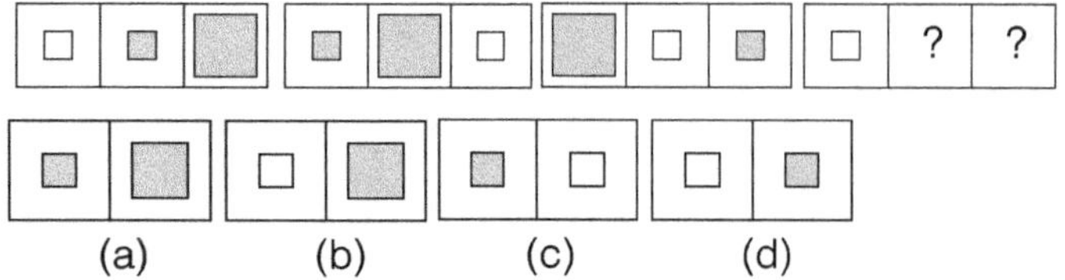

(a) (b) (c) (d)

Think After observing we see that, in each successive step, each figure is moving from right to left in the set.

Sol. Here, starting from the extreme right first figure becomes second, second figure becomes third and the third figure becomes first. On the following this pattern, option figure (a) will complete the series as shown below

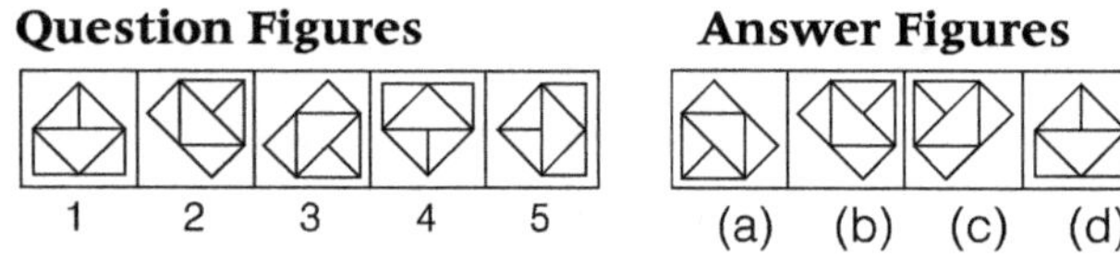

Hence, option (a) is correct.

EXAMPLE 3 Find the next term in the series given below.

Question Figures   Answer Figures

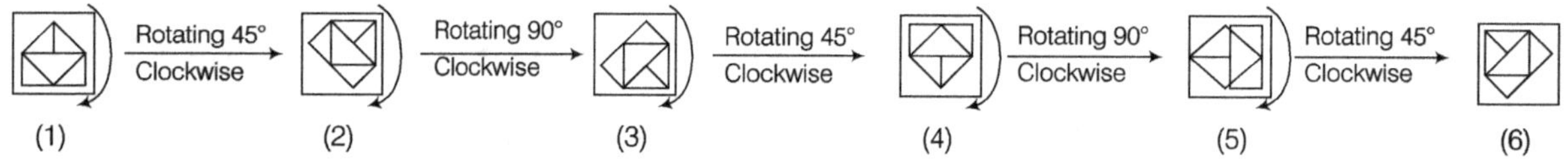

1   2   3   4   5   (a) (b) (c) (d)

Think After observing we see that, figures are following rotation pattern.

Sol. Here, the previous figure is rotated 45° and 90°, alternatively in clockwise direction to obtain the next figure as shown below

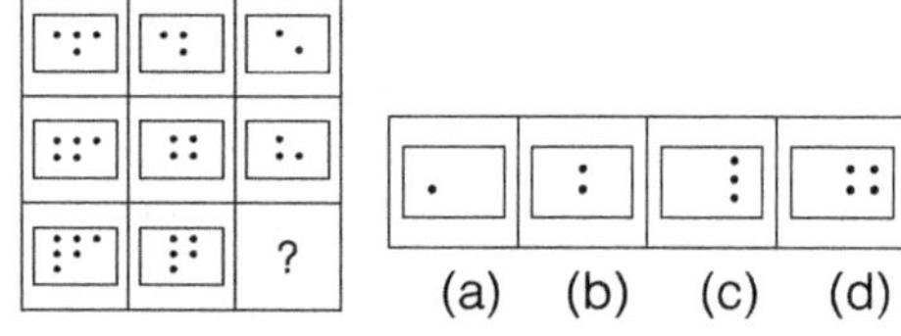

(1)   (2)   (3)   (4)   (5)   (6)

So, option figure (c) will be the next term.
Hence, option (c) is correct.

Figure Matrix

In figure matrix, figures or shapes are arranged in cells of the matrix. This arrangement of figures or shapes follows a certain pattern. The students are required to identify the pattern and find out the missing figure or shape that will complete the given matrix.

'Figure matrix' is also known as 'Grid completion'.

In figure matrix, following types of questions are generally asked

EXAMPLE 1 Select a figure from the options that will complete the following figure matrix.

(a) (b) (c) (d)

Think After observing we see that, the matrix follow both columnwise and rowwise pattern.

Sol. Consider columnwise, a dot is removed from column (I) to column (II) and column (II) to column (III).
Consider rowwise, a dot is added from row (I) to row (II) and row (II) to row (III).
So, it will be four dots in the last block of third column and third row.

Hence, option (d) is correct.

Practice
Centre

 Direction (Q. Nos. 1-16) Find the next term in the series given below.

1. 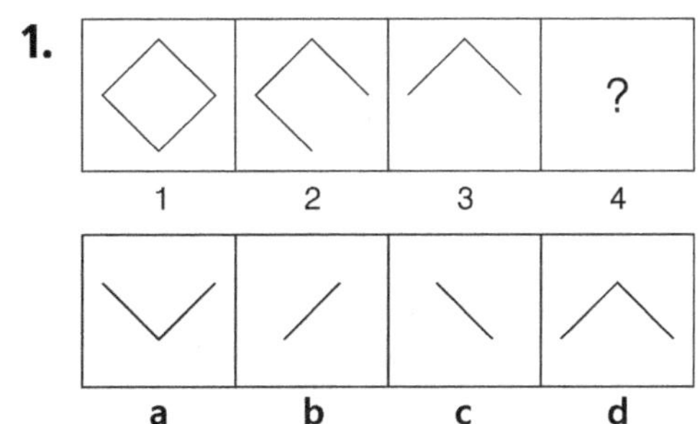

2. 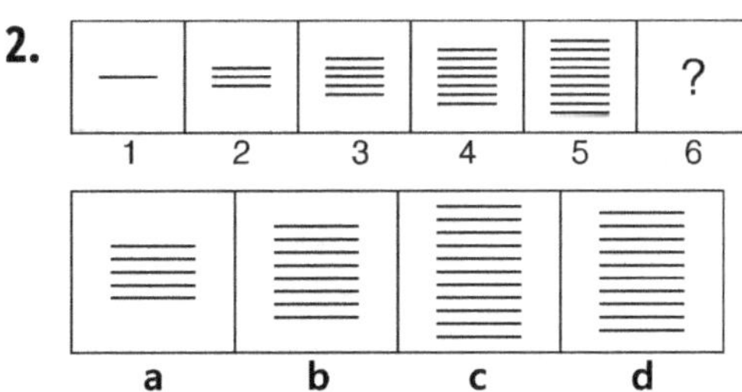

3. 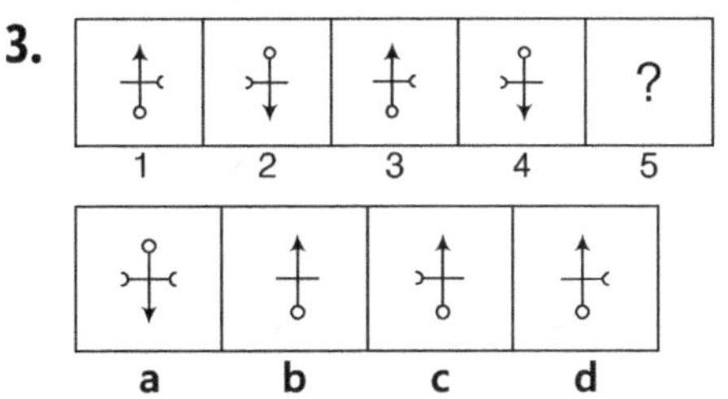

4. 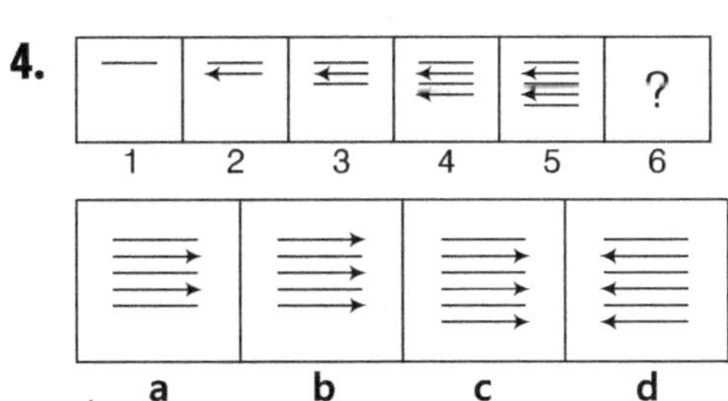

5. 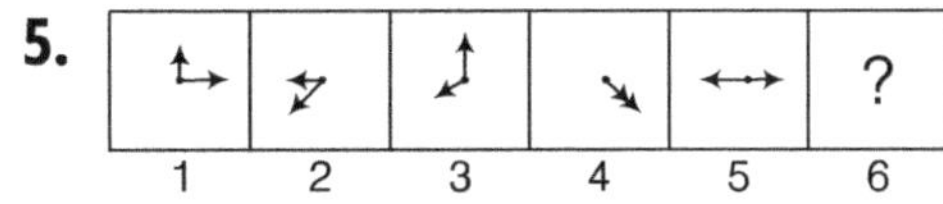

6. 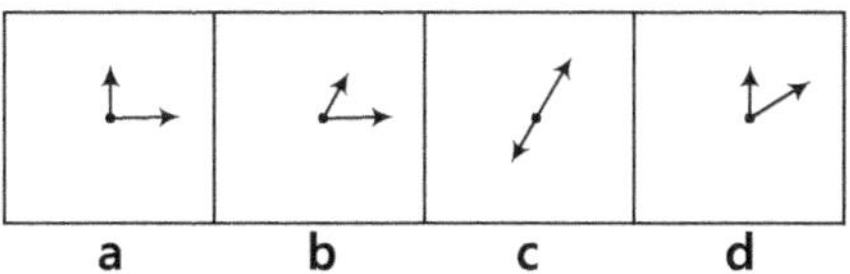

7. 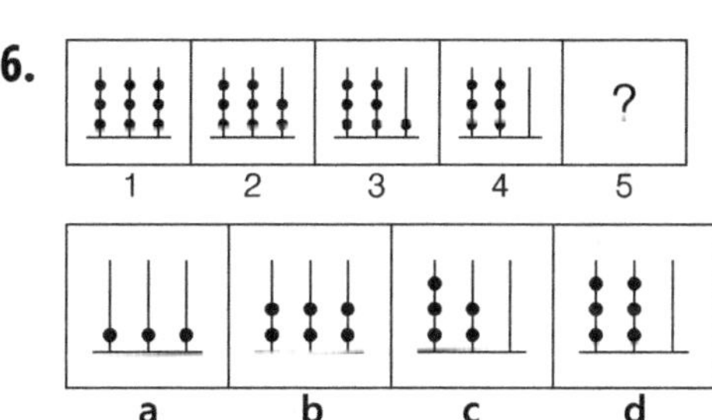

8. 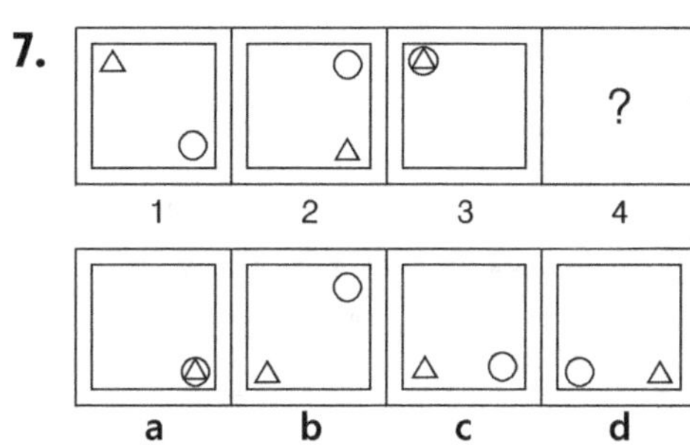

9. 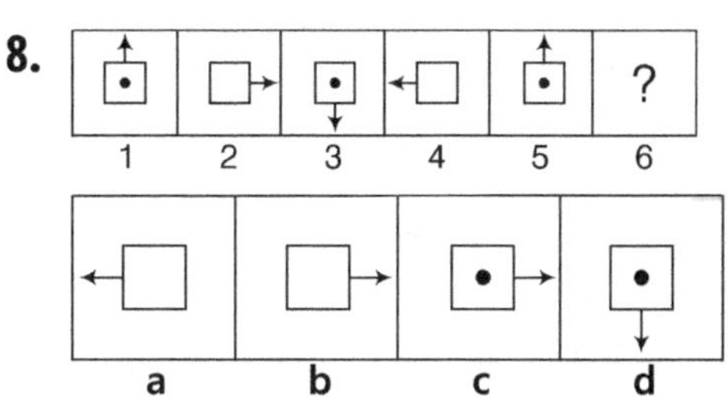

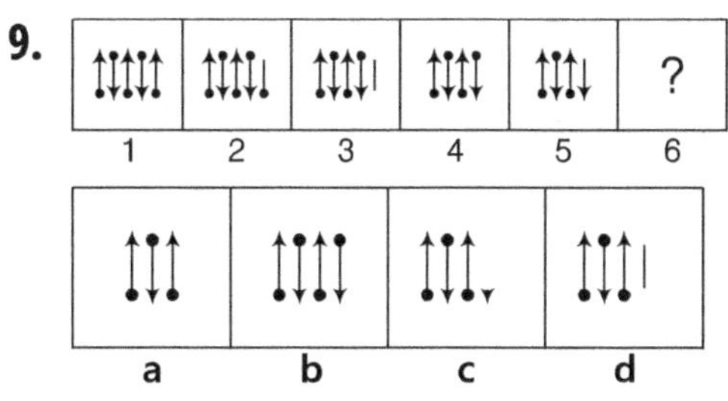

10.

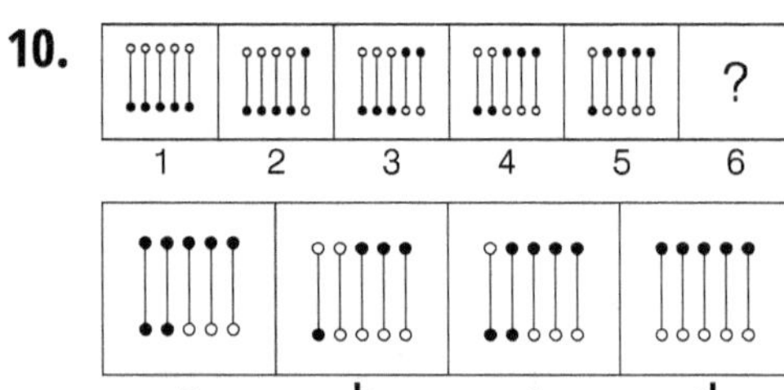

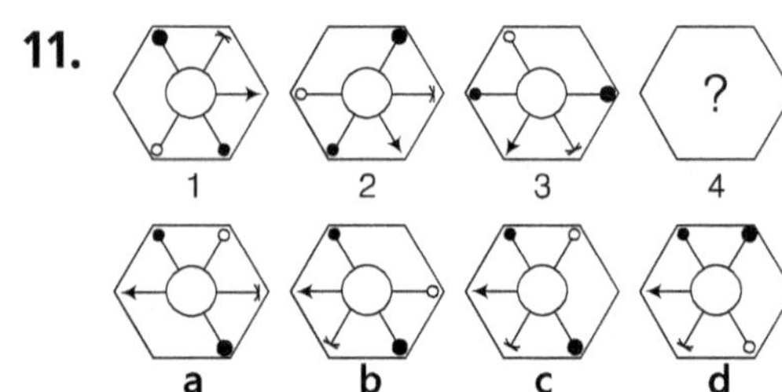

11.

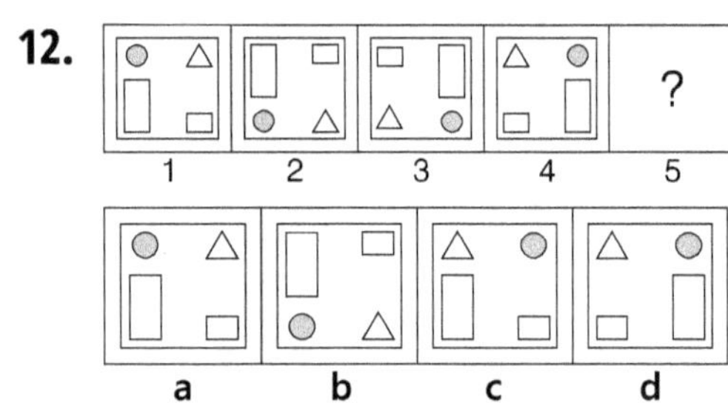

12.

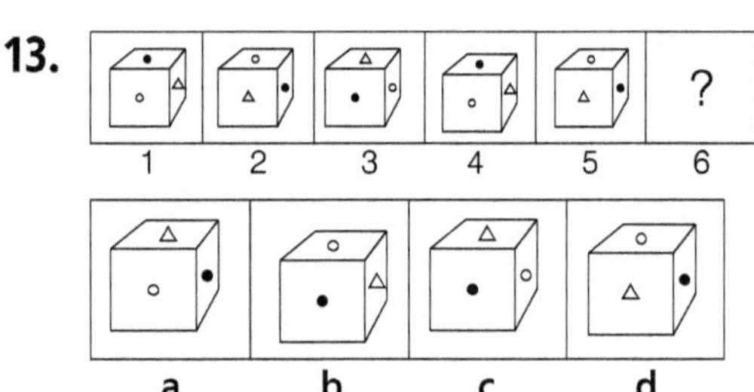

13.

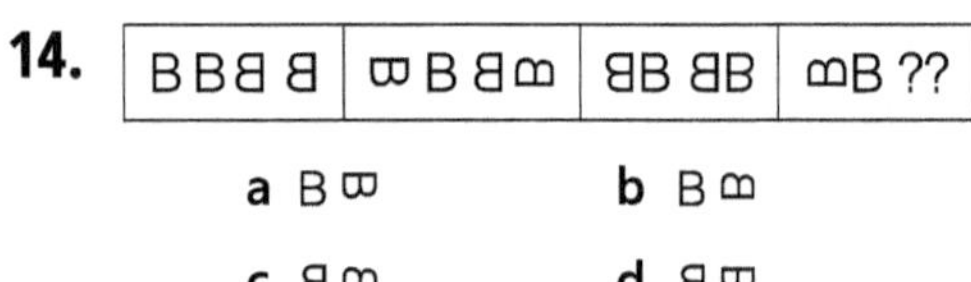

14.

BBBB	BBBB	BB BB	BB ??

a BB   **b** BB

c BB   **d** BB

15.

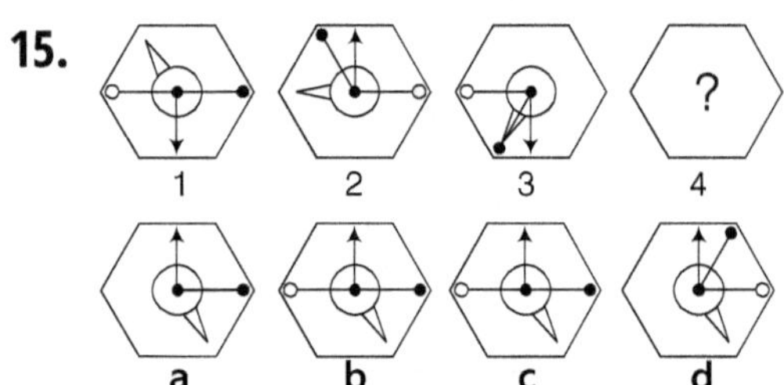

16.

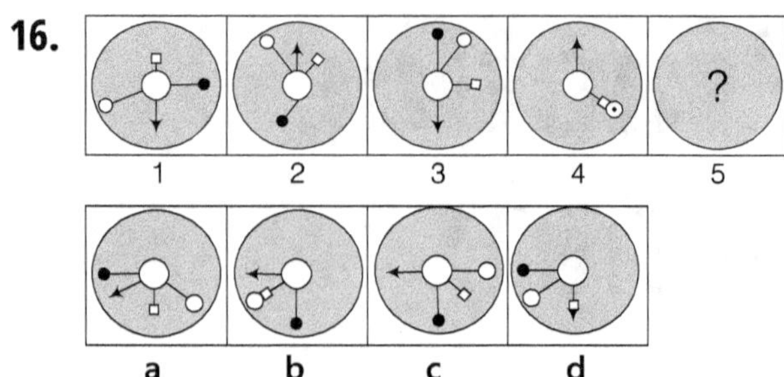

Direction (Q. Nos. 17-20) Find the missing term in the series given below.

17.

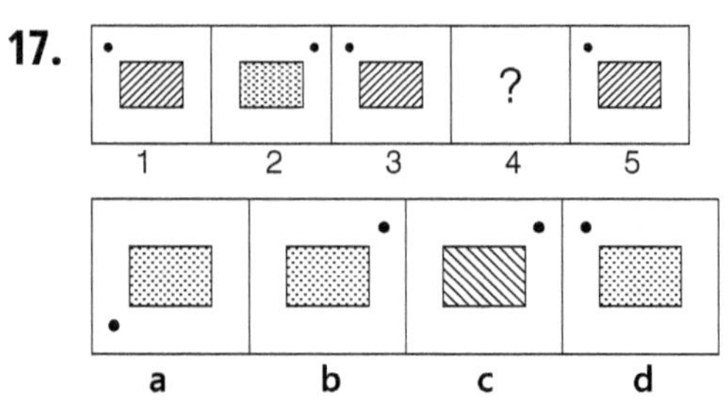

18.

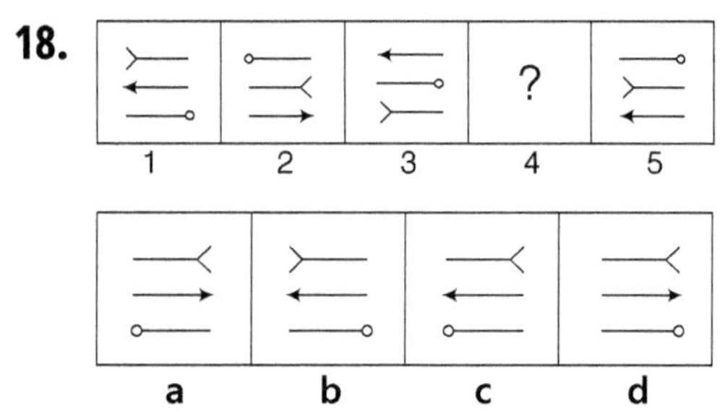

19.

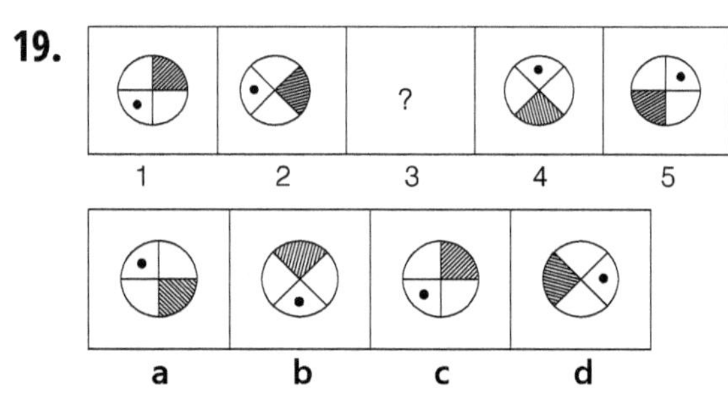

20.

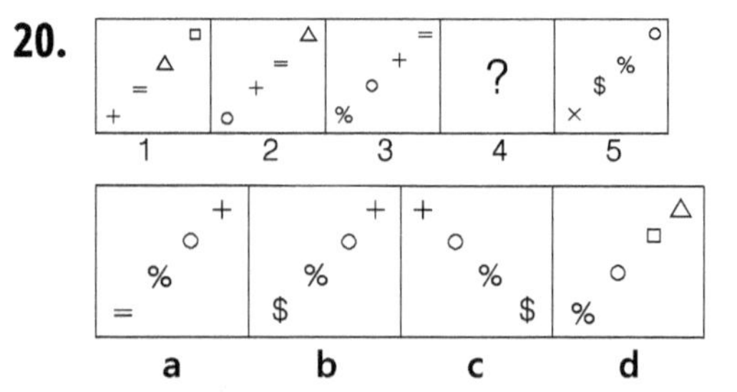

Direction (Q. Nos. 21-34) In each of the following questions, select a figure from the options that will complete the following figure matrix.

21.

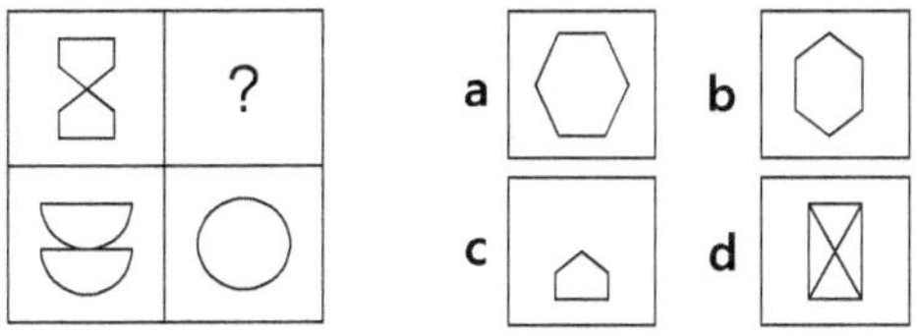

22.

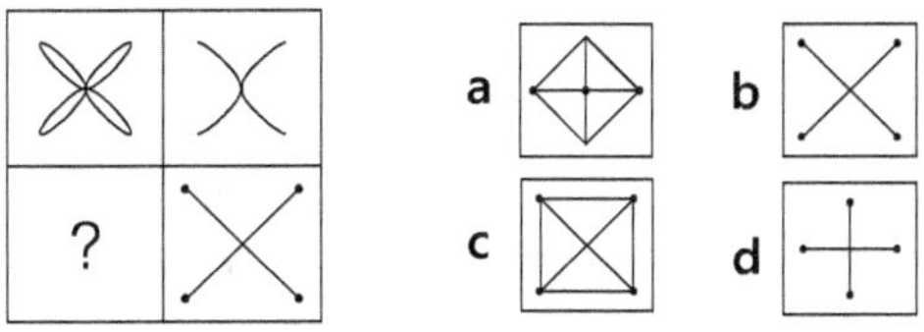

23.

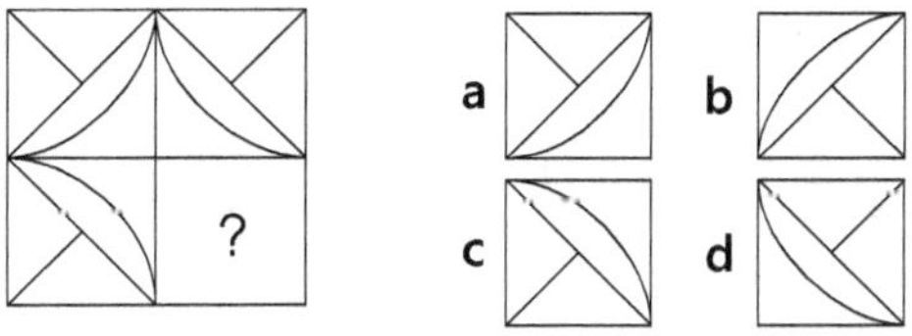

24.

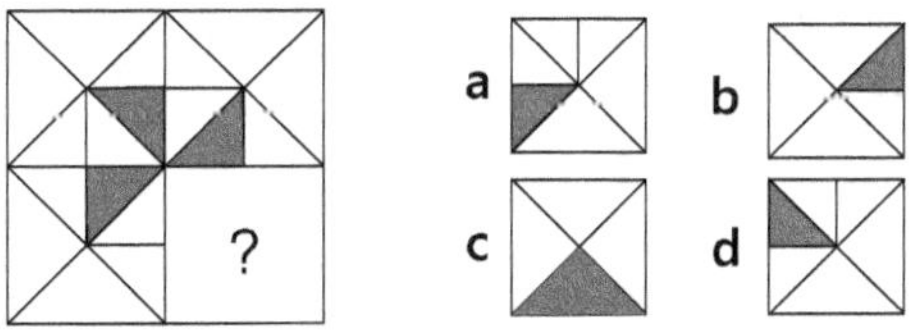

25.

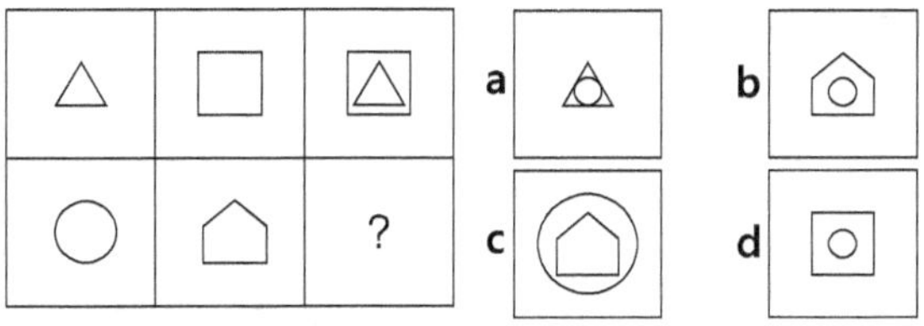

26.

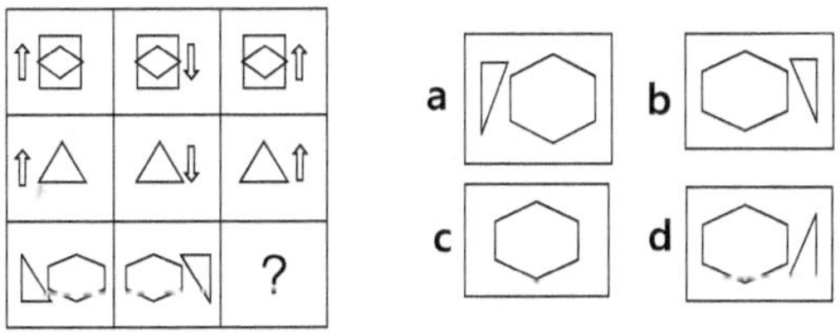

27.

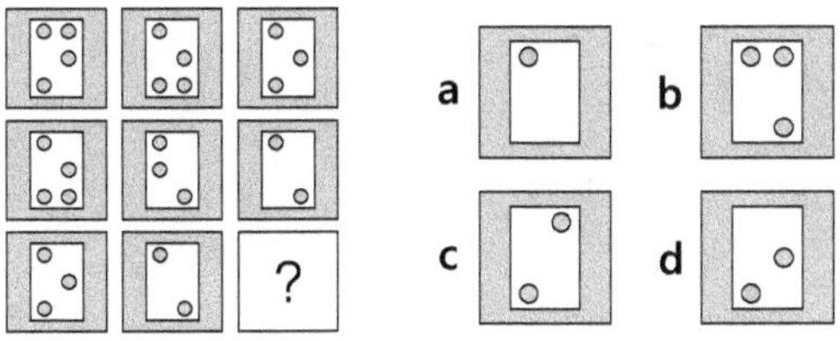

28.

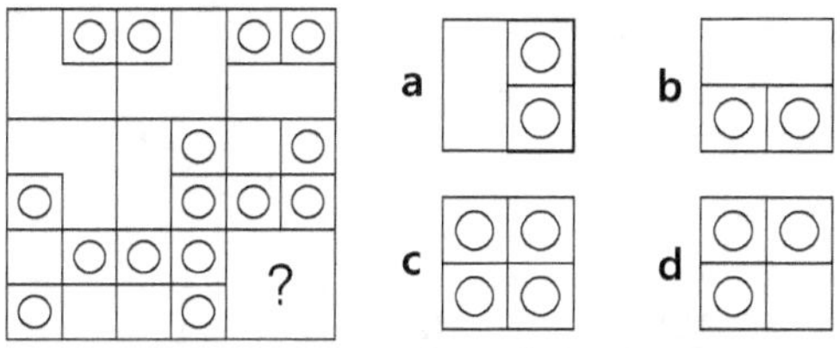

29.

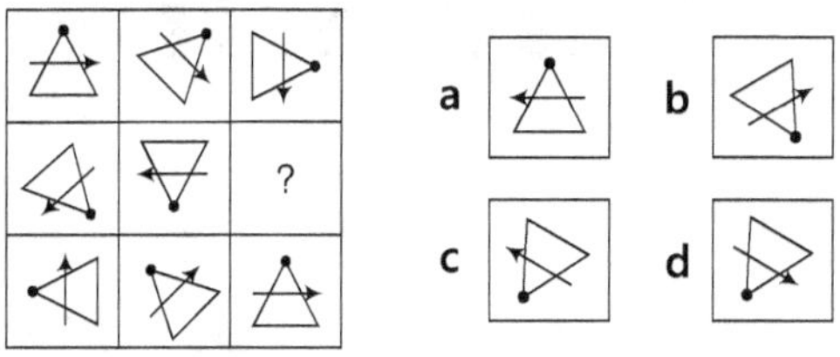

30.

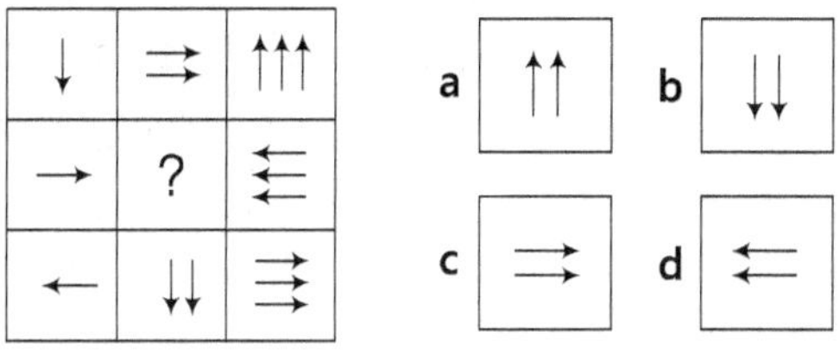

31.

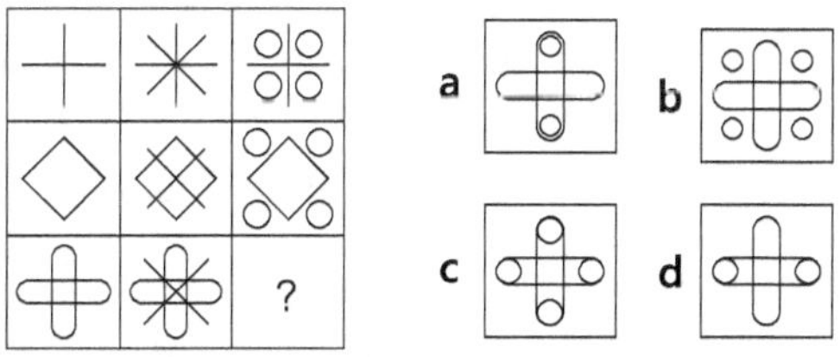

32.

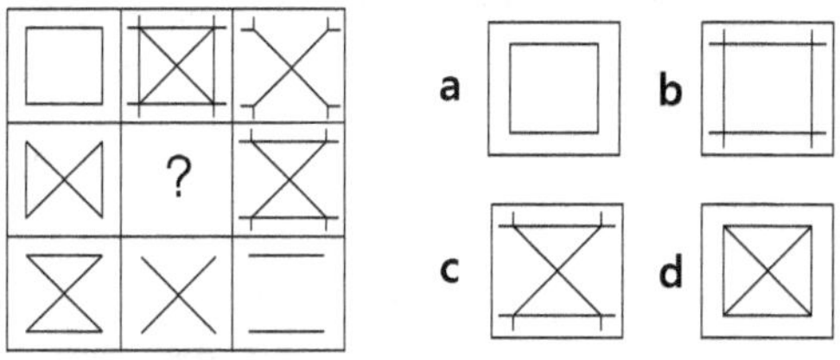

33.

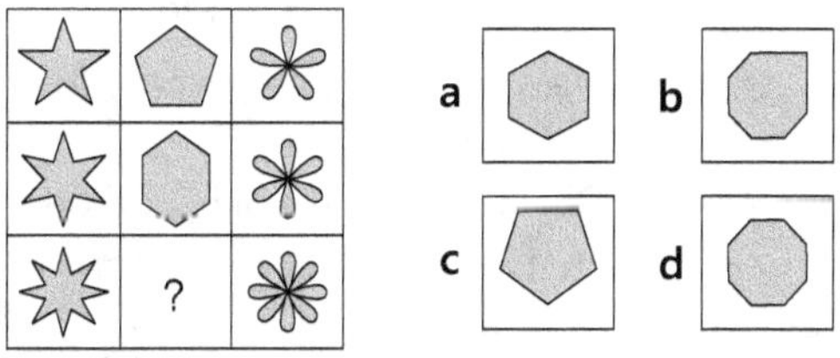

34.

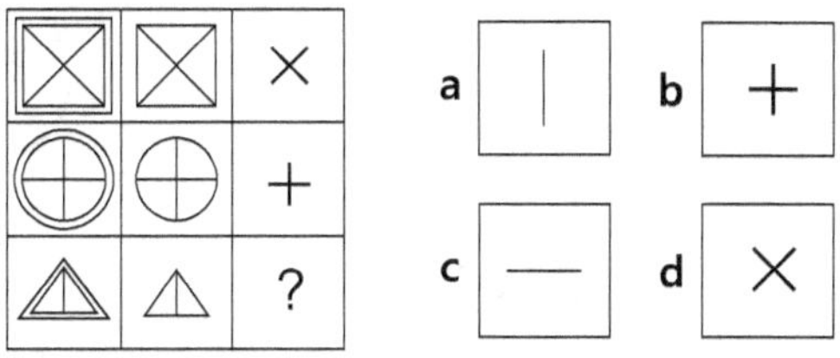

Chapter 14

Odd One Out

'Odd One Out' means to find out a different figure or shape from a given set of figures or shapes in accordance with certain common quality or qualities possessed by them.

'Odd One Out' is also known as 'Classification'.

For example, Choose the figure which is different from the rest.

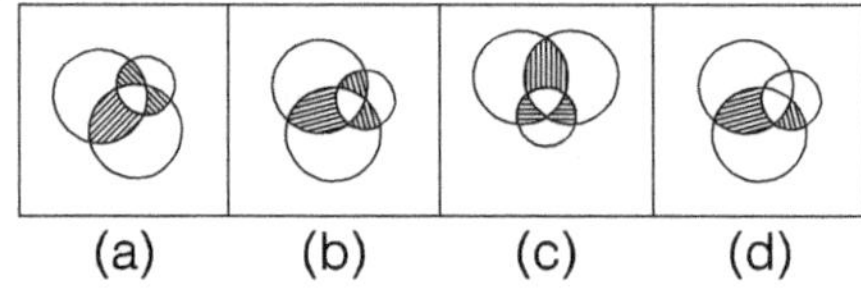

(a)   (b)   (c)   (d)

Here, in all the figures except figure (d) the areas common to only two circles are shaded, but in figure (d) one such area is not shaded.

Hence, figure (d) is odd one out.

In odd one out, following types of questions are generally asked

EXAMPLE 1 Choose a figure which is different from others.

× +	✓ ×	+ ✓	0 ✓
✓	+	×	=
0 =	÷ 0	0 =	+ ×
(a)	(b)	(c)	(d)

Think • Analyse the given figures carefully and try to find out the common characteristics, which is possessed by most of the figures.

• After analysing we find that, most of the figures have common elements in it.

Sol. Here, all the figures except (b) have common elements, but option figure (b) has division (÷) instead of equal (=).

So, option figure (b) is odd one out.

Hence, option (b) is correct.

EXAMPLE 2 Choose a figure which is different from others.

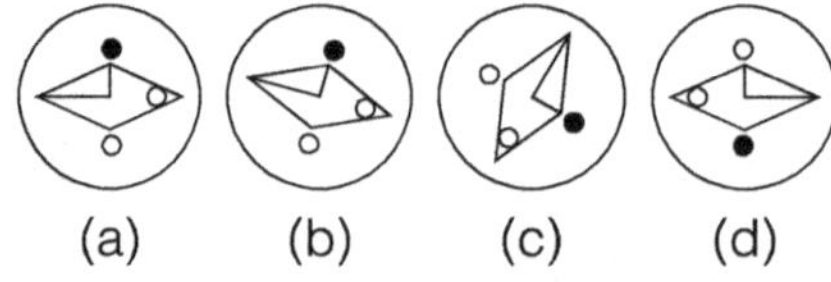

(a)   (b)   (c)   (d)

Think After observing carefully, we see that most of the figures have same pattern.

Sol. All the figures except figure (d) are same when rotated. But option figure (d) does not have same pattern as others.

So, option figure (d) is odd one out.

Hence, option (d) is correct.

Practice
Centre

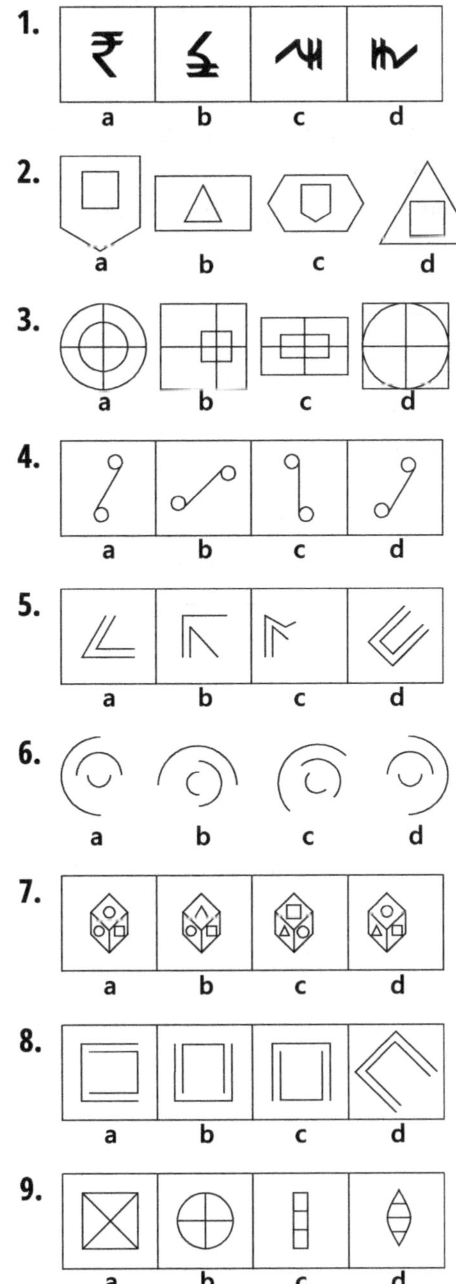

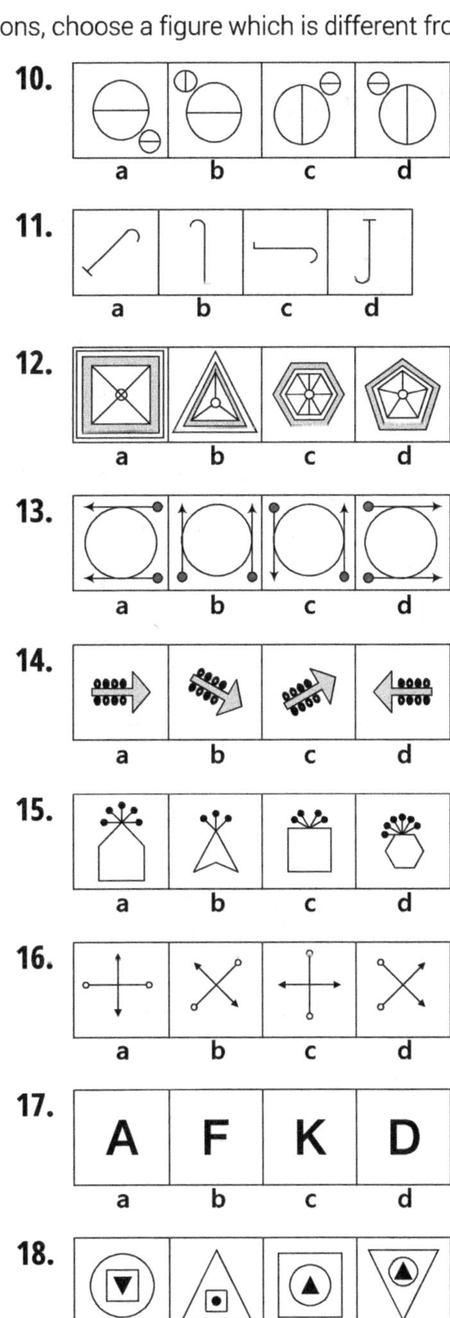

Chapter 15

Mirror and Water Images

Mirror Image

A mirror image is a reflected duplication of an object into a plane mirror that appears identical but reversed. It is of same size as the object but the left half of the object becomes the right half and the right half of the object becomes the left half of the mirror image.

For example, Consider the following figure and find out its mirror image from the given four alternatives.

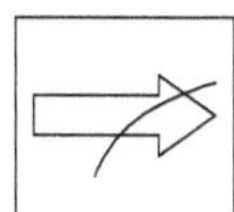   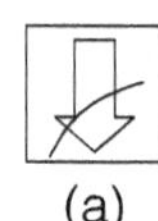   

                                 (a)   (b)   (c)   (d)

Here, in mirror image, the right half of the original image will become the left half and *vice-versa* as shown in adjacent figure Hence, option (c) is correct.

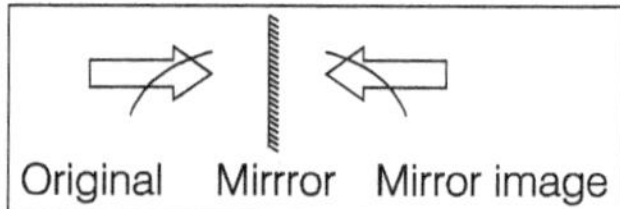

Original   Mirrror   Mirror image

Let us observe the mirror image of

(i) Digits   (ii) Capital letters   (iii) Small letters

Mirror image					
Digits	**Capital Letters**			**Small Letters**		

The table shows each character paired with its mirror image:

Digits: 0, 1, 2, 3, 4, 5, 6, 7, 8, 9

Capital Letters: A, B, C, D, E, F, G, H, I — J, K, L, M, N, O, P, Q, R — S, T, U, V, W, X, Y, Z

Small Letters: a, b, c, d, e, f, g, h, i — j, k, l, m, n, o, p, q, r — s, t, u, v, w, x, y, z

In mirror image, following types of questions are generally asked

EXAMPLE 1 Identify the correct mirror image of the given figure.

 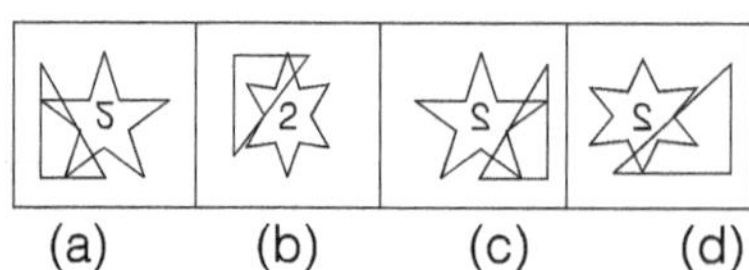

                                 (a)   (b)   (c)   (d)

Think Look at the figure carefully and use your visualisation power to reverse the object.

Sol. Here, the triangle placed to the left of the star will be shown to the right of the star in mirror image and the digit will be inverted horizontally as shown in adjacent figure

Hence, option (c) is correct.

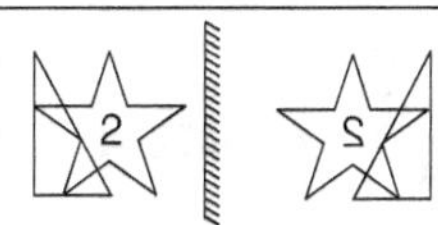

Water Image

The reflection of an object, as seen in water is called its water image. It is the upside down or vertically inverted image of an object.

For example, Consider the following figure and find out its water image.

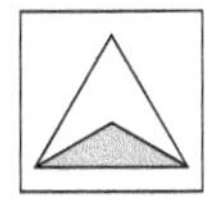 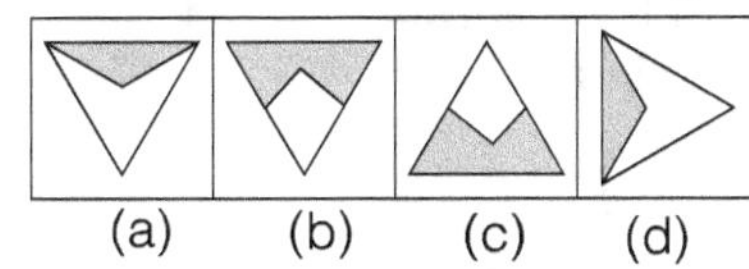

(a) (b) (c) (d)

Here, in water image, the triangle pointing upward in original figure will point downward and the shaded portion at the bottom in original figure will show at the top in water image as shown in adjacent figure

Hence, option (a) is correct.

Let us observe the water image of

(i) Digits

Digits	0	1	2	3	4	5	6	7	8	9
Water images	0	ɟ	ϛ	Ɛ	ⱴ	ϛ	℮	⅄	8	ə

(ii) Capital letters

Digits	A	B	C	D	E	F	G	H	I	J	K	L	M	N	O	P	Q	R	S	T	U	V	W	X	Y	Z
Water images	∀	B	C	D	E	Ⅎ	Ϭ	H	I	⅂	K	Γ	W	И	O	Ь	Ø	Я	Ƨ	⊥	Ո	∧	M	X	⅄	Ƨ

(iii) Small letters

Digits	a	b	c	d	e	f	g	h	i	j	k	l	m	n	o	p	q	r	s	t	u	v	w	x	y	z
Water images	ɑ	p	c	q	℮	ɟ	ā	μ	!	!	ʞ	ⵑ	ɯ	u	o	b	d	ⵏ	ƨ	ɟ	∩	∧	ʍ	x	⅄	Ƨ

In water image, following types of questions are generally asked

EXAMPLE 1 Choose the correct water image of the figure below.

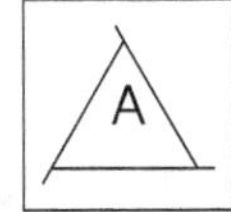 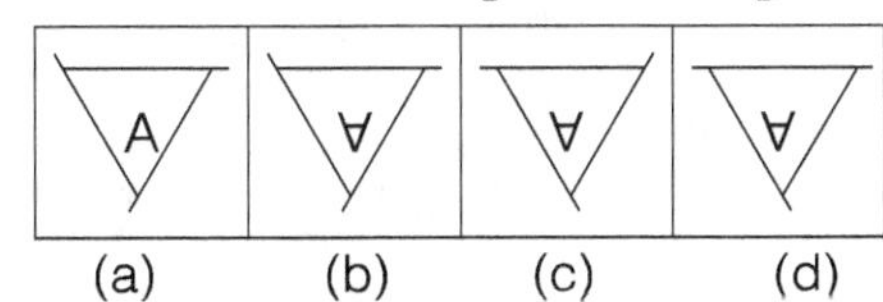

(a) (b) (c) (d)

(Think) Here, after looking carefully and we find that the top edge will become the bottom edge and the bottom edge will become the top edge in water image.

Sol. The water image can be obtained as

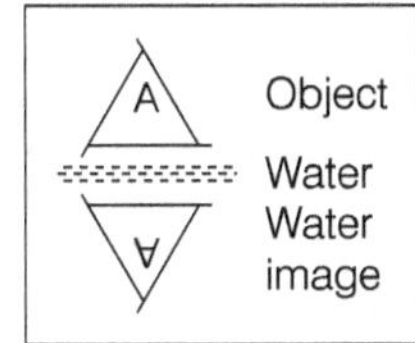

Hence, option (b) is correct.

Practice Centre

 Direction (Q. Nos. 1-5) In each of the following questions, choose the correct mirror image of the given word/number from the four given alternatives.

1. VERBAL

   a LABREV   **b** LRVEBA **c** REVBAL **d** JABR3V

2. QUALITY

   a YTIJAUQ **b** YUALITQ **c** YTILAUQ **d** QUALITY

3. 24759

   a 95742   **b** 54759   **c** 92457   **d** 24759

4. DL3N469F

   a DL3469FB **b** F964N3LD **c** DL3N469F **d** F964N3DL

5. disturb

   a dhutsib **b** disturb **c** brutsid **d** bdistur

6. Which of the following group of letters will look the same in the mirror?

   a ALONE **b** HEAD   **c** TOOTH **c** SCHOOL

Direction (Q. Nos. 7-12) In each of the following question, choose the correct mirror image of the given figure (X) among the four given alternatives.

7. 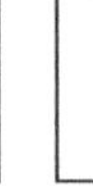 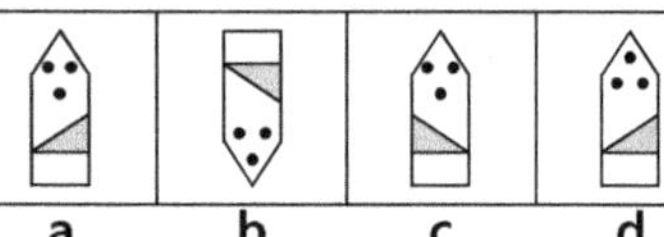

8. 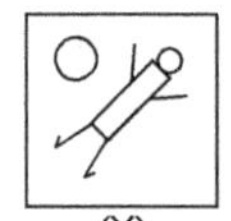 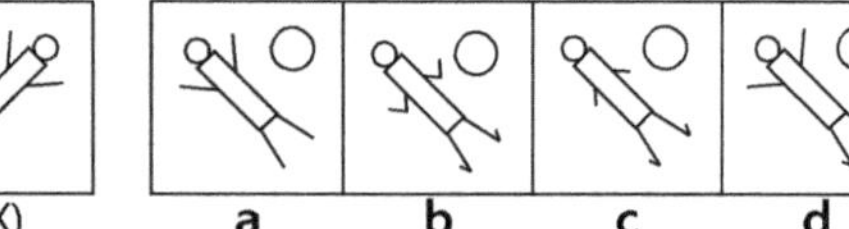

9. 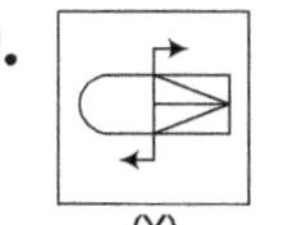 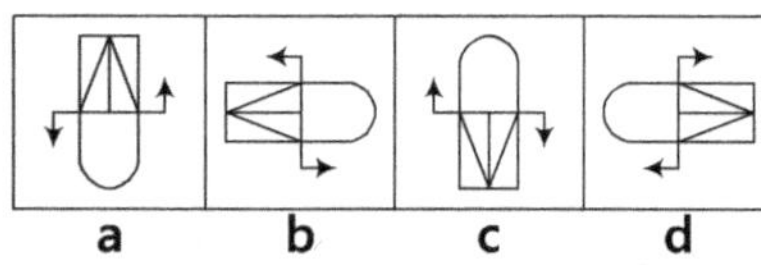

10. 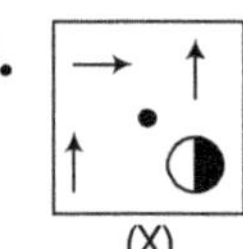 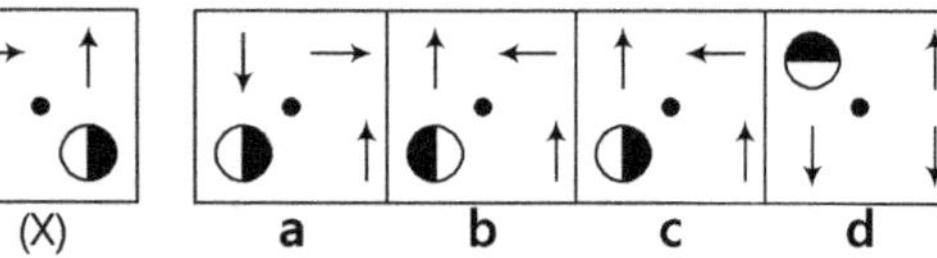

11. 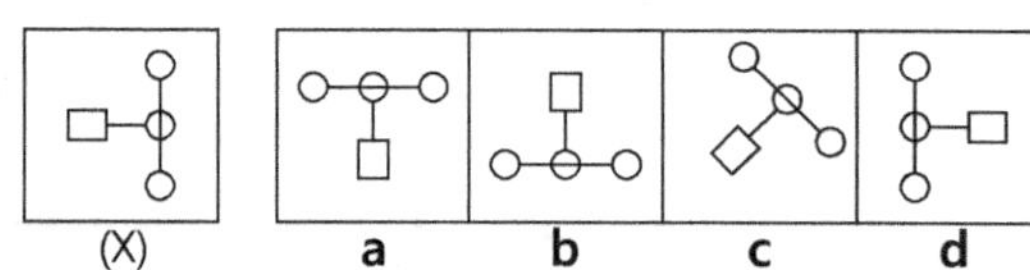

12. 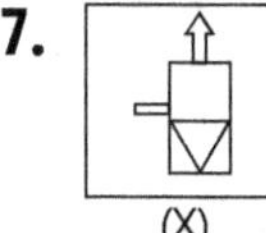 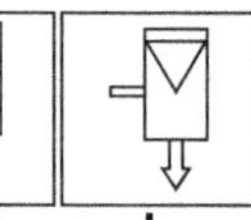 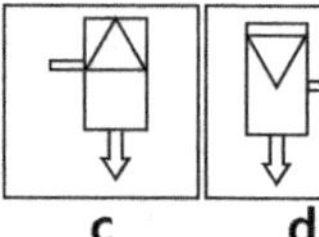

Direction (Q. Nos. 13-16) In each of the following questions choose the correct water image of the given word/number from among the four given alternatives.

13. SURFACE

   a ƎƆAℲЯUƧ **b** SURFACE **c** SURFACE **d** SURFACE

14. 1942

   a 2491   **b** 1942   **c** 1942   **d** 1942

15. rise

   a rise   **b** esir   **c** rise   **d** rise

16. U4P15B7

   a U4P15B7 **b** Z8S1P4U **c** U4P15B7 **d** U4P15B7

Direction (Q.Nos. 17-20) In each of the following question, choose the correct water image of the given figure (X).

17. 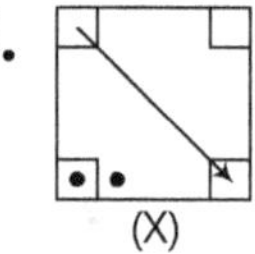 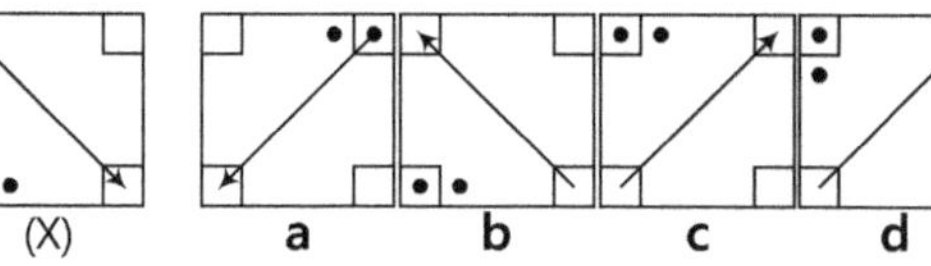

18. 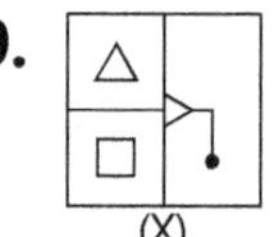 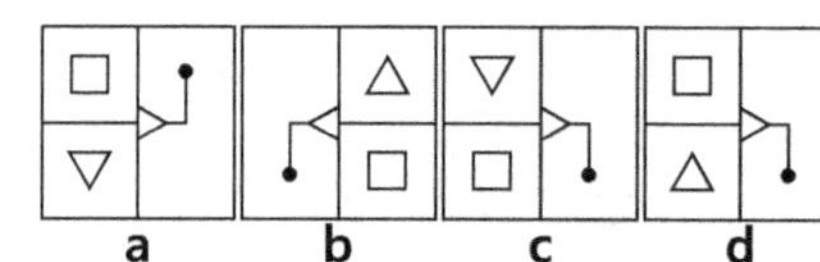

19. 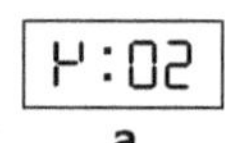

20. (X) 4:05 **a** **b** **c** **d**

Chapter 16

Cubes and Dice

Cubes A 'Cube' is a three-dimensional solid piece with 6 faces, 8 corners and 12 edges, in which a particular face is joined with another four faces and the remaining sixth face is opposite to a particular face.

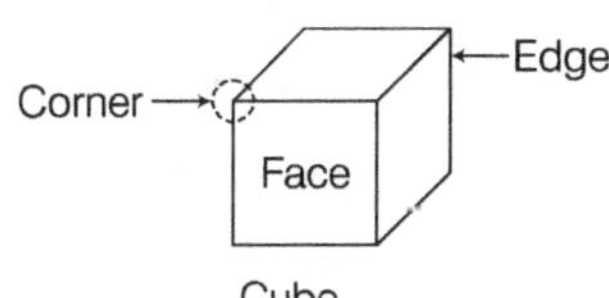

Dice A 'Dice' is a cube having numbers or dots from 1 to 6 marked on its different faces.

In this section, three types of questions are covered
   (i) Counting of number of small cubes
  (ii) Construction of cube (or dice) from a given net (unfolded dice)
 (iii) Finding the element on the face opposite to a particular face

(i) Counting of number of small cubes

In this topic, a stack of cubes is given and students are required to count the number of small cubes given in the stack.

In cubes and dice, following types of questions are generally asked

EXAMPLE 1 Count the number of cubes in the given figure.

    (a) 8   (b) 12   (c) 20   (d) 10

Think Mark the numbers on each cube and count the cubes carefully to avoid the repetition

Sol.

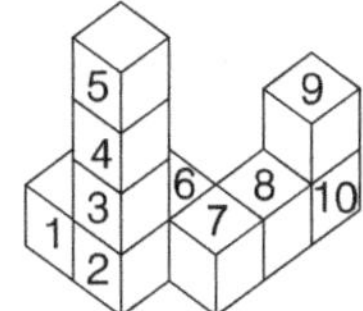

Number of cubes in the given figure = 10
Hence, option (d) is correct.

(ii) Construction of cube (or dice) **from a given net** (unfolded dice)

In this topic, one of the net or unfolded dice is given as shown below and we have to find out the cube or dice which can be formed by folding the given net. Various formats of net can be obtained by unfolding a dice in different ways. Four such nets are shown below

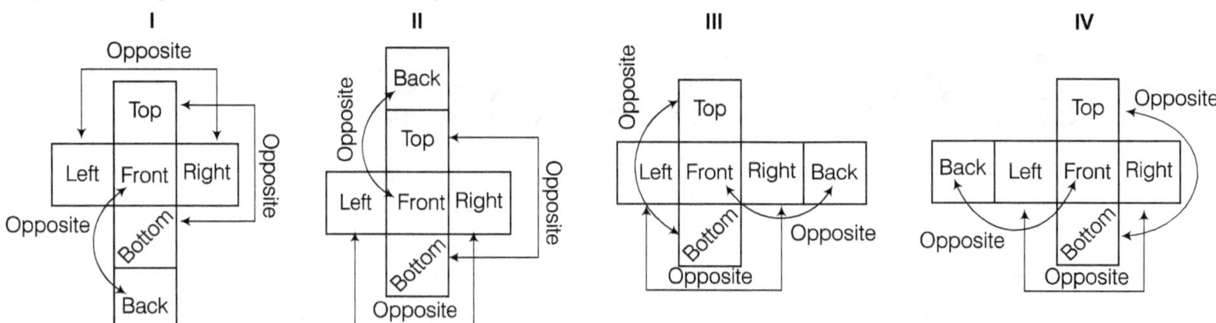

As seen in the above figures, the top face is opposite to the bottom face, the left face is opposite to the right face and the front face is opposite to the back face.

EXAMPLE 2 Which cube can be formed by folding the given sheet of paper (X)?

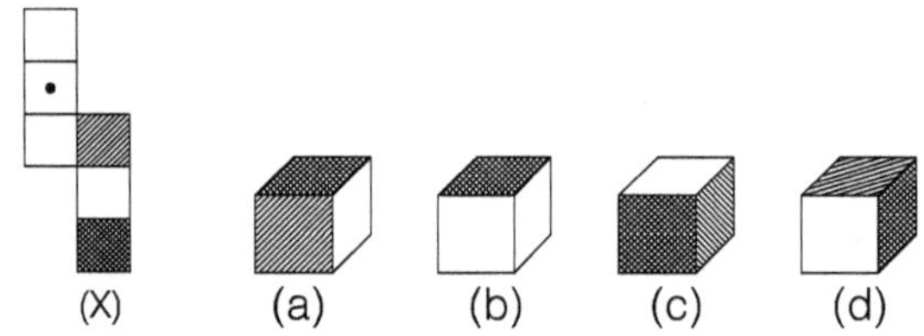

Think • First of all, find out the opposite faces from the net.
• Now, analyse each alternative cube to see that no opposite faces are shown adjacent to each other.

Sol. When the sheet of paper represented by figure (X) is folded to form a cube, then the pairs of opposite faces will be (□,□) , (□,□) and (▨,▨). Now, in figure (a), (c) and (d), patterns (▨,▨) are shown on adjacent faces. So, these cubes cannot be formed from the given sheet of paper (X), the only cube (b) will be formed.

Hence, option (b) is correct.

(iii) Finding the element on the face opposite to a particular face

In this topic, two or more dice having numbers/letters/symbols are given and we have to find out the number/letter/symbol opposite to a particular face.

EXAMPLE 3 From the given two positions of a single dice, find the digit opposite to the face having digit 1.

    2 | 5
4 1   3 1
(I)   (II)

(a) 4   (b) 6   (c) 5   (d) 2

Think • First of all, analyse the figures and find out the common number.
• After this, consider both positions and write down the adjacent faces of the common number from both positions to find out the remaining face.

Sol. Here, we see that number '1' is common in both the positions.

Now, the adjacent faces of '1' are 2, 4, 5 and 3. So, the remaining face having number '6' will be opposite to the face having number '1'.

Hence, option (b) is correct.

Practice Centre

Direction (Q. Nos. 1-4) Count the number of cubes in the following figures.

1.

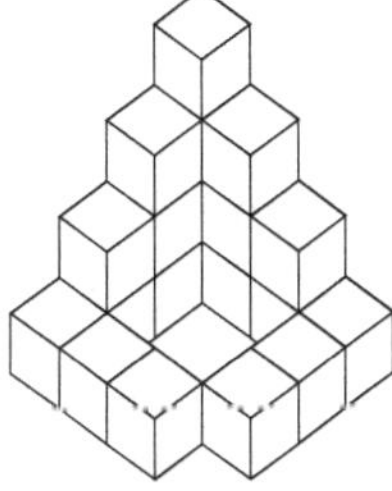

   a 25   **b** 20
   c 22   **d** 18

2.

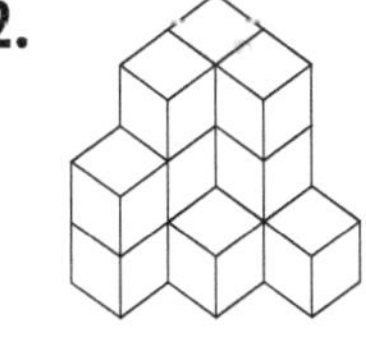

   a 10   **b** 23
   c 19   **d** 13

3.

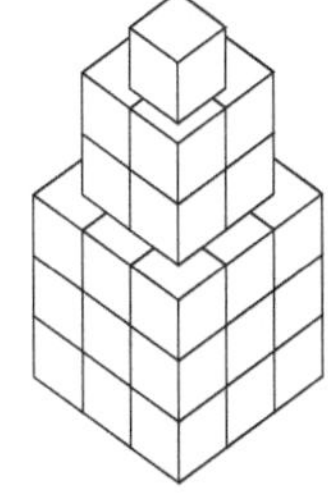

   a 35
   b 36
   c 26
   d 34

4.

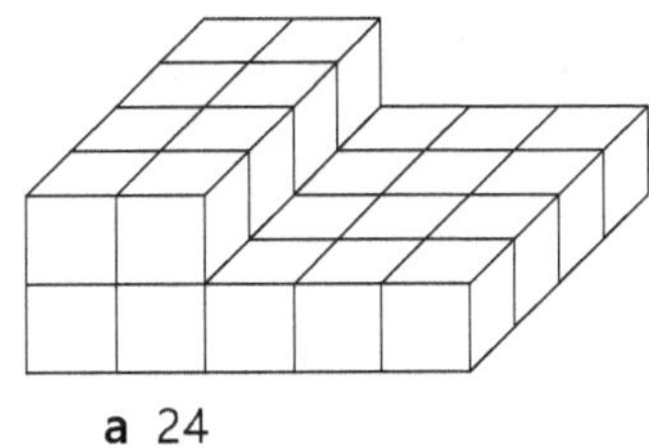

   a 24
   b 35
   c 28
   d 30

Direction (Q. Nos. 5-12) In each of the following questions, a sheet of paper represented as fig. (X) is folded to form a cube. From amongst the four alternatives (a), (b), (c) and (d), choose the cube which can be formed after folding the net.

5.

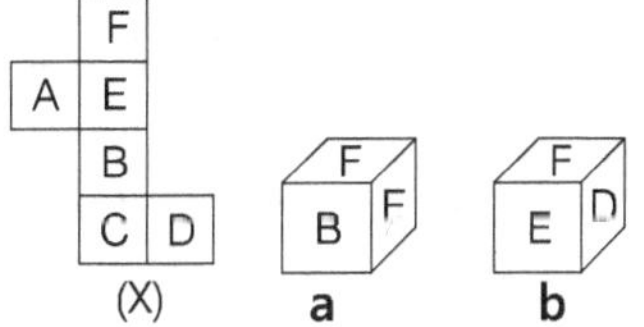
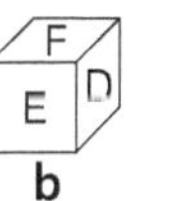
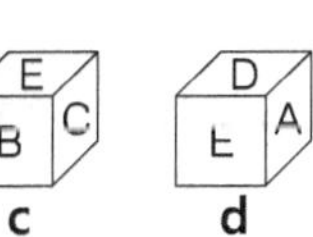

  (X)   **a**   **b**   **c**   **d**

6.

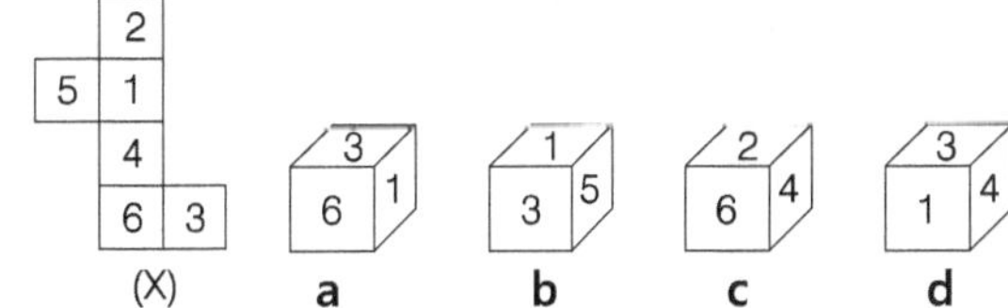

  (X)   **a**   **b**   **c**   **d**

7.

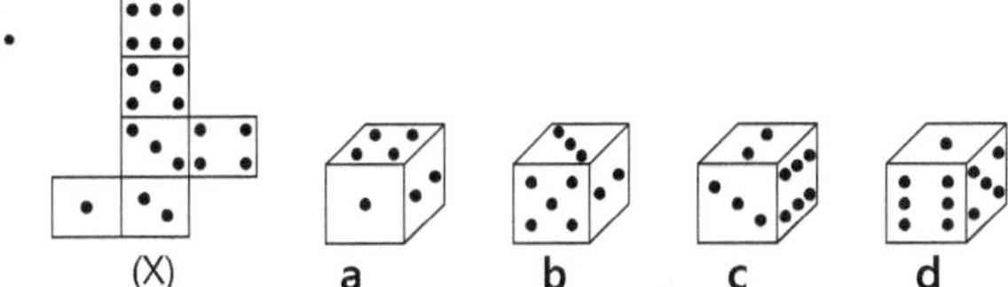

  (X)   **a**   **b**   **c**   **d**

8.

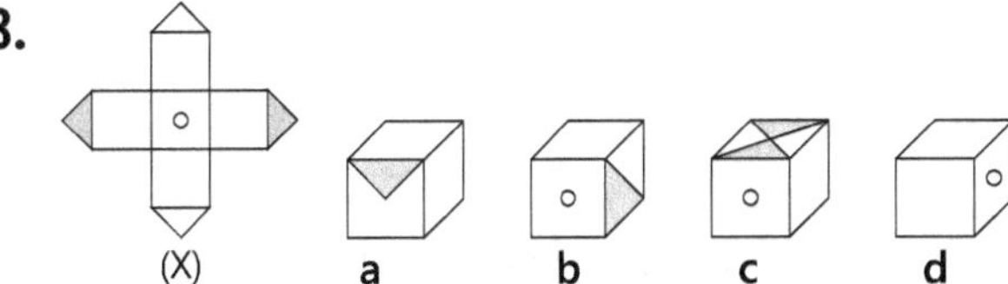

  (X)   **a**   **b**   **c**   **d**

9.

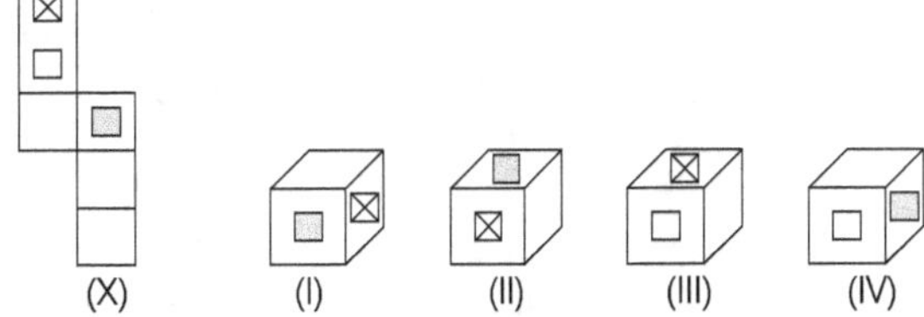

  (X)   (I)   (II)   (III)   (IV)

   a I and II   **b** II and III
   c III and IV   **d** I, II, III and IV

10.

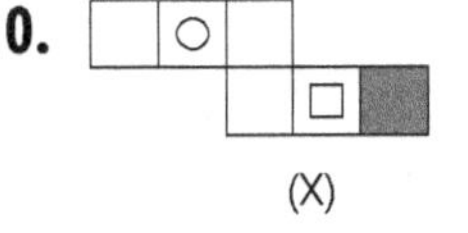
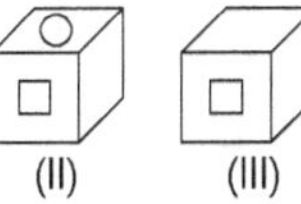
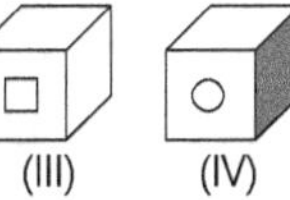

      (X)   (I)   (II)   (III)   (IV)

   a I and II   **b** II and IV
   c I and IV   **d** III and IV

11.

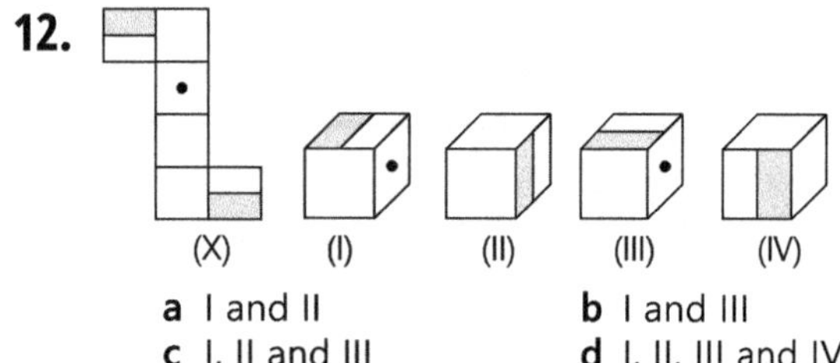

    (X)   (I)   (II)   (III)   (IV)

  a I and II   **b** II and III
  c III and IV   **d** I and IV

12.

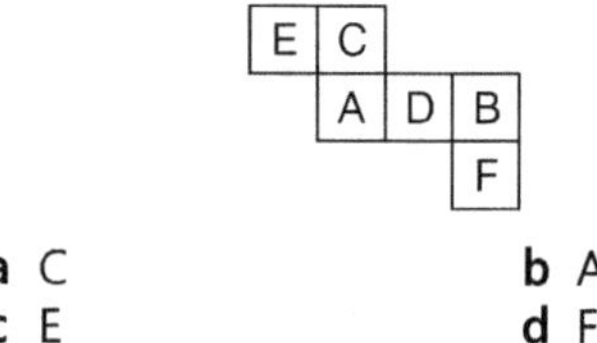

    (X)   (I)   (II)   (III)   (IV)

  a I and II   **b** I and III
  c I, II and III   **d** I, II, III and IV

13. The given figure shows the net of a cube. The cube is placed on the table with face "D" on the top of the cube. Which face is at the bottom of the cube?

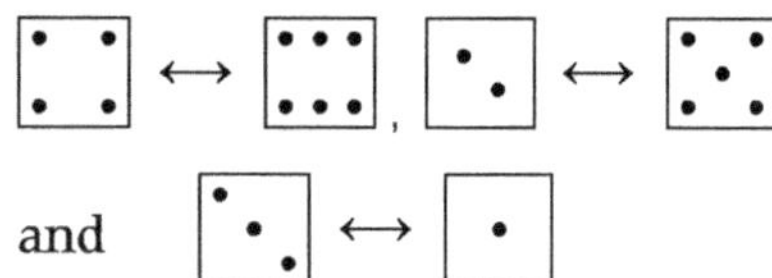

  a C   **b** A
  c E   **d** F

14. The opposite faces of a cube are as shown

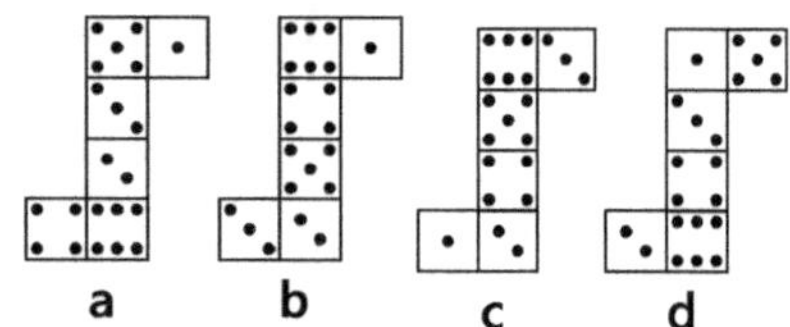

Which of the following options represents the unfolded cube?

    a   **b**   **c**   **d**

15. Two positions of a dice are shown below. When the number 6 will be at the bottom, then which number will be at the top?

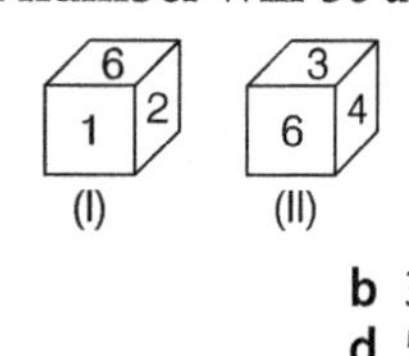

    (I)   (II)

  a 2   **b** 3
  c 4   **d** 5

16. Two different positions of a dice are shown in figures given below

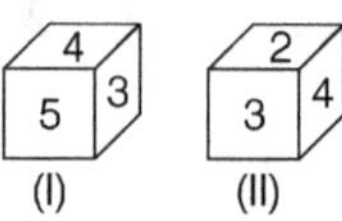

    (I)   (II)

Which number lies opposite to number 2?

  a 5   **b** 4
  c 3   **d** 1

17. Two positions of a dice are shown below.

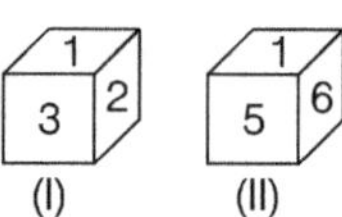

    (I)   (II)

When 4 is at the bottom, what number will be on the top?

  a 5   **b** 6
  c 2   **d** 1

18. Two positions of a dice with 1 to 6 dots on its sides are shown below. If the dice is resting on the side with two dots, what will be the number of dots on the side at the top?

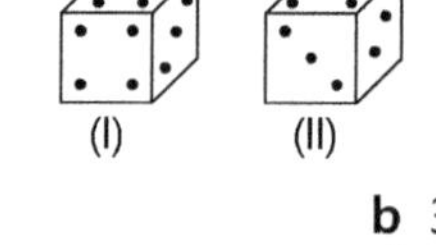

    (I)   (II)

  a 2   **b** 3
  c 6   **d** 1

19. Two positions of a dice has been shown here.

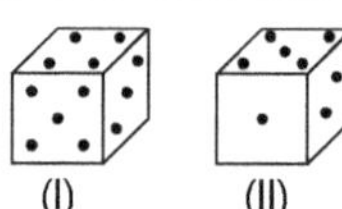

    (I)   (II)

What digit will be just opposite of 5?

  a 1
  b 2
  c 4
  d 6

20. Four faces of a dice are shown below.

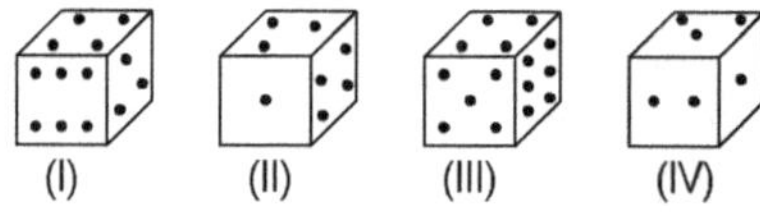

    (I)   (II)   (III)   (IV)

How many dots will be on the face opposite to the face which contains 3 dots?

  a 2
  b 5
  c 4
  d 6

Chapter 17

Counting of Figures

In 'Counting of Figures', a complex figure consisting of several small geometrical figures such as lines, triangles, squares, circles, rectangles etc, is given and students are required to count these small geometrical figures.

For example, How many squares are there in the figure given below?

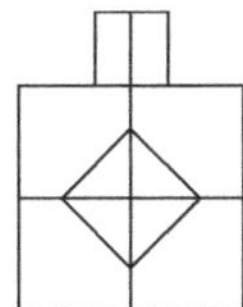

(a) 6   (b) 7   (c) 8   (d) 5

Here, the figure may the labelled as shown in adjacent figure.

The number of squares composed of single unit are □ANIJ, □ROPQ, □ NBKI, □JILD, □IKCL and □EFGH i.e. 6.

The number of squares composed of more than one unit is □ABCD, i.e. 1.

So, the total number of squares $= 6 + 1 = 7$

Hence, option (b) is correct.

In counting of figures, following types of questions are generally asked

EXAMPLE 1 How many triangles are there in the following figure?

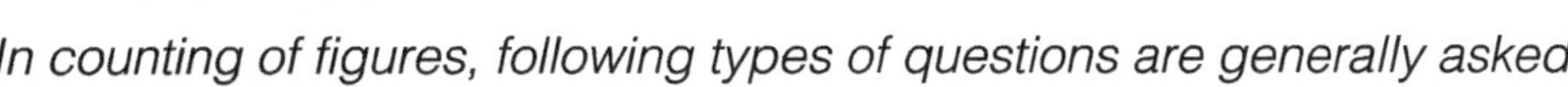

(a) 5   (b) 6   (c) 4   (d) 3

Think • After observing the given figure, we find two different forms of the triangle, i.e. triangle composed of one unit and the triangle composed of two units.

• Now, we will label the given figure and count the triangles of different forms.

Sol. On labelling the figure, we get

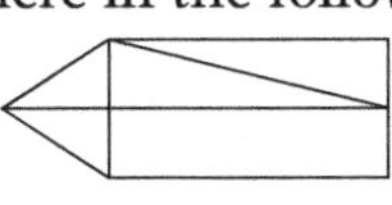

The number of triangles composed of one unit are ΔABF, ΔAFE, ΔBCG, ΔBFG, i.e. 4.

The number of triangles composed of two units are ΔABG and ΔABE, i.e. 2.

Therefore, the total number of triangles $= 4 + 2 = 6$

Hence, option (b) is correct.

Practice Centre

1. How many straight lines are there in the figure given below?

    a 7   **b** 8
    c 9   **d** 12

2. How many straight lines are there in a given figure?

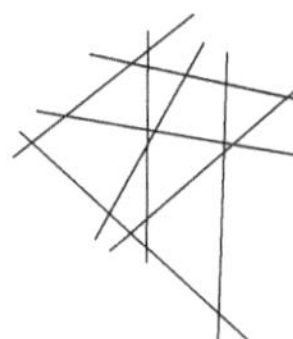

    a 10   **b** 6
    c 8   **d** None of these

3. How many circles are there in the figure given below?

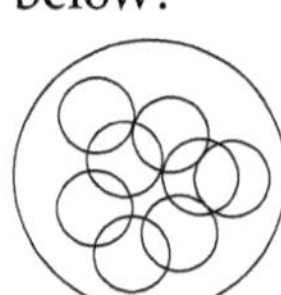

    a 11   **b** 9
    c 7   **d** 5

4. How many triangles are there in the figure given below?

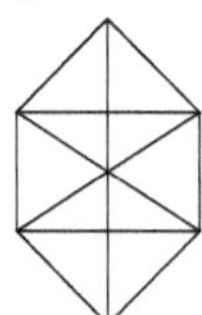

    a 22   **b** 25
    c 20   **d** 18

5. Find the number of triangles in the figure given below?

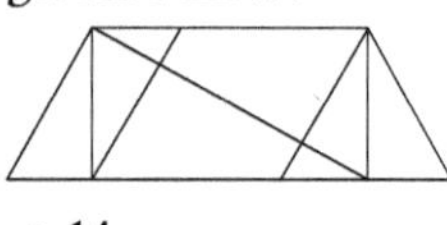

    a 14   **b** 16
    c 12   **d** 18

6. How many squares are there in the figure given below?

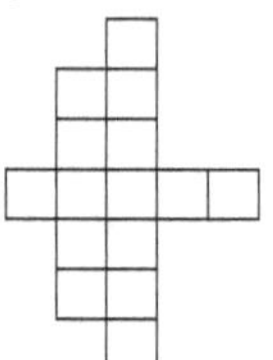

    a 16   **b** 20
    c 25   **d** 19

7. How many squares are there in the given figure?

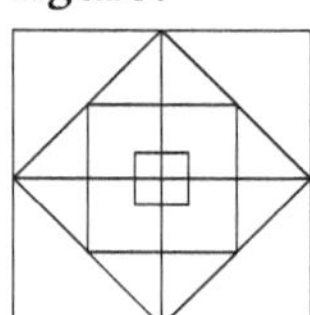

    a 15   **b** 18
    c 16   **d** 12

8. Find the number of rectangles in the given figure.

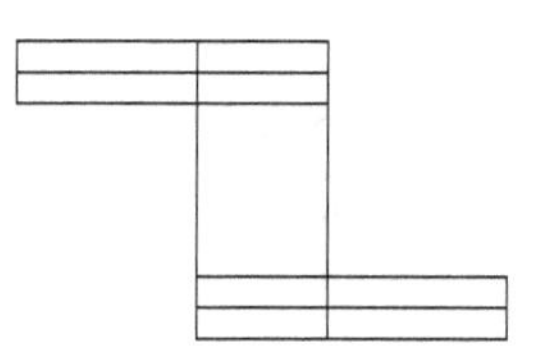

    a 12   **b** 27   **c** 20   **d** 22

9. How many triangles and squares are there in the figure?

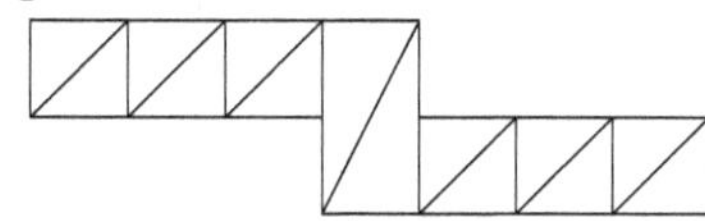

    a Triangles = 10, squares = 8
    b Triangles = 8, squares = 6
    c Triangles = 14 , squares = 6
    d None of the above

10. Find the number of triangles in the given figure.

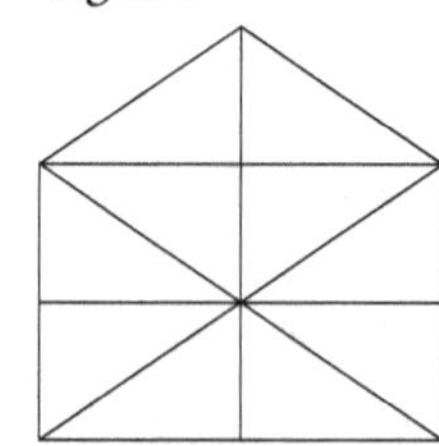

    a 20   **b** 19
    c 21   **d** 24

11. How many straight lines are there in the given figure?

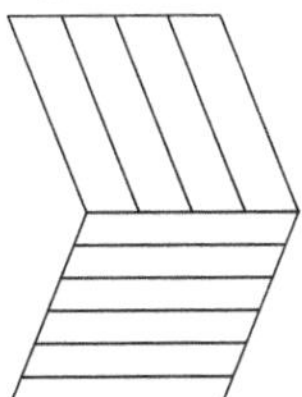

a 15   **b** 14
c 17   **d** 18

12. How many circles are there in the figure given below?

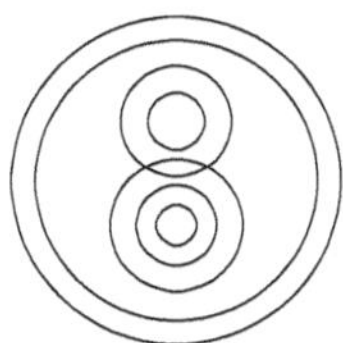

a 5   **b** 7
c 8   **d** 6

13. How many triangles are there in the given figure?

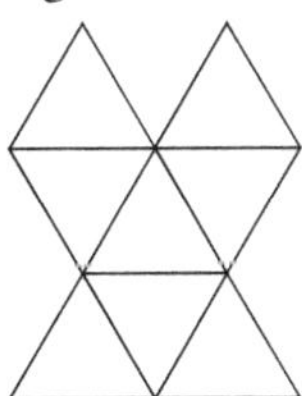

a 10   **b** 1
c 15   **d** 8

14. How many squares are there in the given figure?

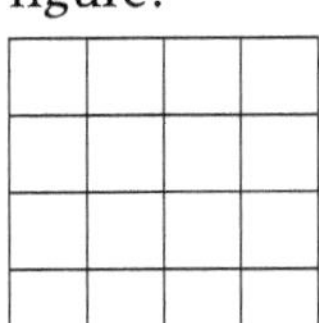

a 20   **b** 30
c 16   **d** 24

15. Count the number of triangles in the given figure.

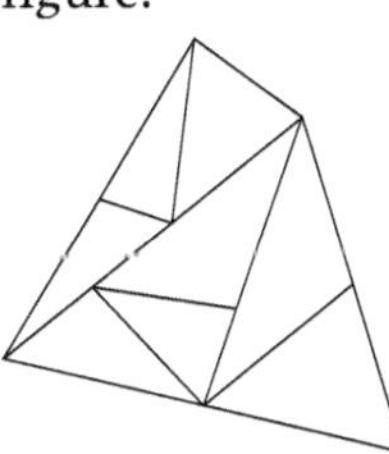

a 10
b 12
c 14
d None of the above

16. How many triangles are there in the given figure below?

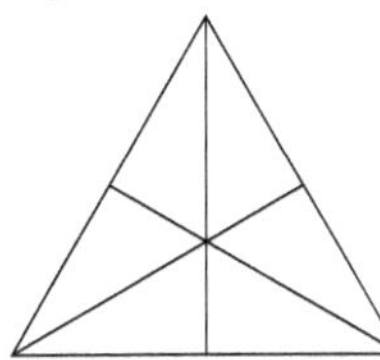

a 16
b 18
c 21
d None of the above

17. How many triangles are there in the given figure?

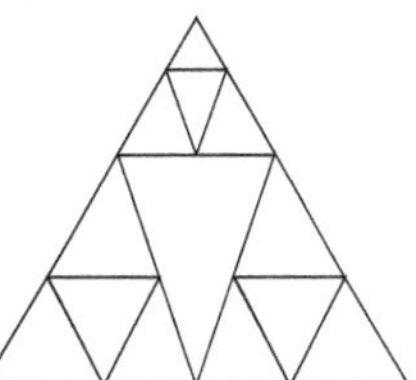

a 10   **b** 17
c 12   **d** 15

18. How many triangles are there in the given figure?

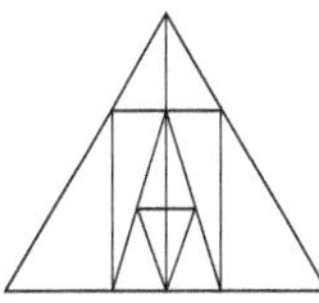

a 11   **b** 18
c 21   **d** 23

19. How many squares are there in a given figure?

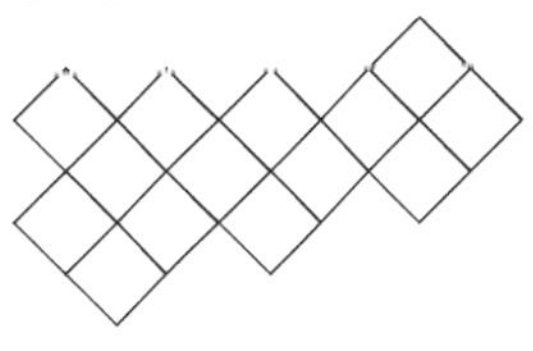

a 12   **b** 18
c 20   **d** None of these

20. How many straight lines are there in the given figure below?

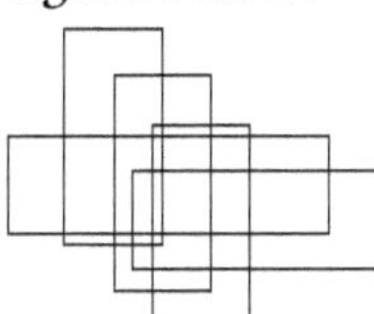

a 19   **b** 21
c 20   **d** 18

21. How many straight lines are there in the given figure?

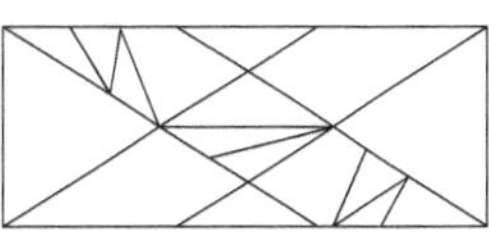

a 10   **b** 15
c 18   **d** 16

22. How many rectangles are there in the given figure?

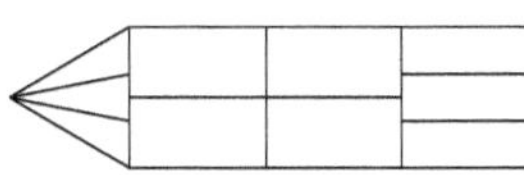

a 12
b 13
c 15
d None of the above

Practice Sets

7

Practice Set (1)

A Whole Content Based Test for Class 7th Reasoning Olympiad

1. Country is related to President in the same way as school is related to
   a Teacher   b Peon
   c Principal   d Students

2. In the following question, find the one letter that will complete the word in front of the circle and begin the word after the circle. The same letter must fit into both sets.

TIM ⑦ GO, HAL ⑦ ARTH

   a O   b E
   c A   d F

3. In the following question, find the two words, one from each group, that together make a new, meaningful word. The word from the first group always comes first.

1	2	3	P	Q	R
HIGH	DARK	TEA	DOOR	CAR	HORSE

   a 2P   b 3R   c 1Q   d 2R

4. Choose one letter that can be moved from the word on the left to the word on the right, making two new words

RANGE	OWE

   a N   b A   c E   d R

5. Pick up the correct option that makes the given series complete.

A AAA ……… AAAAAAA

   a AA   b AAAAA
   c AAAA   d AAAAAAAA

6. If T = 52, Q = 13, J = 9, A = 3 and U = 31, then find the value of following expression. A × J + T ÷ Q = ?
   a C   b Q
   c U   d T

7. 79 is related to 63 in the same way as 21 is related to
   a 2   b 3
   c 1   d 0

8. Sudiksha wants to go to school. She starts from her home which is in the West and comes to the crossing. The road to the left, ends in a park, straight ahead is the theater. In which direction is the school?
   a South   b East
   c West   d North

9. If cow is called lion, lion is called cat, cat is called rat and rat is called donkey, then who is the king of jungle?
   a Cow   b Donkey   c Lion   d Cat

10. Find the missing term which replaces the question mark.

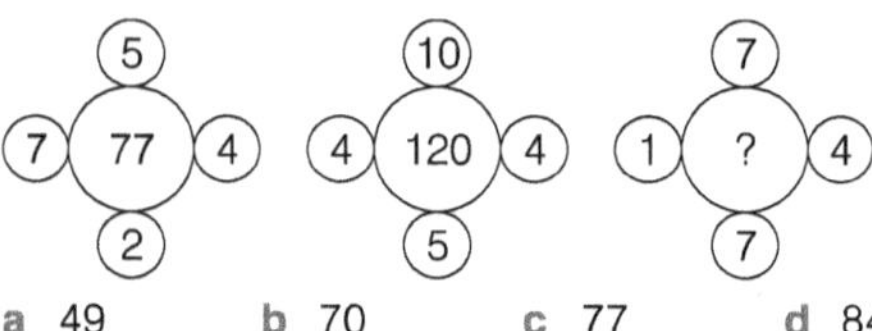

   a 49   b 70   c 77   d 84

11. Pointing to Yana, Daksh says, "I am the son of the only son of her grandfather." How is Daksh related to Yana?
   a Sister   b Brother   c Son   d Cousin

Direction (Q. No. 12) Study the given information carefully and answer the question that follows.

- P, Q, R, S, T and U are sitting around a circle facing towards the centre.
- T is sitting on the immediate left of R but is not the neighbour of S or U.
- Q is sitting opposite to T.
- S is sitting between P and Q.

12. Who is sitting between S and U?
   a T   b Q
   c P   d R

13. Which of the following diagrams best depits the relationship among Pencil, chair and stationery?

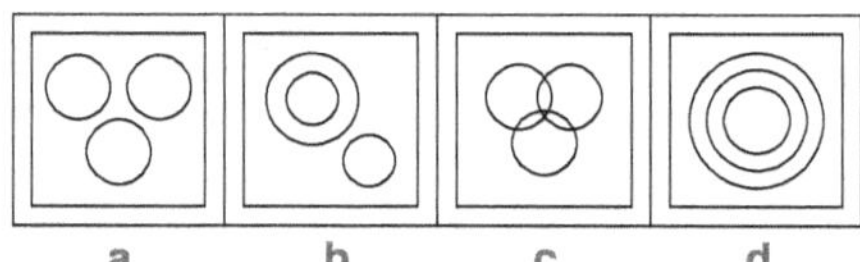

   a   b   c   d

14. If '+' means '÷', '÷' means '×' and '×' means '+', then 20 × 10 ÷ 6 + 2 = ?
   a 60   b 10
   c 0   d 50

15. Which of the following is odd one out?
   a India
   b Sri Lanka
   c Asia
   d England

16. Find the correct figure which replaces the question mark.

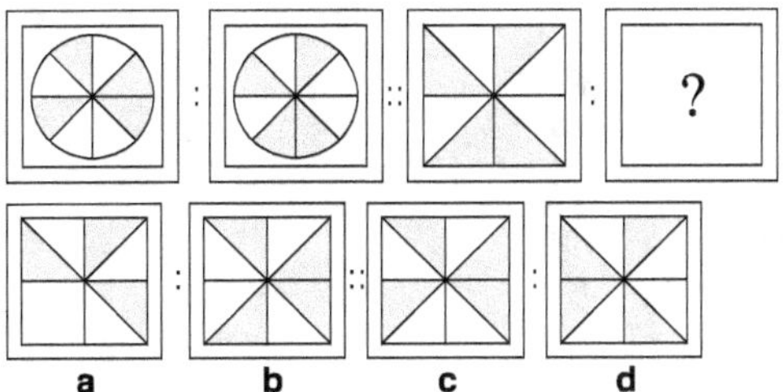

17. Find the odd one out.
a JOPK
b AOPB
c TOPU
d TOPS

18. Select a figure from the options which forms the correct mirror image of fig. (X).

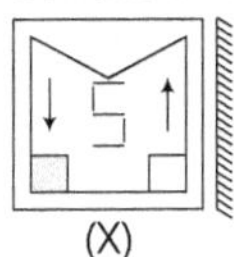

(X)

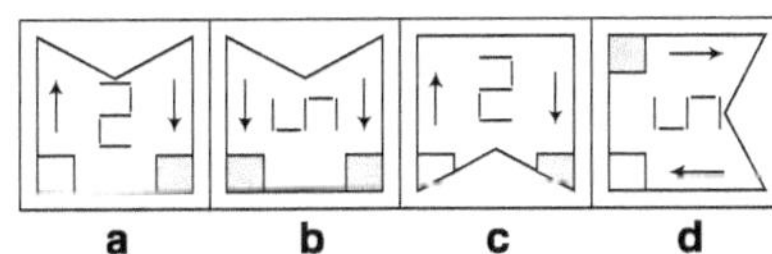

19. Select a figure from amongst the options which will continue the series established by the given problem figures?

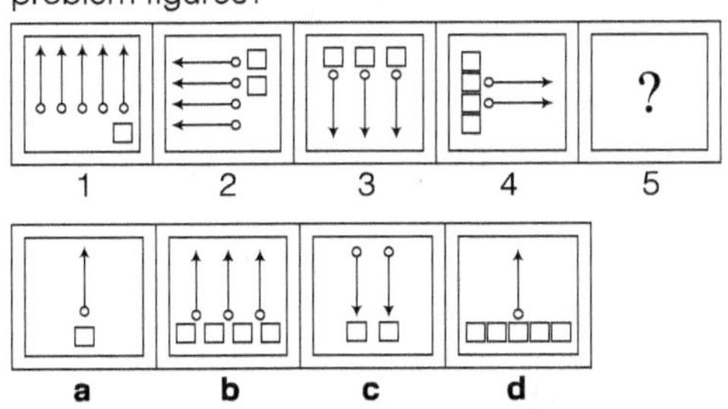

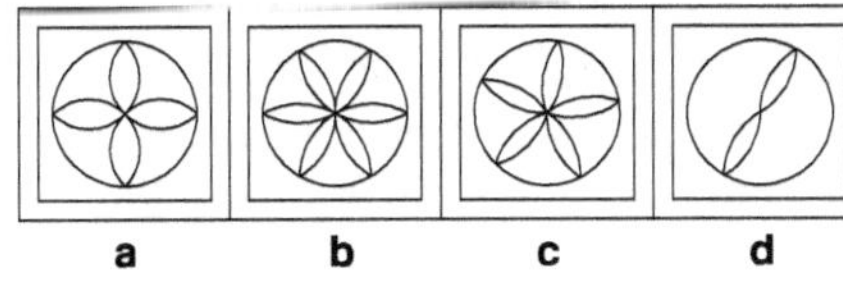

20. In this question, there are four figures as given in options (a), (b), (c) and (d). Out of these four figures, three are similar in a certain way. Choose the figure which is different from the rest.

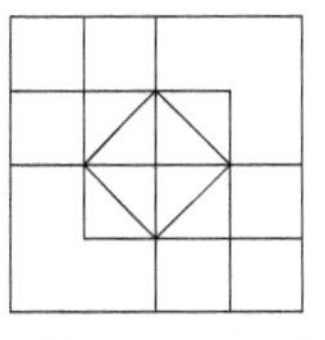

21. How many squares are there in the given figure?

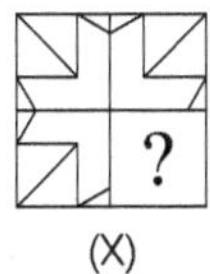

a 17   b 16   c 15   d 19

22. Find the figure from the options which completes the fig. (X).

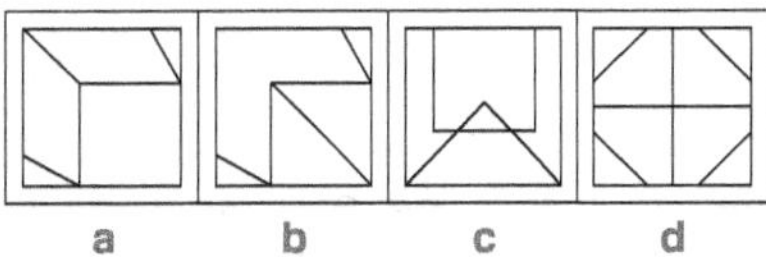

(X)

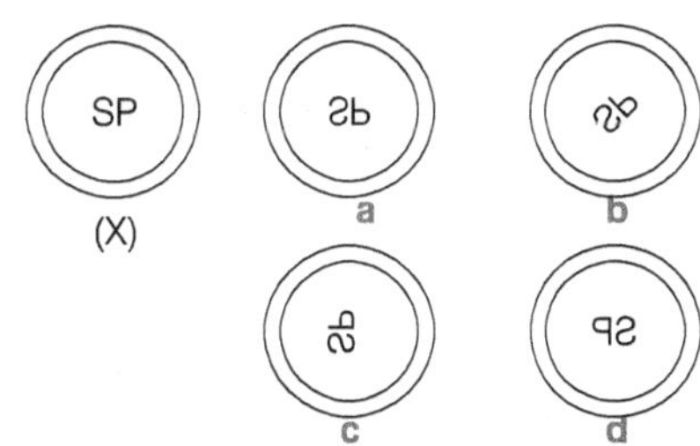

23. Choose the correct water image of the given figure (X)

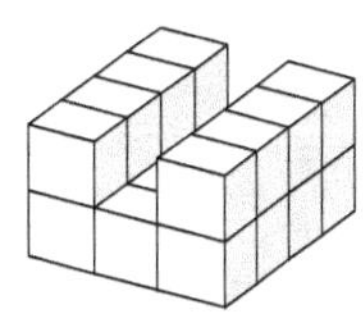

24. Count the number of cubes in the given figure.

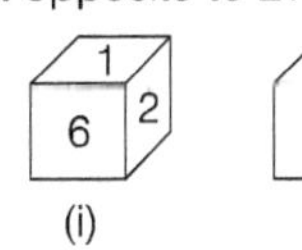

a 25   b 30   c 20   d 10

25. Two positions of a dice has been shown here. What digit will be just opposite to 2?

(i)   (ii)

a 1   b 6   c 3   d 4

Practice Set ②

A Whole Content Based Test for Class 7th Reasoning Olympiad

1. What comes next in the series given below?

   4, 8, 24, 48, 144, 288, ?

   a 576　　b 864　　c 432　　d 648

2. Find the correct set of letters which replaces the question mark.

   BAG : CDL :: TOM :?

   a URR　　b VQO　　c UST　　d YRN

3. Identify the letter to be moved from the first word to the second word, making two new words.

   | TOOLS | | LOW |

   a T　　b L　　c O　　d S

4. In the following question, find the two words, one form each group, that together make a new, meaningful word. The word from the first group always comes first.

P	Q	R
CAN	HOT	COLD

1	2	3
OR	LINE	RAIN

   a Q2　　b P3　　c Q1　　d R2

5. Insert a letter in the below figure to complete the two words.

   L
   E
   ? A T C H
   O
   N

   a O　　　　　　b M
   c A　　　　　　d B

6. If A = 6, O = 18, R = 27 and Q = 3, then $\dfrac{R \times A}{Q}$ = ?

   a O × Q　　b R　　c $\dfrac{R}{Q}$　　d A × Q

7. Choose the odd one out.

   a 400　　b 100　　c 900　　d 200

8. Akanksha walked 10 m towards East. She turned left and walked 4 m. She again turned left and walked 10 m. Now, she turned right and walked 2 m. How far and in which direction is she now from the starting point?

   a 6 m, North　　　　b 20 m, North
   c 14 m, East　　　　d 4 m, South

9. Choose the word which is different from others.

   a Aunt　　　　　　b Niece
   c Brother　　　　　d Mother

10. Find the missing term that will replace the question mark (?).

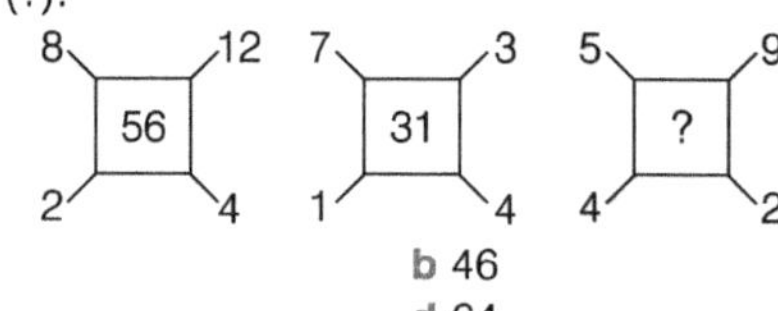

    a 20　　　　　　b 46
    c 49　　　　　　d 64

11. If '+' means '−', '−' means, '×', '×' means '÷' and '÷' means '+', then 4 − 4 ÷ 24 × 8 + 2 = ?

    a 15　　　　　　b 20
    c 17　　　　　　d 27

12. Study the given figure and answer the following question.

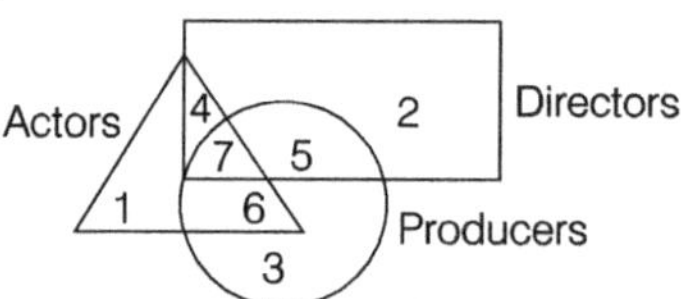

    How many actors are both directors and producers?

    a 7　　　　　　b 4 + 5 + 6
    c 6　　　　　　d 5

13. A is the father of B and C is the brother of B. How is B related to A?

    a Son　　　　　　b Daughter
    c Mother　　　　　d Cannot be determined

14. Abhishek, Parag and Vaibhav play football, hockey and cricket. Abhishek and Arpit play hockey, cricket and basketball. Abhishek, Parag, Shantanu and Vaibhav play football and cricket.

    Which game is played by all the boys?

    a Hockey　　　　　b Basketball
    c Football　　　　　d Cricket

15. Find the code for ALONE, if the code for TRAIN is BZIQV.

    a JUVWN　　　　　b ITWVM
    c HUVWM　　　　　d MITVW

16. Pick up the term which does not belong to the series.

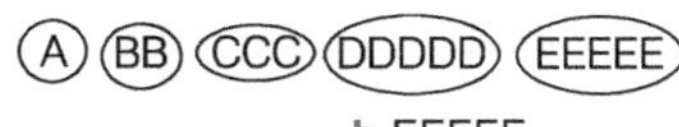

a BB	**b** EEEEE
c DDDDD	**d** CCC

17. Count the number of triangle in the figure given below.

a 3 **b** 6 **c** 4 **d** 8

18. Choose a figure that will complete the second pair in the same way as first pair.

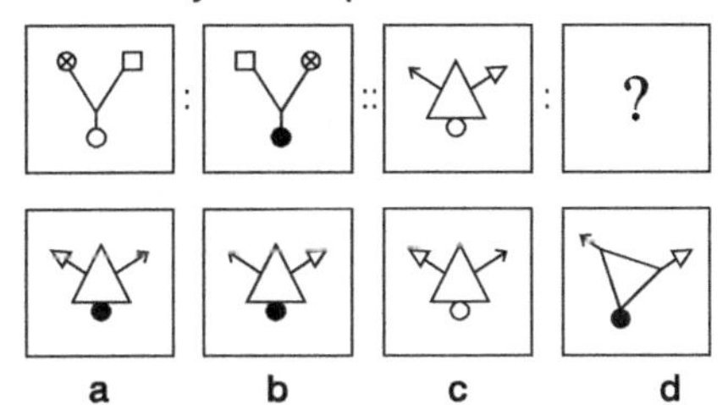

a **b** **c** **d**

19. Select the correct water image of the figure given below.

Question figure

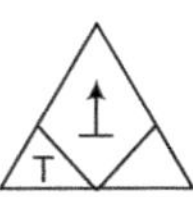

Answer Figures

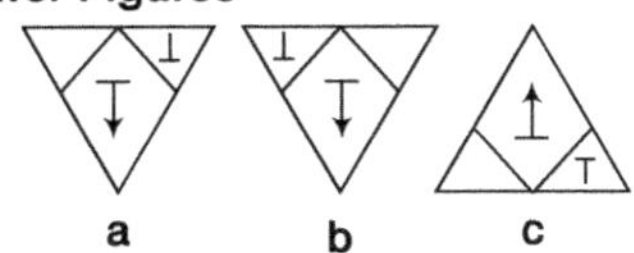

a **b** **c** **d**

20. What comes next in the series given below?

Question figures

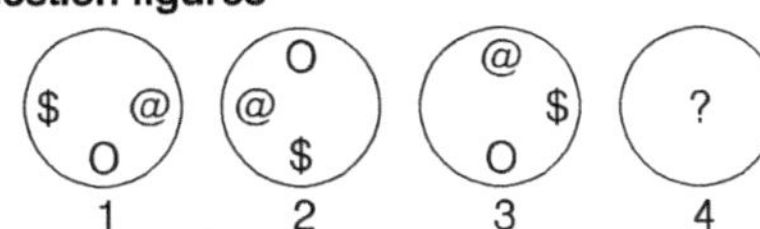

1 2 3 4

Answer figures

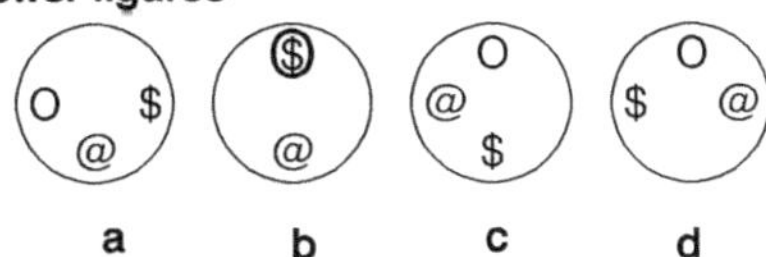

a **b** **c** **d**

21. Choose a figure which does not belong to the group.

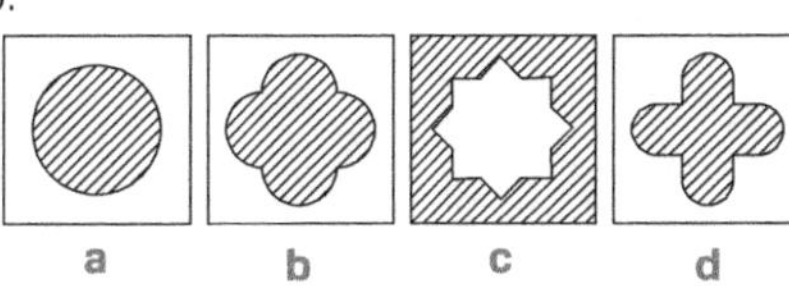

a **b** **c** **d**

22. Choose the pair in which the words bear the same relationship to each other as similar to the words of the given pair bear.

Building : Vertical

a Room : Big	**b** Lane : Wide
c Street : Horizontal	**d** Road : Narrow

23. Select the correct mirror image of the figure given below.

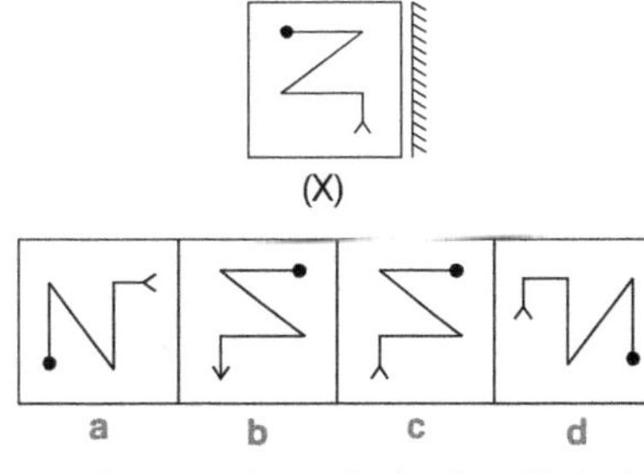

(X)

a **b** **c** **d**

24. The sheet of paper shown in the fig. (X), is folded to form a box. Choose a box from the options, that is similar to the box that is formed.

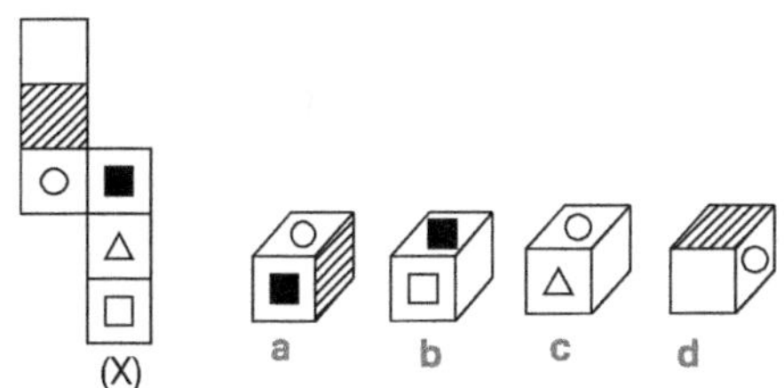

(X)

a **b** **c** **d**

25 Count the number of cubes in the following figure.

a 48
b 20
c 12
d 24

Answer & Explanations

7

Answer Sheet

Chapter_1 Playing with Words

1. (b)	**2.** (d)	**3.** (c)	**4.** (a)	**5.** (b)	**6.** (d)	**7.** (a)	**8.** (c)	**9.** (b)	**10.** (a)
11. (a)	**12.** (b)	**13.** (c)	**14.** (d)	**15.** (a)	**16.** (c)	**17.** (a)	**18.** (a)	**19.** (a)	**20.** (d)
21. (c)	**22.** (a)	**23.** (d)	**24.** (b)	**25.** (c)	**26.** (d)	**27.** (c)	**28.** (a)	**29.** (c)	**30.** (c)
31. (c)	**32.** (b)	**33.** (c)	**34.** (b)	**35.** (c)	**36.** (a)	**37.** (d)	**38.** (b)	**39.** (b)	

Chapter_2 Using Letters for Numbers

1. (b)	**2.** (c)	**3.** (d)	**4.** (c)	**5.** (d)	**6.** (a)	**7.** (c)	**8.** (c)	**9.** (d)	**10.** (c)
11. (a)	**12.** (b)	**13.** (c)	**14.** (d)	**15.** (b)	**16.** (a)	**17.** (c)	**18.** (c)	**19.** (d)	**20.** (b)

Chapter_3 Similar of Pairs

1. (d)	**2.** (b)	**3.** (a)	**4.** (a)	**5.** (d)	**6.** (b)	**7.** (b)	**8.** (c)	**9.** (a)	**10.** (d)
11. (d)	**12.** (a)	**13.** (b)	**14.** (a)	**15.** (b)	**16.** (b)	**17.** (c)	**18.** (a)	**19.** (d)	**20.** (b)
21. (c)	**22.** (b)	**23.** (d)	**24.** (a)	**25.** (c)	**26.** (c)	**27.** (c)	**28.** (c)	**29.** (a)	**30.** (b)
31. (d)	**32.** (b)	**33.** (a)	**34.** (c)	**35.** (d)	**36.** (b)	**37.** (b)	**38.** (b)	**39.** (a)	

Chapter_4 What Comes Next?

1. (b)	**2.** (c)	**3.** (d)	**4.** (c)	**5.** (c)	**6.** (d)	**7.** (b)	**8.** (c)	**9.** (c)	**10.** (c)
11. (d)	**12.** (c)	**13.** (b)	**14.** (a)	**15.** (c)	**16.** (d)	**17.** (c)	**18.** (b)	**19.** (c)	**20.** (a)
21. (d)	**22.** (b)	**23.** (c)	**24.** (d)	**25.** (d)	**26.** (b)	**27.** (b)	**28.** (a)	**29.** (d)	**30.** (a)
31. (c)	**32.** (d)	**33.** (b)	**34.** (a)						

Chapter_5 Odd One Out

1. (d)	**2.** (a)	**3.** (b)	**4.** (d)	**5.** (c)	**6.** (a)	**7.** (c)	**8.** (b)	**9.** (b)	**10.** (c)
11. (d)	**12.** (c)	**13.** (b)	**14.** (a)	**15.** (d)	**16.** (d)	**17.** (d)	**18.** (a)	**19.** (c)	**20.** (c)
21. (c)	**22.** (d)	**23.** (d)	**24.** (d)	**25.** (b)	**26.** (d)	**27.** (d)	**28.** (c)	**29.** (b)	**30.** (c)
31. (b)	**32.** (c)	**33.** (b)	**34.** (b)	**35.** (a)					

Chapter_6 Coding Decoding

1. (b)	**2.** (c)	**3.** (d)	**4.** (b)	**5.** (b)	**6.** (d)	**7.** (d)	**8.** (c)	**9.** (d)	**10.** (a)
11. (c)	**12.** (b)	**13.** (b)	**14.** (b)	**15.** (d)	**16.** (c)	**17.** (c)	**18.** (b)	**19.** (a)	**20.** (c)
21. (b)	**22.** (c)	**23.** (a)	**24.** (d)	**25.** (a)	**26.** (a)	**27.** (b)	**28.** (c)	**29.** (d)	**30.** (a)
31. (c)	**32.** (c)	**33.** (b)							

Chapter_7 Mathematical Reasoning

1. (a)	**2.** (d)	**3.** (a)	**4.** (c)	**5.** (d)	**6.** (c)	**7.** (a)	**8.** (d)	**9.** (a)	**10.** (a)
11. (c)	**12.** (c)	**13.** (d)	**14.** (b)	**15.** (a)	**16.** (a)	**17.** (a)	**18.** (c)	**19.** (d)	**20.** (a)
21. (d)	**22.** (b)	**23.** (c)	**24.** (a)	**25.** (d)	**26.** (c)	**27.** (c)	**28.** (b)	**29.** (a)	**30.** (b)
31. (c)	**32.** (d)	**33.** (b)	**34.** (b)	**35.** (a)					

Chapter_8 Puzzle Test

1. (d)	**2.** (d)	**3.** (c)	**4.** (c)	**5.** (b)	**6.** (a)	**7.** (c)	**8.** (c)	**9.** (b)	**10.** (a)
11. (c)	**12.** (a)	**13.** (c)	**14.** (b)	**15.** (c)	**16.** (b)	**17.** (c)	**18.** (b)	**19.** (a)	**20.** (d)
21. (b)	**22.** (c)								

Chapter_9 Direction Sense Test

1. (b)	**2.** (c)	**3.** (a)	**4.** (d)	**5.** (b)	**6.** (c)	**7.** (b)	**8.** (a)	**9.** (b)	**10.** (b)
11. (c)	**12.** (b)	**13.** (b)	**14.** (a)	**15.** (c)	**16.** (c)	**17.** (d)	**18.** (c)	**19.** (a)	**20.** (b)
21. (b)	**22.** (d)								

Chapter_10 Venn Diagram

1. (b)	**2.** (a)	**3.** (d)	**4.** (a)	**5.** (b)	**6.** (c)	**7.** (a)	**8.** (b)	**9.** (b)	**10.** (a)
11. (b)	**12.** (d)	**13.** (b)	**14.** (b)						

Chapter_11 Blood Relations

1. (b)	**2.** (c)	**3.** (a)	**4.** (d)	**5.** (a)	**6.** (a)	**7.** (d)	**8.** (b)	**9.** (b)	**10.** (a)
11. (d)	**12.** (a)	**13.** (b)	**14.** (b)	**15.** (a)	**16.** (d)	**17.** (c)	**18.** (d)	**19.** (a)	**20.** (c)
21. (b)	**22.** (d)	**23.** (a)	**24.** (c)						

Chapter_12 Similar Pairs

1. (d)	**2.** (c)	**3.** (b)	**4.** (d)	**5.** (a)	**6.** (c)	**7.** (a)	**8.** (b)	**9.** (c)	**10.** (c)
11. (a)	**12.** (d)	**13.** (b)	**14.** (d)	**15.** (a)	**16.** (a)	**17.** (c)	**18.** (a)	**19.** (b)	**20.** (b)
21. (b)	**22.** (c)	**23.** (b)	**24.** (b)						

Chapter_13 What Comes Next?

1.(c)	**2.**(c)	**3.**(d)	**4.**(d)	**5.**(d)	**6.**(c)	**7.**(d)	**8.**(b)	**9.**(d)	**10.**(d)
11.(c)	**12.**(b)	**13.**(c)	**14.**(d)	**15.**(a)	**16.**(d)	**17.**(b)	**18.**(a)	**19.**(a)	**20.**(b)
21.(b)	**22.**(c)	**23.**(b)	**24.**(d)	**25.**(b)	**26.**(d)	**27.**(a)	**28.**(c)	**29.**(c)	**30.**(a)
31.(b)	**32.**(b)	**33.**(d)	**34.**(a)						

Chapter_14 Odd One Out

1. (b)	**2.** (d)	**3.** (d)	**4.** (d)	**5.** (c)	**6.** (d)	**7.** (a)	**8.** (d)	**9.** (d)	**10.** (a)
11. (c)	**12.** (a)	**13.** (c)	**14.** (c)	**15.** (b)	**16.** (d)	**17.** (d)	**18.** (d)		

Chapter_15 Mirror Image and Water Image

1. (d)	**2.** (c)	**3.** (b)	**4.** (b)	**5.** (a)	**6.** (c)	**7.** (d)	**8.** (d)	**9.** (b)	**10.** (b)
11. (d)	**12.** (b)	**13.** (d)	**14.** (c)	**15.** (a)	**16.** (c)	**17.** (d)	**18.** (c)	**19.** (a)	**20.** (c)
21. (a)	**22.** (c)	**23.** (a)	**24.** (c)	**25.** (a)	**26.** (a)	**27.** (c)			

Chapter_16 Cubes and Dice

1. (b)	**2.** (d)	**3.** (b)	**4.** (c)	**5.** (b)	**6.** (d)	**7.** (d)	**8.** (d)	**9.** (d)	**10.** (d)
11. (a)	**12.** (d)	**13.** (c)	**14.** (c)	**15.** (d)	**16.** (a)	**17.** (d)	**18.** (c)	**19.** (d)	**20.** (b)
21. (d)									

Chapter_17 Counting of Figures

1. (c)	**2.** (c)	**3.** (b)	**4.** (a)	**5.** (a)	**6.** (d)	**7.** (c)	**8.** (b)	**9.** (c)	**10.** (c)
11. (a)	**12.** (b)	**13.** (a)	**14.** (b)	**15.** (c)	**16.** (a)	**17.** (b)	**18.** (d)	**19.** (b)	**20.** (c)
21. (d)	**22.** (d)								

Practice Set_1

1. (c)	**2.** (b)	**3.** (d)	**4.** (a)	**5.** (b)	**6.** (c)	**7.** (a)	**8.** (a)	**9.** (d)	**10.** (b)
11. (b)	**12.** (b)	**13.** (b)	**14.** (d)	**15.** (c)	**16.** (c)	**17.** (c)	**18.** (a)	**19.** (d)	**20.** (c)
21. (d)	**22.** (b)	**23.** (a)	**24.** (c)	**25.** (d)					

Practice Set_2

1. (b)	**2.** (a)	**3.** (d)	**4.** (a)	**5.** (b)	**6.** (a)	**7.** (d)	**8.** (a)	**9.** (c)	**10.** (b)
11. (c)	**12.** (a)	**13.** (d)	**14.** (d)	**15.** (b)	**16.** (c)	**17.** (b)	**18.** (a)	**19.** (b)	**20.** (c)
21. (c)	**22.** (c)	**23.** (c)	**24.** (a)	**25.** (d)					

1. The words are NEWS and PAPER, because when joined together, they make a new word 'NEWSPAPER'.
   So, the answer is A1.
   Hence, option (b) is correct.

2. The words are EYE and BALL, because when joined together they make a new word 'EYEBALL'. So, the answer is 2Z.
   Hence, option (d) is correct.

3. The words are BED and ROOM, because when joined together they make a new word 'BEDROOM'.
   So, the answer is 3P.
   Hence, option (c) is correct.

4. The words are AIR and PLANE, because when joined together they make a new word 'AIRPLANE'.
   So, the answer is L3.
   Hence, option (a) is correct.

5. The words are CLASS and ROOM, because when joined together they make a word 'CLASSROOM'.
   So, the answer is 2Z.
   Hence, option (b) is correct.

6. The words are DOOR and BELL, because when joined together they make a word 'DOORBELL'.
   So, the answer is B2.
   Hence, option (d) is correct.

7. The words are GOOD and NIGHT, because when joined together they make a new word 'GOODNIGHT'.
   So, the answer is 3Q.
   Hence option (a) is correct.

8. The words are IN and TO, because when joined together they make a new word 'INTO'.
   So, the answer is L3.
   Hence, option (c) is correct.

9. The words are KEY and BOARD, because when joined together they make a new word 'KEYBOARD'.
   So, the answer is 1Q.
   Hence, option (b) is correct.

10. The words are MY and SELF, because when joined together they make a new word 'MYSELF'.
    So, the answer is A3.
    Hence, option (a) is correct.

11. 'E' moves from the first word WHEAT to leave the new word WHAT and is placed into the second word to make another new word 'MEAT'.
    Hence, option (a) is correct.

12. 'N' moves from the first word SAND to leave the new word SAD and is placed into the second word to make another new word 'NEVER'.
    Hence, option (b) is correct.

13. 'A' moves from the first word READ to leave the new word RED and is placed into the second word to make new word 'ROAD'.
    Hence, option (c) is correct.

14. 'P' moves from first word PAGE to leave new word AGE and is placed into the second word to make new word 'PLAN'.
    Hence, option (b) is correct.

15. 'S' moves from the first word NEWS to leave the new word NEW and is placed into the second word to make another new word 'STEPS'.
    Hence, option (a) is correct.

16. 'O' moves from the first word COAT to leave the new word CAT and is placed into the second word to make another new word 'HELLO'.
    Hence, option (c) is correct.

17. 'L' moves from the first word BLANK to leave the new word BANK and is placed into the second word to make another new word 'LAND'.
    Hence, option (a) is correct.

18. 'R' moves from first word TIRE to leave new word TIE and is placed into second word to make new word 'RASH'.
    Hence, option (a) is correct.

19. 'M' moves from first word 'MAN' to leave a new word 'AN' and is placed into second word to make a new word 'TIME'.
    Hence, option (a) is correct.

20. 'T' moves from the first word WET to leave the new word WE and is placed into the second word to make another new word 'TEAR'.
    Hence, option (d) is correct.

21. The four words are AREA?, ?INGS, RISE? and ?HOUT.
    Here, the letter 'S' will complete all the four words as AREAS, SINGS, RISES and SHOUT
    Hence, option (c) is correct.

22. The four words are REWAR?, ?OWRY, TREA? and ?EBAR
    Here, the letter 'D' will complete all the four words as REWARD, DOWRY, TREAD and DEBAR
    Hence, option (a) is correct.

23. The four words are BRONZ?, ?NOUGH, HURDL? and ?MPLOY
    Here, the letter 'E' will complete all the four words as BRONZE, ENOUGH, HURDLE and EMPLOY.
    Hence, option (d) is correct.

24. The four words are CHANNE?, ?ESSONS, QUARRE? and ?EARNER
    Here, the letter 'L' will complete all the four words as CHANNEL, LESSONS, QUARREL and LEARNER
    Hence, option (b) is correct.

25. The four words are CAR?, ? ASE, DIC? and ? VEN
    Here, the letter 'E' will complete all the four words as shown below CARE, EASE, DICE and EVEN
    Hence, option (c) is correct.

26. The four words are PANI?, ?AVIL, CIVI? and ?ABLE
    Here, the letter 'C' will complete all the four words as PANIC, CAVIL, CIVIC and CABLE
    Hence, option (d) is correct.

27. The four words are CRO?, ?IND, FLE? and ?ORM Here, the letter 'W' will complete all the four words as CROW, WIND, FLEW and WORM
Hence, option (c) is correct.

28. The four words are DEM?, ?PEN, RED? and ?VAL
Here, the letter 'O' will complete all the four words as DEMO, OPEN, REDO and OVAL
Hence, option (a) is correct.

29. The four words are ABAC?, ?NOBS, QUIC? and ?NEEL
Here, the letter 'K' will complete all the four words as ABACK, KNOBS, QUICK and KNEEL
Hence, option (c) is correct.

30. The two words are LAUG ? and C?ANT. Here, the lettor 'H' will complete both the words as LAUGH and CHANT.
Hence, option (c) is correct.

31. The three words are COP?, ?EV? and ?OLT. Here, the letter B and Y will complete all the words as shown in following figure.

The words are COPY, BEVY and BOLT.
Hence, option (c) is correct.

32. The three words are BOR?, K?O?, ?EAR.
Here, the letters 'NW' will complete all the words as shown in the following figure.

Hence, option (b) is correct.

33. The three words are V?NUS, M?RC?RY and PL?TO.
Here, the letters 'EU' will complete all the three words in the figure as shown below

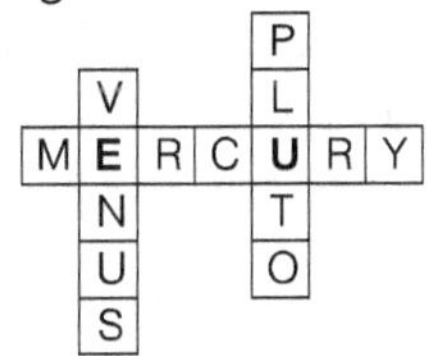

Therefore, the complete words are VENUS, MERCURY and PLUTO
Hence, option (c) is correct.

34. The three words are ?HEA?, ?HEFS and ALER?
Here, the letters 'CT' will complete all the three words in figure as shown below

Therefore, the complete words are CHEAT, CHEFS and ALERT.
Hence, option (b) is correct.

35. The two words are ST? and ?PLE
Here, the letters 'RIP' will complete both the words as STRIP and RIPPLE.
Hence, option (c) is correct.

36. The two words are TEA? and ?ORE
Here, the letters 'CH' will complete both words as TEACH and CHORE.
Hence, option (a) is correct.

37. The two words are TOR? and ?AIR
Here, the letters 'CH' will complete both the words as TORCH and CHAIR.
Hence, option (d) is correct.

38. The two words are ST? and ?ER
Here, the letters 'RING' will complete both the words as STRING and RINGER.
Hence, option (b) is correct.

39. The two words are GRAVI? and? PING
Here, the letters 'TY' will complete both the words as GRAVITY, TYPING.
Hence, option (b) is correct.

(2) Using Letters for Numbers

1. On putting the values of the letters in the given equation, we get

$$C \div I \times P - H$$
$$\downarrow \quad \downarrow \quad \downarrow \quad \downarrow$$
$$12 \quad 3 \quad 4 \quad 13$$

(By using the rule of BODMAS)
$= 12 \div 3 \times 4 - 13$
$= 4 \times 4 - 13 = 16 - 13 = 3$
Here, we can see that the value '3' represents the letter 'I'.

[as given in question]
So, the missing letter is 'I'.
Hence, option (b) is correct.

2. On putting the values of the letters in the given equation, we get

$$F - W + R + F$$
$$\downarrow \quad \downarrow \quad \downarrow \quad \downarrow$$
$$7 \quad 6 \quad 4 \quad 7$$

$= 7 - 6 + 4 + 7 = 12 = 18 - 6 = 12$
Here, we can see that the value '12' represents the letter 'O'.

[as given in question]
So, the missing letter is 'O'.
Hence, option (c) is correct.

3. On putting the values of the letters in the given equation, we get

$$W \times W \div X - Y$$
$$\downarrow \quad \downarrow \quad \downarrow \quad \downarrow$$
$$6 \quad 6 \quad 4 \quad 3$$

$= 6 \times 6 \div 4 - 3 = 6 \times \dfrac{6}{4} - 3$
$= 6 \times 1.5 - 3 = 9 - 3 = 6$
Here, we can see that the value '6' represents the letter 'W'.

[as given in question]
So, the missing value is W'.
Hence, option (d) is correct.

4. On putting the values of the letters in the given equation, we get

X ÷ F + G – K
↓   ↓   ↓   ↓
18   9   4   2

$= 18 \div 9 + 4 - 2$
$= 2 + 4 - 2 = 6 - 2 = 4$

Here, the value '4' represents the letter 'G'.　[as given in question]
So, the missing value is 'G'.
Hence, option (c) is correct.

5. On putting the values of the letters in the given equation, we get

R ÷ S + U ÷ T
↓   ↓   ↓   ↓
81   9   20   10

$= 81 \div 9 + 20 \div 10 = 9 + 2 = 11$

Here, the value '11' does not represent any letter.
Hence, option (d) is correct.

6. On putting the values of the letters, we get

B E A D
↓ ↓ ↓ ↓
2 5 1 4

Now, $2 + 5 + 1 + 4 = 12$
Hence, option (a) is correct.

7. On putting the values of the letters, we get

S E E K
↓ ↓ ↓ ↓
19 5 5 11

Now, $19 + 5 + 5 + 11 = 40$
Hence, option (c) is correct.

8. On putting the values of the letters, we get

T E L L
↓ ↓ ↓ ↓
20 5 12 12

Now, $20 + 5 + 12 + 12 = 49$
Hence, option (c) is correct.

9. On putting the values of the letters in the given expression, we get

O ÷ C – B + T
↓   ↓   ↓   ↓
15   3   2   20

Now, $15 \div 3 - 2 + 20$
$= 5 - 2 + 20 = 23$
Hence, option (d) is correct.

10. On putting the values of the letters in the given expression, we get

Y ÷ E × J – O
↓   ↓   ↓   ↓
25   5   10   15

Now, $25 \div 5 \times 10 - 15$
$= 5 \times 10 - 15 = 50 - 15 = 35$
Hence, option (c) is correct.

11. On putting the values of the letters in the given expression, we get

N ÷ G × B + P – J
↓   ↓   ↓   ↓   ↓
14   7   2   16   10

Now, $14 \div 7 \times 2 + 16 - 10$
$= 2 \times 2 + 16 - 10$
$= 4 + 16 - 10 = 10$
Hence, option (a) is correct.

12. Given equation,

$$R \times R + R = Q \times Q - [?]$$

Consider it as LHS and RHS
On taking, LHS $= R \times R + R$
On putting the values of the letters, we get

LHS = R × R + R
     ↓   ↓   ↓
     9   9   9

$= 9 \times 9 + 9 = 81 + 9 = 90$
On taking RHS, $= Q \times Q - [?]$
On putting the values of the letters in RHS equation, we get

RHS = Q × Q – [?]
     ↓   ↓
     10 × 10 – [?]

Now, if we put LHS = RHS, then
$90 = 10 \times 10 - [?]$
$\Rightarrow 90 = 100 - [?] \Rightarrow 100 - 90 = [?]$
$\therefore [?] = 10 = Q$
So, the missing letter is 'Q'.
Hence, option (b) is correct.

13. Given equation,

$V \times X + Q = P + O + [?]$

Consider it, as LHS and RHS
On taking LHS $= V \times X + Q$
On putting the values of the letters in LHS equation, we get

LHS = V × X + Q
     ↓   ↓   ↓
     5 × 3 + 10

$= 5 \times 3 + 10 = 15 + 10 = 25$
Now taking, RHS $= P + O + [?]$
On putting the values of the letters in RHS equation, we get

RHS = P + O + [?]
     ↓   ↓
     11   12

$= 11 + 12 + [?] = 23 + [?]$
Now, if we put LHS = RHS, then
$25 = 23 + [?] \Rightarrow 25 - 23 = [?]$
$\Rightarrow 2 = [?] = Y$ [as given in question]
Thus, the missing letter is 'Y'.
Hence, option (c) is correct.

14. Given equation,

$$Y + X + [?] = S$$

Consider it as LHS = RHS
On, taking, LHS $= Y + X + [?]$
On putting the values of the letters in LHS equation, we get

LHS = Y + X + [?]
     ↓   ↓
     2 + 3 + [?]

$= 2 + 3 + [?] = 5 + [?]$
Now taking, RHS $= S$
On putting the value of the letter in RHS equation, we get

RHS = S
     ↓
     8

Now, LHS = RHS
$\Rightarrow 5 + [?] = 8 \Rightarrow [?] = 8 - 5$
$\therefore [?] = 3 = X$ [as given in question]
So, the missing letter is 'X'.
Hence, option (d) is correct.

15. Given equation,

$Y \times (N + Y) = Q + [?] + L$

Consider it, as LHS and RHS
On taking, LHS $= Y \times (N + Y)$
On putting the values of the letters in LHS equation, we get

LHS = Y × (N + Y)
     ↓   ↓   ↓
     2   13   2

$= 2 \times (13 + 2) = 2 \times 15 = 30$
Now taking, RHS $= Q + [?] + L$
On putting the values of the letters in RHS equation, we get

RHS = Q + [?] + L
     ↓   ↓
     10 + [?] + 15

Now, LHS = RHS
$\Rightarrow 30 = 10 + [?] + 15$
$\Rightarrow 30 = 25 + [?] \Rightarrow 30 - 25 = [?]$
$\therefore 5 = [?] = V$ [as given in question]
Thus, the missing letter is 'V'.
Hence, option (b) is correct.

16. On putting the values of the letters in the given equation, we get

$$\frac{N \times V}{K} = \frac{14 \times 2}{7} = \frac{28}{7} = 4$$

Here, the value '4' represents the letter 'I'.

[as given in question]

So, the missing value is 'I'.
Hence, option (a) is correct.

17. On putting the values of letters in the given equation, we get

$$X \div Z \times S + H - T \times Y$$
$$= 13 \div 26 \times 20 + 50 - 6 \times 2$$
$$= \frac{1}{2} \times 20 + 50 - 6 \times 2$$

$$= 10 + 50 - 12 = 60 - 12 = 48$$

Here, the value '48' represents the letter 'W'.   [as given in question]
So, the missing letter is 'W'.
Hence, option (c) is correct.

18. On putting the values of the letters in given equation, we get

$$T \div S \times W - P = 10 \div 5 \times 12 - 4$$
$$= 2 \times 12 - 4$$
$$= 24 - 4 = 20$$

Here, the value 20 represents the letter 'N'.
Hence, option (c) is correct.

19. On putting the values of the letters in the given equation, we get

$$S - P + Q = 16 - 9 + 15$$
$$= 7 + 15 = 22$$

Here, the value '22' does not represents any letter.
Hence, option (d) is correct.

20. On putting the values of the letters in the given equation, we get

$$A \times D - B - C = 1 \times 20 - 3 - 14$$
$$= 20 - 3 - 14 = 3$$

Here, the value '3' represents the letter 'B'.
Hence, option (b) is correct.

3 Similar Pairs

Similarity of Numbers

1. As, $6^2 = 36$
Similarly, $9^2 = 81$
So, 9 is to 81.
Hence, option (d) is correct.

2. The relation is as $5 - 3 = 2$
In the same way, $7 - 4 = 3$
Hence, option (b) is correct.

3. The relation is as $6 \times 5 = 30$
In the same way, $8 \times 8 = 64$
Hence, option (a) is correct.

4. Here sum of digits of 81 is
$$8 + 1 = 9$$
Similarly, sum of digits of 64 is
$$6 + 4 = 10$$
Hence, option (a) is correct.

5. In this question, we just reverse the digits of the given number and starting from the unit's place of digit

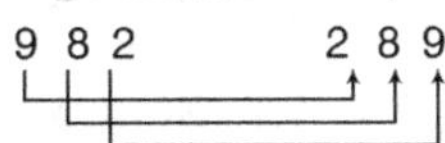

982 becomes 289
Similarly in case of 761 starting from unit's place, which is, 1 i.e.
$$761 \rightarrow 167$$
761 becomes 167.
Hence, option (d) is correct.

6. In this question,

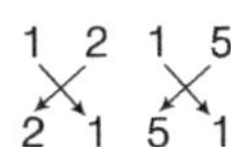

We change the positions of digits in a pair of two digits each.
Similarly,

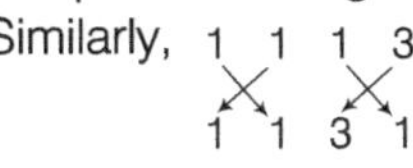

$$1113 \rightarrow 1131$$
1113 becomes 1131
Hence, option (b) is correct.

7. The relation is as $48 \div 3 = 16$
In the same way, $72 \div 3 = 24$
Hence, option (b) is correct.

8. The relation is as
$$8 \times 5 + 0 = 40 + 0 = 40$$
In the same way,
$$7 \times 8 + 2 = 56 + 2 = 58$$
Hence, option (c) is correct.

9. The relation is as
$$6^3 = 6 \times 6 \times 6 = 216$$
In the same way,
$$5^3 = 5 \times 5 \times 5 = 125$$
Hence, option (a) is correct.

10. The relation is as
$$64 = 8^2, \; 8 + 2 = 10$$
In the same way,
$$81 = 9^2, \; 9 + 2 = 11$$
Hence, option (d) is correct.

Similarity of Letters

11. The relation can be shown as

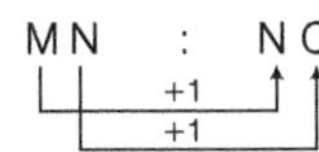

Hence, option (d) is correct.

In the same way,

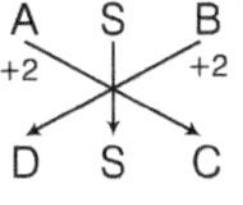

Hence, option (d) is correct.

12. The relation can be shown as

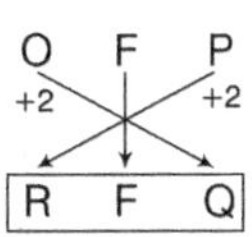

In the same way,

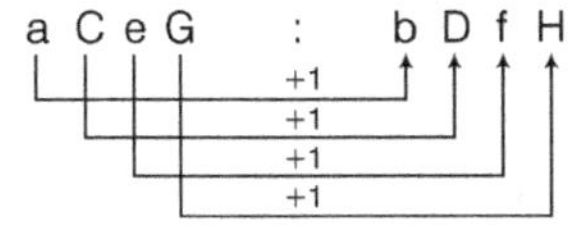

Hence, option (a) is correct.

13. The relation can be shown as

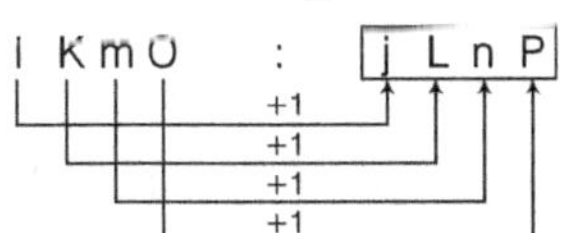

In the same way,

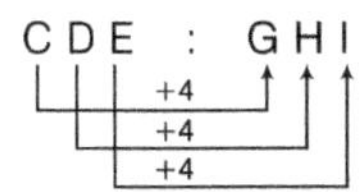

Hence, option (b) is correct.

14. The relation can be shown as

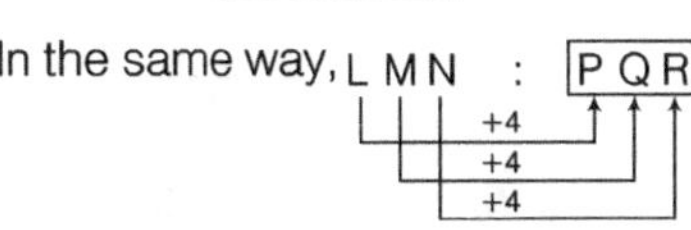

In the same way,

Hence, option (a) is correct.

15. The relation can be shown as

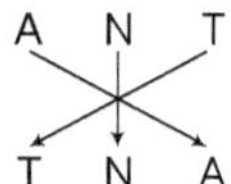

In the same way,

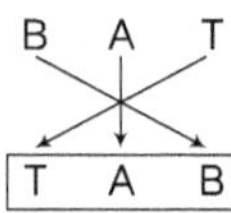

Hence, option (b) is correct.

16. The relation can be shown as

H O R S E
↓ +2↓ ↓ +2↓ ↓
H Q R U E

In the same way,

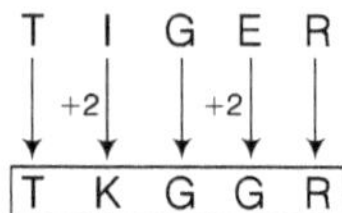

Hence, option (b) is correct.

17. The relation can be shown as

S I M I L A R
M I S I R A L

In the same way,

Hence, option (c) is correct.

18. The relation can be represented as

T O M
−2↓ −2↓ −2↓
R M K

Similarly,

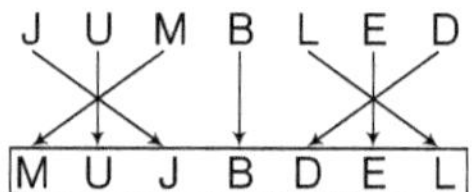

Hence, option (a) is correct.

19. The relation can be represented as

P A C E
+1↓ +2↓ +3↓ +4↓
Q C F I

Similarly,

O A T H
+1↓ +2↓ +3↓ +4↓
P C W L

Hence, option (d) is correct.

20. The relation can be represented as

D F H J
+3↓ −3↓ +3↓ −3↓
G C K G

Similarly,

Hence, option (b) is correct.

21. The relation can be represented as

N A T I O N
A N I T N O

Similarly,

H U N G R Y
U H G N Y R

Hence, option (c) is correct.

Similarity of Words

22. As, TREE originates from ROOT, in the same way SMOKE originates from FIRE.
Hence, option (b) is correct.

23. As, GOOD is the word opposite in meaning to BAD, in the same way FLOOR is opposite to ROOF.
Hence, option (d) is correct.

24. As, OVAL is the figure which is similar to the CIRCLE, in the same way RECTANGLE is the figure which is similar to SQUARE as both of them have four corners.
Hence, option (a) is correct.

25. As, the function of EYE is to SEE, in the same way the function of EAR is to HEAR.
Hence, option (c) is correct.

26. Oxygen is inhaled by us to survive, similarly we exhale carbon dioxide in the process of breathing.
Hence, option (c) is correct.

27. Feeling of guilt comes with mistakes done in past and that of hope for a better future.
Hence, option (c) is correct.

28. As, RAINING follows SUMMER season, in the same way JANUARY follows DECEMBER.
Hence, option (c) is correct.

29. As, WATER is the medium to SWIM, in the same way GROUND is the place to PLAY.
Hence, option (a) is correct.

30. As, JACKAL and DOG belong to the same class, in the same way ORANGE and LEMON belong to the same class.
Hence, option (b) is correct.

31. As, NEST is made up of STRAWS, in the same way CLOTH is made up of THREADS.
Hence, option (d) is correct.

32. Cricket is an outdoor game is correct, so we have to find out the correct match from the given options.
Squash, Chess are indoor games. Badminton is also an indoor game. Tennis is an outdoor game.
Hence, option (b) is correct.

33. Book is published by Publisher. Similarly, the film is directed by director.
Hence, option (a) is correct.

34. Oven keeps the food hot, similarly Refrigerator keeps the food cold.
Hence, option (c) is correct.

35. As, YEAST is used to make BREAD, in the same way BACTERIA is used to make CURD.
Hence, option (d) is correct.

36. As, PULL is opposite to PUSH, in the same way PICK is opposite to THROW.
Hence, option (b) is correct.

37. As, man wears trousers, in the same way woman wears skirt.
Hence, option (b) is correct.

38. As, court is a place, where there must be truthfulness, in the same way Restaurant is a place, where there must be cleanliness.
Hence, option (b) is correct.

39. As, arrival is the opposite of departure, in the same way life is the opposite of death.
Hence, option (a) is correct.

4 What Comes Next?

Number Series

1. The series can be represented as

45   44   42   39   35   [30]

with differences −1, −2, −3, −4, −5.

So, the next term will be 30.
Hence, option (b) is correct.

2. The series can be represented as

$$1 \longrightarrow 9 \longrightarrow 25 \longrightarrow 49 \longrightarrow \boxed{81}$$
$$(1)^2 \longrightarrow (3)^2 \longrightarrow (5)^2 \longrightarrow (7)^2 \longrightarrow (9)^2$$

The series consists of the square of consecutive odd numbers. So, the next term will be 81.
Hence, option (c) is correct.

3. The series can be represented as

234   236   239   243   248   [254]

with differences +2, +3, +4, +5, +6.

So, the next term will be 254.
Hence, option (d) is correct.

4. The series can be represented as

[3003]   3006   3009   3012

with differences +3, +3, +3.

So, the missing term will be 3003.
Hence, option (c) is correct.

5. The given series is a combination of two series based on two different pattern.

1st series can be represented as

5   4   3   2   1

with differences −1, −1, −1, −1.

2nd series can be represented as

6   7   8   9   10

with differences +1, +1, +1, +1.

So, next terms will be 1, 10.
Hence, option (c) is correct.

6. The series can be represented as

$$11 \to 13 \to 17 \to 19 \to 23 \to \textcircled{29}$$

Here, we can see that, the series contain consecutive prime numbers.
So, the next term will be 29.
Hence, option (d) is correct.

7. The series can be represented as

$$32 \xrightarrow{\div 2} 16 \xrightarrow{\div 2} 8 \xrightarrow{\div 2} 4 \xrightarrow{\div 2} \textcircled{2}$$

So, the next term will be 2.
Hence, option (b) is correct.

8. The series can be represented as

$66 \Rightarrow 6 + 6 = 12$, $75 \Rightarrow 7 + 5 = 12$
$84 \Rightarrow 8 + 4 = 12$, $93 \Rightarrow 9 + 3 = 12$

So, the next term will be $\boxed{93\text{-}12}$.
Hence, option (c) is correct.

9. The series can be represented as

$$8 \xrightarrow{+5} 13 \xrightarrow{+5} 18 \xrightarrow{+5} \overset{\boxed{23}}{24} \xrightarrow{+5} 28 \xrightarrow{+5} 33$$

Here, 23 should come in place of 24.
Hence, option (c) is correct.

10. The series can be represented as

$$52 \xrightarrow{+1} 53 \xrightarrow{+2} 55 \xrightarrow{+1} 56 \xrightarrow{+2} \underset{59}{\boxed{58}}$$

Here, 58 should come in place of 59.
Hence, option (c) is correct.

11. The series can be represented as

8   27   64   [125]/126   216
$(2)^3$ $(3)^3$ $(4)^3$ $(5)^3$ $(6)^3$

The series contain the cube of consecutive numbers.
Therefore, 125 should come in place of 126. So, 126 does not belong to the series.
Hence, option (d) is correct.

12. The series can be represented as

$$96 \quad 48 \quad 24 \quad \underset{}{\overset{\boxed{12}}{13}} \quad 6$$

with differences +2, +2, +2, +2.

Here, 12 should come in place of 13. So, 13 does not belong to the series.
Hence, option (c) is correct.

13. The series can be represented as

$$3 \xrightarrow{\times 3} 9 \xrightarrow{\times 3} \underset{27}{\boxed{26}} \xrightarrow{\times 3} 81 \xrightarrow{\times 3} 243$$

Here, 27 should come in place 26. So, 26 does not belong to the series.
Hence, option (b) is correct.

14. The series can be represented as

$$12 \xrightarrow{+1} 13 \xrightarrow{+1} 14 \xrightarrow{+1} 15 \xrightarrow{+1} 16 \xrightarrow{+1} 17$$
$$21 \xrightarrow{-2} 19 \xrightarrow{-2} 17 \xrightarrow{-2} 15 \xrightarrow{-2} \underset{13}{\boxed{12}} \xrightarrow{-2} 11$$

Here, 13 should come in place of 12.
So, $\boxed{\dfrac{16}{12}}$ does not belong to the series.
Hence, option (a) is correct.

15. The series can be represented as

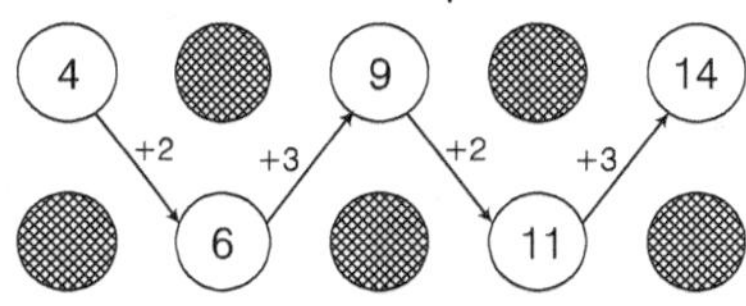

So, the missing term will be 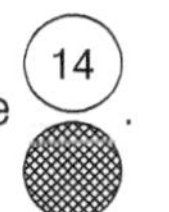 14 .

Hence, option (c) is correct.

Letter Series

16. The series can be represented as

$$U \xrightarrow{+2} W \xrightarrow{+2} Y \xrightarrow{+2} A \xrightarrow{+2} \boxed{C}$$

So, the next term will be C.
Hence, option (d) is correct.

17. The series can be represented as

$$M \xrightarrow{-1} L \xrightarrow{-1} K \xrightarrow{-1} J \xrightarrow{-1} \boxed{I}$$
$$N \xrightarrow{+1} O \xrightarrow{+1} P \xrightarrow{+1} Q \xrightarrow{+1} \boxed{R}$$

Therefore, the next term will be IR.
Hence, option (c) is correct.

18. The series can be represented as

$$AB \xrightarrow{+1} CD \xrightarrow{+1} EF \xrightarrow{+1} GH \xrightarrow{+1} \boxed{IJ}$$
$$Z \xrightarrow{-1} Y \xrightarrow{-1} X \xrightarrow{-1} W \xrightarrow{-1} \boxed{V}$$

Therefore, the next term will be IJV.
Hence, option (b) is correct.

19. The series can be represented as

$$Y \xrightarrow{-1} X \xrightarrow{-1} W \xrightarrow{-1} V \xrightarrow{-1} \boxed{U}$$
$$Z \xrightarrow{-1} Y \xrightarrow{-1} X \xrightarrow{-1} W \xrightarrow{-1} \boxed{V}$$

So, the next term will be UV.
Hence, option (c) is correct.

20. The series can be represented as

$$E \xrightarrow{+3} \boxed{H} \xrightarrow{+3} K \xrightarrow{+3} N \xrightarrow{+3} Q$$
$$G \xrightarrow{+3} \boxed{J} \xrightarrow{+3} M \xrightarrow{+3} P \xrightarrow{+3} S$$

Therefore, the missing term will be HJ.
Hence, option (a) is correct.

21. The series can be represented as

$$J \xrightarrow{+3} M \xrightarrow{+3} P$$
$$\xrightarrow{+3} \boxed{S} \xrightarrow{+3} V \xrightarrow{+3} Y$$

First letter of the group of alphabet change in order of (+ 3) and the second letter of the group of alphabet change as shown below

$$K \xrightarrow{+3} N \xrightarrow{+3} Q$$
$$\xrightarrow{+3} \boxed{T} \xrightarrow{+3} W \xrightarrow{+3} Z$$

Therefore, missing term will be ST.
Hence, option (d) is correct.

22. The series can be represented as

$$J \xrightarrow{+2} L \xrightarrow{+2} N \xrightarrow{+2}$$
$$\underset{\boxed{P}}{O} \xrightarrow{+2} R$$

Here, P should come in place of O.
So, O does not belong to the series
Hence, option (b) is correct.

23. The series can be represented as

$$Nn \xrightarrow{+1} Oo \xrightarrow{+1} \underset{\boxed{PP}}{PP}$$
$$\xrightarrow{+1} Qq \xrightarrow{+1} Rr$$

Here, Pp should come in place of PP.
So, PP does not belong to the series
Hence, option (c) is correct.

24. The series can be represented as

Hh   Ii   Jj   Kk   Ll

Here, the first letter is in capital alphabetical order and the second letter is in small alphabetical order. Therefore, Jj should come in place of JJ.
So, JJ does not belong to the series.
Hence, option (d) is correct.

25. The series can be represented as

$$H \xrightarrow{-4} D \xrightarrow{-3} A$$
$$\xrightarrow{-2} Y \xrightarrow{-1} X$$
$$h \xrightarrow{+1} i \xrightarrow{+2} k$$
$$\xrightarrow{+3} n \xrightarrow{+4} \underset{\boxed{r}}{s}$$

Here, in the first letter series the number to be subtracted is

decreased by 1 to obtain the next letter.
And in second letter series each time the number to be added is increased by 1 to get the next letter.
Therefore, Xr should come in place of Xs.
So, Xs does not belong to the series.
Hence, option (d) is correct.

26. The series can be represented as

$$TUV \xrightarrow{+2} XYZ \xrightarrow{+2} BCD$$
$$\xrightarrow{+2} \underset{EFG}{\boxed{FGH}} \xrightarrow{+2} JKL$$

Therefore, FGH should come in place of EFG.
So, EFG does not belong to the series.
Hence, option (b) is correct.

Alpha-Numeric Series

27. The series can be represented as

$$E \xrightarrow{+1} F \xrightarrow{+1} G \xrightarrow{+1} H \xrightarrow{+1} \boxed{I}$$
$$6 \xrightarrow{+2} 8 \xrightarrow{+2} 10 \xrightarrow{+2} 12 \xrightarrow{+2} \boxed{14}$$

Therefore, the next term will be 14.
Hence, option (b) is correct.

28. The series can be represented as

$$L \xrightarrow{+2} N \xrightarrow{+2} P \xrightarrow{+2} R \xrightarrow{+2} \boxed{T}$$
$$4 \longrightarrow 9 \longrightarrow 16 \longrightarrow 25 \longrightarrow \boxed{36}$$
$$(2)^2 \xrightarrow{+1} (3)^2 \xrightarrow{+1} (4)^2 \xrightarrow{+1} (5)^2 \xrightarrow{+1} (6)^2$$

Therefore, the next term will be $\dfrac{T}{36}$.
Hence, option (a) is correct.

29. The series can be represented as

EF	GH	IJ	KL	MN
24	22	20	18	16

Therefore, the missing term will be $\dfrac{GH}{22}$.
Hence, option (d) is correct.

30. The series can be represented as

P	O	N	M	L
1	3	9	27	81

Therefore, the missing term will be $\dfrac{M}{27}$.
Hence, option (a) is correct.

31. The series can be represented as

$$A \xrightarrow{+2} C \xrightarrow{+2} E \xrightarrow{+2} G \xrightarrow{+2} \boxed{I}$$
$$3 \xrightarrow{+6} 9 \xrightarrow{-3} 6 \xrightarrow{+6} 12 \xrightarrow{-3} \boxed{9}$$

So, the next term will be I/9.
Hence, option (c) is correct.

32. The series can be represented as

$$A \xrightarrow{+5} F \xrightarrow{+5} \boxed{K} \xrightarrow{+5} P$$
$$1 \xrightarrow{+1} 2 \xrightarrow{+1} \boxed{3} \xrightarrow{+1} 4$$

So, the next term will be K/3.
Hence, option (d) is correct.

33. The series can be represented as

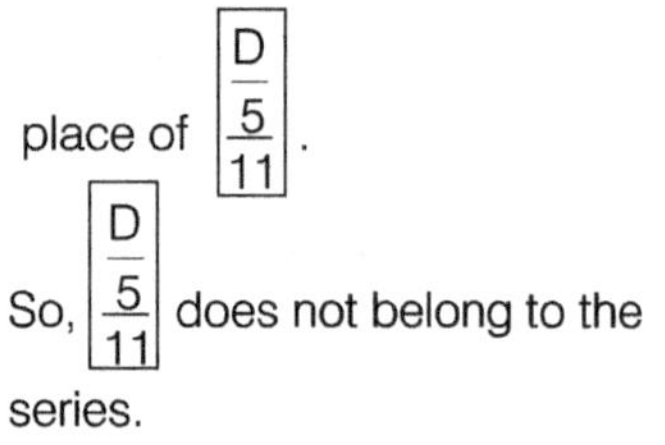

$$A \xrightarrow{+1} B \xrightarrow{+1} \underset{\boxed{C}}{D}$$
$$\xrightarrow{+1} D \xrightarrow{+1} E$$
$$3 \xrightarrow{+1} 4 \xrightarrow{+1} 5$$
$$\xrightarrow{+1} 6 \xrightarrow{+1} 7$$
$$8 \xrightarrow{+2} 10 \xrightarrow{+2} \underset{12}{\boxed{11}}$$
$$\xrightarrow{+2} 14 \xrightarrow{+2} 16$$

Therefore, $\boxed{\dfrac{C}{\dfrac{5}{12}}}$ should come in

place of $\boxed{\dfrac{D}{\dfrac{5}{11}}}$.

So, $\boxed{\dfrac{D}{\dfrac{5}{11}}}$ does not belong to the series.
Hence, option (b) is correct.

34. The series can be represented as

$$PQR \xrightarrow{+1} STU \xrightarrow{+1} VWX$$
$$\xrightarrow{+1} \underset{ZAB}{\boxed{YZA}} \xrightarrow{+1} BCD$$
$$1 \xrightarrow{+2} 3 \xrightarrow{+2} 5$$
$$\xrightarrow{+2} \underset{6}{\boxed{7}} \xrightarrow{+2} 9$$

Therefore, YZA7 should come in place of ZAB6.
So, ZAB6 does not belong to the series.
Hence, option (a) is correct.

Word Classification

1. Except square, all others are three-dimensional and square is two-dimensional. So, square is odd one out.
Hence, option (d) is correct.

2. Except universe, all others are the part of the universe. So, universe is different from others.
Hence, option (a) is correct.

3. Except fox, all others are belong to the cat family. So, fox is different from the others.
Hence, option (b) is correct.

4. Except foul, all others are synonyms. So, foul does not belong to the group.
Hence, option (d) is correct.

5. Except home, all others are human settlements. So, home does not belong to the group.
Hence, option (c) is correct.

Number Classification

6. Here, $49 = 7^2$, $36 = 6^2$ and $25 = 5^2$, but 32 is not a perfect square of any number. So, 32 is odd one out.
Hence, option (a) is correct.

7. Numbers 6, 12 and 18 are multiples of 6, but 25 is not a multiple of 6.
$6 \times 1 = 6, \quad 6 \times 2 = 12$
$6 \times 3 = 18, \quad 6 \times 4 = 24 \neq 25$
So, 25 is odd one out.
Hence, option (c) is correct.

8. Here, in all the options except (b) the sum of digits is 10.
As, $7 + 3 = 10$, $6 + 4 = 10$,
$5 + 5 = 10$, but $8 + 1 = 9 \neq 10$
So, 81 is odd one out.
Hence, option (b) is correct.

9. The addition of two digits give an odd number but in option (b) the addition of two digits give an even number i.e. 8.
So, $\boxed{35,\ 8}$ is the odd one out
Hence, option (b) is correct.

10. Here, $\dfrac{24}{12} = 2$, $\dfrac{26}{13} = 2$, $\dfrac{28}{14} = 2$
and $\dfrac{32}{15} = 2.13$
As, we can see that 2 is common among three but 2.13 is different from the others. So, 32-15 is odd one out.
Hence, option (c) is correct.

11. Except 121, all others are even numbers and 121 is an odd number. So, 121 does not belong to the group.
Hence, option (c) is correct.

12. Here, we see that the numbers are written as many times as the count value is
$1 \rightarrow$ written one time
$2 \rightarrow$ written two times
$4 \rightarrow$ written four times
Similarly, '3' should be written three times but it is written four times. So, 3333 is odd one out.
Hence, option (c) is correct.

13. Except 25, all others are cubes of numbers. But 25 is the square of a number i.e. 5.
Here, $(2)^3 = 8$, $(3)^3 = 27$, $(4)^3 = 64$
But $(5)^2 = 25 \neq (5)^3$
So, 25 does not belong to the group.
Hence, option (b) is correct.

14. Except 81, all others are prime numbers, but 81 is not a prime number. So, 81 does not belong to the group.
Hence, option (a) is correct.

15. Here, $36\text{-}12 \Rightarrow 36 \div 12 = 3$
$39\text{-}13 \Rightarrow 39 \div 13 = 3$
$45\text{-}15 \Rightarrow 45 \div 15 = 3$
But $50\text{-}16 \Rightarrow 50 \div 16$
$= 3.125 \neq 3$
So, 50-16 is odd one out.
Hence, option (d) is correct.

16. Here, $\dfrac{42}{3} = 14$, $\dfrac{27}{3} = 9$,
$\dfrac{75}{3} = 25$ and $\dfrac{57}{3} = 19$

Here, 14, 9 and 25 are composite numbers and 19 is a prime number. So, $\dfrac{57}{3}$ is odd one out.
Hence, option (d) is correct.

17. Except $\dfrac{85}{5}$, all others give even numbers but $\dfrac{85}{5}$ gives an odd/prime number.
As, $\dfrac{36}{2} = 18$, $\dfrac{48}{3} = 16$, $\dfrac{56}{4} = 14$
and $\dfrac{85}{5} = 17$
Here, 18, 16 and 14 are even numbers, but 17 is an odd/prime number. So, $\dfrac{85}{5}$ is odd one out.
Hence, option (d) is correct.

Letter Classification

18. Letters C, F and G are consonants, but letter A is not a consonant, it is a vowel. So, A is different from others.
Hence, option (a) is correct.

19. Letters, E, I and O are vowels, but letter H is not a vowel, it is a consonant. So, H is different from the others.
Hence, option (c) is correct.

20. Here we see that, first and third alphabets are of lower case and the alphabet in the middle is of upper case. But in option (c), letter 'm' in the middle is also in lower case. So, lmn is different from the others.
Hence, option (c) is correct.

21. The relation between the letters is shown as

So, AB is different from the others.
Hence, option (c) is correct.

22. The relation between the group of letters is shown as

A   B   D   E   F   H
+1 +2   +1 +2

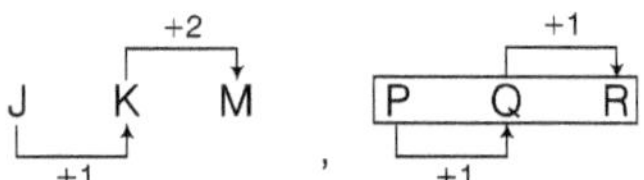

Here, we see that letters groups ABD, EFH and JKM follow a similar pattern, but letters group PQR do not follow the same pattern. So, PQR is different from the others.

Hence, option (d) is correct.

23. The relation between the group of letters is shown as

Here, $A = 1, D = 4, E = 5$

$$A + D = E$$
$$\Rightarrow \quad 1 + 4 = 5$$
$$B = 2, E = 5, G = 7$$
$$B + E = G$$
$$\Rightarrow \quad 2 + 5 = 7$$
$$E = 5, A = 1, F = 6 \Rightarrow E + A = F$$
$$5 + 1 = 6$$

But, $F = 6, B = 2, I = 9$

$$F + B = H \text{ not } I$$
$$\Rightarrow \quad 6 + 2 = 8 \neq 9$$

Hence, option (d) is correct.

24. The relation between the letters is shown as

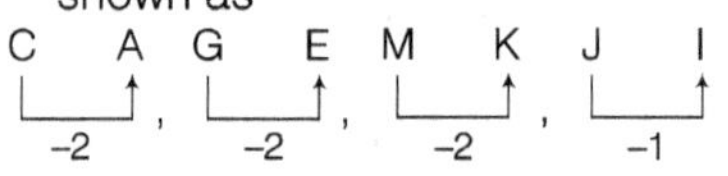

Here, we see that letters CA, GE and MK follow a similar relationship, but letters JI do not follow the similar relationship.

So, JI is the odd one out.

Hence, option (d) is correct.

25. The relation between the group of letters is shown as

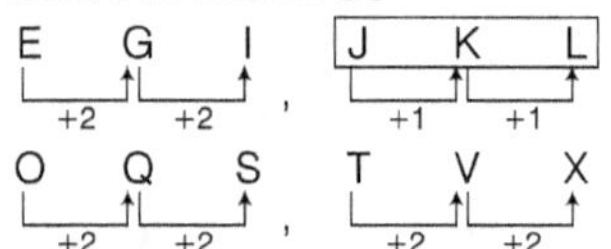

So, JKL is different from the others.

Hence, option (b) is correct.

26. Here, letters are opposite from both the ends i.e. the positional value of first letter from backward is same as the positional value of second letter from forward, but letters SG do not follow this pattern, since the positional value of S from backward is 8 and positional value of G from forward is 7.

Hence, option (d) is correct.

27. All the groups, except NPQR, have atleast one vowel, while group NPQR does not have any vowel

(A) C D F, (E) G H J
Vowel .... Vowel

(I) K L M, [N P Q R] → No vowel
Vowel

So, NPQR does not belong to the group.

Hence, option (d) is correct.

28. The relation between the group of letters is shown as

$$A + B = C, \quad A + C = D,$$
$$1 + 2 = 3 \quad\quad 1 + 3 = 4$$

$$B + C = F \quad C + D = G$$
$$2 + 3 \neq 4 \text{ and } 3 + 4 = 7$$

So, BCF does not belong to the group.

Hence, option (c) is correct.

Mixed Classification

29. The relation between the letter and numbers is shown as

$4 + 1 = 5$ and 5 is the alphabetical order of E. $6 + 2 = 8$ and 8 is the alphabetical order of H.

$5 + 7 = 12$ and 12 is the alphabetical order of L.

$3 + 6 = 9$ and 9 is the alphabetical order of I not J.

We can see that, groups 4E1, 6H2 and 5L7 follow a similar pattern, but group 3J6 does not follow the same pattern. So, 3J6 is odd one out.

Hence, option (b) is correct.

30. As, 14 is the place value of N.

16 is the place value of P.

23 is the place value of W.

But 20 is not the place value of U.

The place value of U is 21.

So, 20U is odd one out.

Hence, option (c) is correct.

31. As, $1 + 5 = 6$, place value of F

$9 + 4 = 13$, place value of M

$7 + 8 = 15$, place value of O

But, $2 + 8 = 10$ and the place value of J not I.

So, 2I8 is odd one out.

Hence, option (b) is correct.

32. As, $26 - 2 = 24$, place value of X

$24 - 2 = 22$, place value of V

$22 - 2 = 20$, place value of T

But $20 - 2 = 18$, place value of R not Q. So, 20Q2 is odd one out.

Hence, option (c) is correct.

33. As, $8 - 3 = 5$, place value of E

$20 - 5 = 15$, place value of O

$10 - 6 = 4$, place value of D not C

$18 - 8 = 10$, place value of J

So, 10C6 is odd one out.

Hence, option (b) is correct.

34. The relation between the numbers and letters is shown as

2 is alphabetical order of B and 4 is alphabetical order of D. 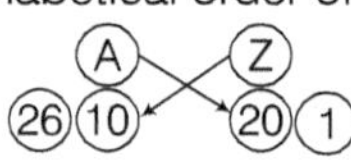

1 is alphabetical order of A and 26 is alphabetical order of Z.

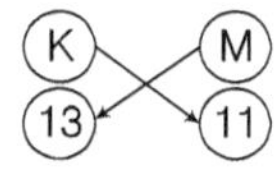

11 is alphabetical order of K and 13 is alphabetical order of M.

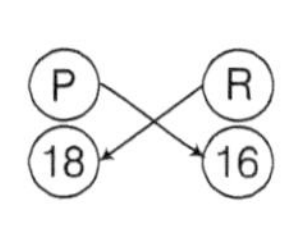

16 is alphabetical order of P and 18 is alphabetical order of R. 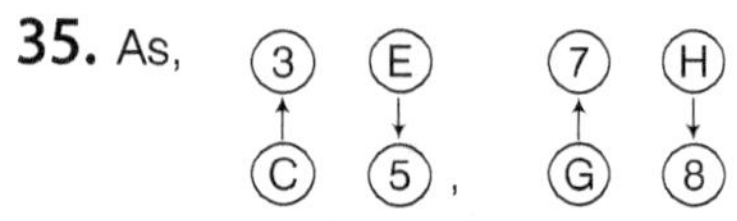

As, we can see that groups in options (a), (c) and (d) follow same pattern, but option (b) does not belong to the group. So, option (b) is odd one out.

Hence, option (b) is correct.

35. As, 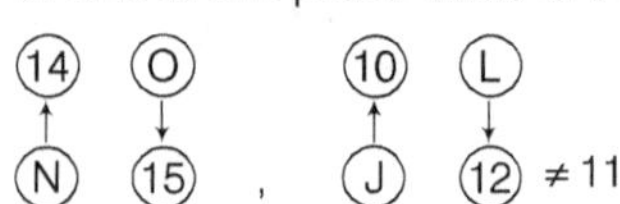

3 is place value of C and 5 is place value of E. 7 is place value of G and 8 is place value of H.

14 is place value of N and 15 is place value of O. 10 is place value of J. But 11 is not the place value of L, place value of L is 12.

So, option (a) is odd one out.

Hence, option (a) is correct.

6 Coding Decoding

1. As,

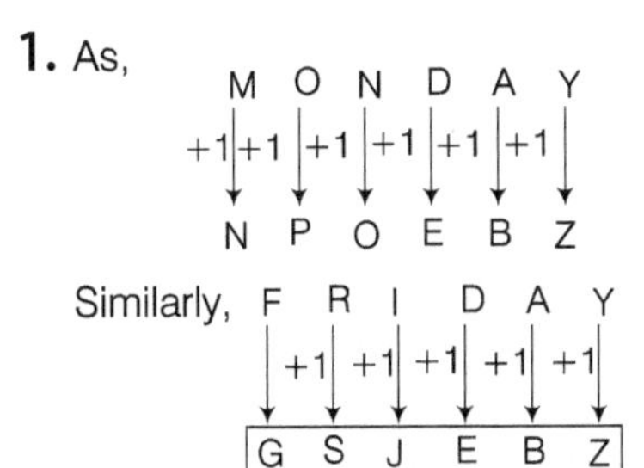

Similarly,

So, 'FRIDAY' would be coded as GSJEBZ.

Hence, option (b) is correct.

2. As,

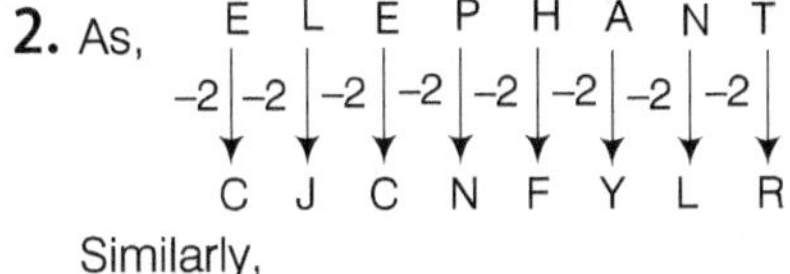

Similarly,

As ELEPHANT is coded as CJCNFYLR Similarly, BIRTHDAY is coded as ZGPRFBYW.

Hence, option (c) is correct.

3. As,

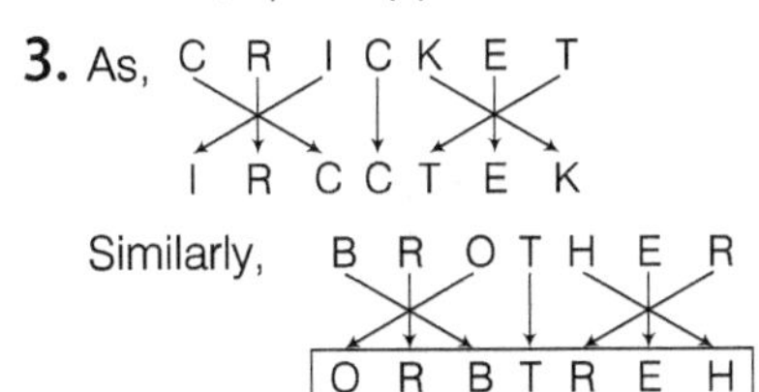

Similarly,

So, BROTHER would be coded as ORBTREH.

Hence, option (d) is correct.

4. As,

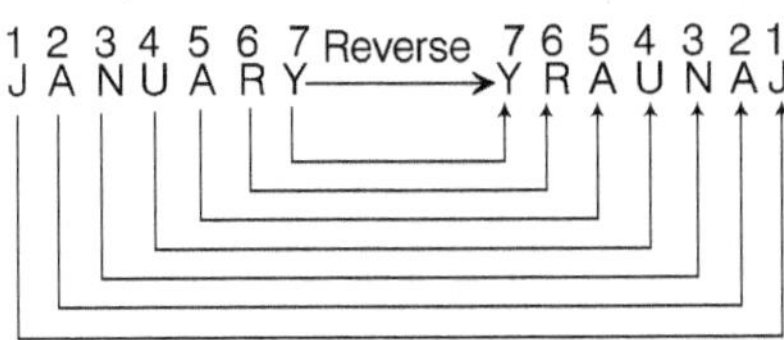

Similarly,

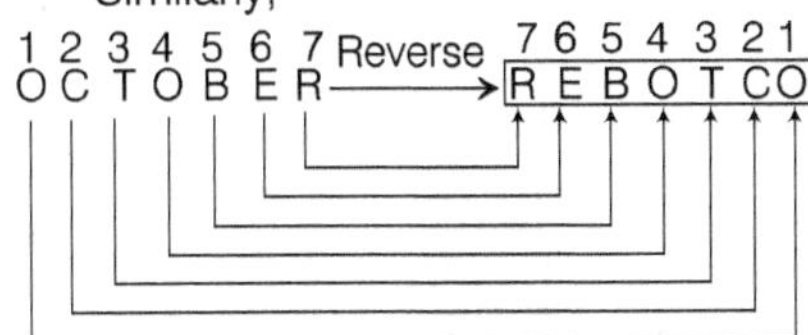

So, OCTOBER would be coded as REBOTCO.

Hence, option (b) is correct.

5. As,

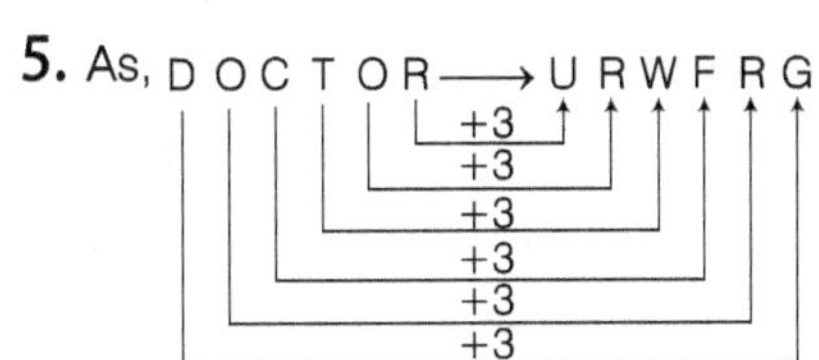

Similarly,

So, JUNGLE would be coded as HOJQXM.

Hence, option (b) is correct.

6. As,

H E N   Similarly,   F A N
+1 −1 +1   +1 −1 +1
I D O   G Z O

So, FAN would be coded as GZO.

Hence, option (d) is correct.

7. As,

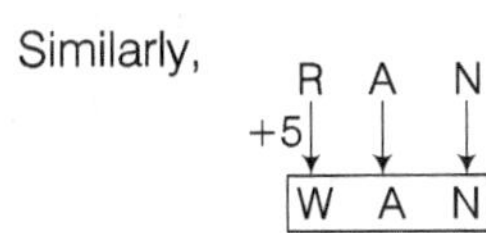

Similarly,

R A N
+5 ↓ ↓
W A N

So, RAN would be coded as WAN.

Hence, option (d) is correct.

8. As,

D U B A I
+3 +2 +3 +2 +3
G W E C L

Similarly,

C H I N A
+3 +2 +3 +2 +3
F J L P D

So, CHINA would be coded as FJLPD.

Hence, option (c) is correct.

9. As,

S E A R C H
−1 −2 −3 −4 −5 −6
R C X N X B

Similarly,

P R E A C H
−1 −2 −3 −4 −5 −6
O P B W X B

So, PREACH would be coded as OPBWXB.

Hence, option (d) is correct.

10. Here, the given letters are coded as

Basic Words	Q	U	A	N	T	U	M
Coded Words	n	A	W	m	k	A	b

Here, A is coded as W. U is coded as A.

N is coded as m. T is coded as k.

Thus, the code for AUNT is WAmk.

Hence, option (a) is correct.

11. As,

D	E	L	H	I	C	A	U	T
6	8	3	4	1	7	5	9	2

Here, C is coded as 7. A is coded as 5.

L is coded as 3. I is coded as 1.

U is coded as 9. T is coded as 2.

C A L I C U T
↓ ↓ ↓ ↓ ↓ ↓ ↓
7 5 3 1 7 9 2

So, the code for CALICUT IS 7531792.

Hence, option (c) is correct.

12. As,

L	I	N	G	E	R
1	2	3	4	5	6

and

F	O	R	C	E
7	8	6	9	5

Here,

F I E R C E
↓ ↓ ↓ ↓ ↓ ↓
7 2 5 6 9 5

So, the code for FIERCE is 725695.

Hence, option (b) is correct.

13. As,

P	A	L	E	R	T	H
2	1	3	4	5	9	0

Here,

P E A R L
↓ ↓ ↓ ↓ ↓
2 4 1 5 3

So, the code for PEARL is 24153.

Hence, option (b) is correct.

14. As,

E	N	G	L	A	D	F	R	C
1	2	3	4	5	6	7	8	9

Here, G $\longrightarrow$ 3, R $\longrightarrow$ 8, E $\longrightarrow$ 1, C $\longrightarrow$ 9

So, the code for GREECE is 381191.
Hence, option (b) is correct.

15. As,

1	3	4	7	9	5	2	6	8
B	R	G	K	M	E	N	Q	O

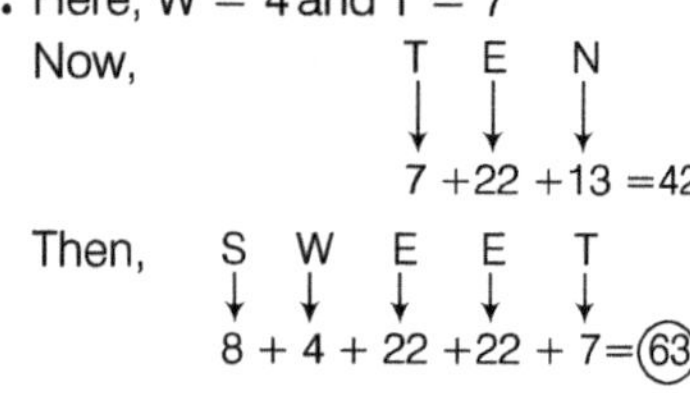

So, the code for 396824 is RMQONG.
Hence, option (d) is correct.

16. As,

1	5	7	8	9	2	3	4	6
X	T	Z	A	L	N	P	S	U

Here,
```
2 3 5 4 9
↓ ↓ ↓ ↓ ↓
N P T S L
```

So, the code for 23549 is NPTSL.
Hence, option (c) is correct.

17. Here,
```
8 7 9 3 4 1
↓ ↓ ↓ ↓ ↓ ↓
D W N I B M
```

So, the code for 879341 is DWNIBM.
Hence, option (c) is correct.

18. Here, E = 5 and GIVE = 43, G = 7, I = 9, V = 22 and E = 5

G + I + V + E

7 + 9 + 22 + 5 = 43

Similarly, THINK
```
T  H  I  N  K
20 + 8 + 9 + 14 + 11 = 62
```
So, code for THINK is 62.
Hence, option (b) is correct.

19. Here, W = 4 and T = 7

Now,
```
T    E    N
↓    ↓    ↓
7  + 22 + 13 = 42
```

Then,
```
S   W   E    E    T
↓   ↓   ↓    ↓    ↓
8 + 4 + 22 + 22 + 7 = 63
```

So, the code for SWEET is 63.
Hence, option (a) is correct.

20. As given, the letters are coded as

Words	A	B	C	D	E	F	G	H	I	J
Codes	2	3	4	5	6	7	8	9	10	11

Here, H is coded as 9, E is coded as 6,
A is coded as 2 and D is coded as 5.
Thus, the code for HEAD is 9625.
Hence, option (c) is correct.

21. As given, the letters are coded as

Letters	G	I	V	E	B	A	T
Symbols	@	*	$	#	+	>	<

Here, B is coded as +, I is coded as *,
T is coded as < and E is coded as #.
So, the code for BITE is + * < #.
Hence, option (b) is correct.

22. As given, the letters are coded as

Letters	C	A	N	D	L	E	S	T
Symbols	+	>	<	*	$	@	?	–

Here, L is coded as $, A is coded as >,
N is coded as < and D is coded as *,
So, the code for LAND is $ > < *.
Hence, option (c) is correct.

23. As given, the symbols are coded as

Symbols	–	*	@	?	+	>	$
Letters	S	T	E	A	D	Y	M

Here, * is coded for T, @ is coded for E,
? is coded for A, $ is coded for M.
So, * @ ? $ is coded for TEAM.
Hence, option (a) is correct.

24. As given, the symbols are coded as

Symbol codes	#	@	?	÷	>	<	+
Letter codes	D	E	S	T	I	N	Y

Here, ÷ is coded for T, @ is coded for E and
? is coded for S.
So, ÷ @ ? ÷ is coded for TEST.
Hence, option (d) is correct.

25. As given, letters are coded as

Letters	N	O	T	I	C	E	S
Codes	5	$	@	6	#	?	7

Here, C is coded as #, O is coded as $,
I is coded as 6 and N is coded as 5.
Thus, the code for COIN is # $ 6 5.
Hence, option (a) is correct.

26. As given, letters are coded as

Letters	C	O	M	P	U	T	E	R
Codes	8	+	*	9	÷	#	2	>

Here, P is coded as 9, E is coded as 2,
T is coded as # and R is coded as >.
Thus, the code for PETER is 9 2 # 2 >.
Hence, option (a) is correct.

27. We know that, 'soap' is used for washing the clothes. But here 'soap' is called 'ink'. So, 'ink' will be used for washing clothes.

Hence, option (b) is correct.

28. We know that, the colour of clear sky is 'blue' and as given, 'blue' is called 'orange'. So, the colour of clear sky is 'orange'.

Hence, option (c) is correct.

29. We know that, aeroplanes fly in the 'sky' and as given, 'sky' is called 'sea'. So, areoplanes fly in the sea.

Hence, option (d) is correct.

30. We know that, person hears with 'ears' and as given, 'ear' is called 'nose'.

So a person hear with nose.

Hence, option (a) is correct.

31. The codes can be written as

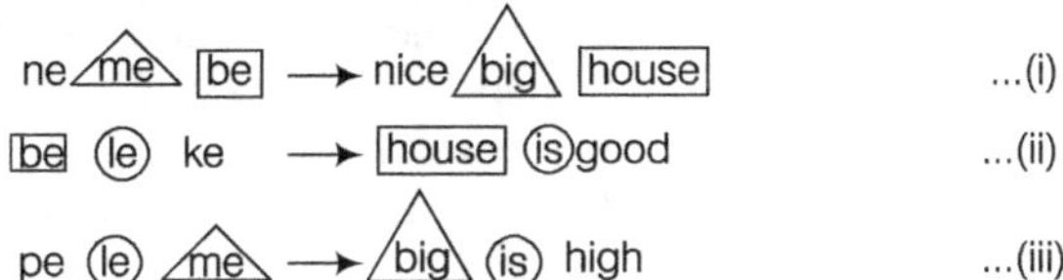

On comparing Eqs. (i) and (ii), we get

$$be \rightarrow house$$

So, the code for 'house' is 'be'.

Hence, option (c) is correct.

32. Here, the codes can be written as

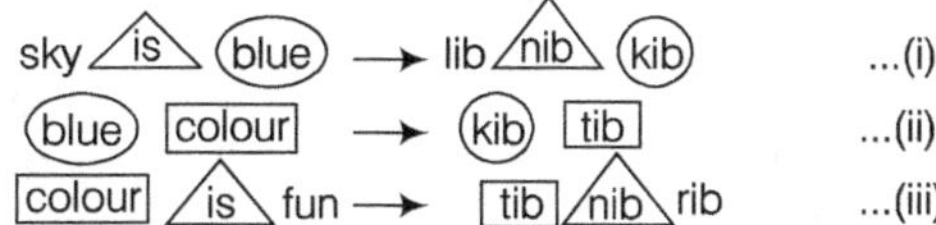

On comparing Eqs. (ii) and (iii), we get

$$colour \rightarrow tib$$

So, the code for 'colour' is 'tib'.

Hence, option (c) is correct.

33. Here, the codes can be written as

On comparing Eqs. (i) and (iii), we get

$$1 \Rightarrow fruit$$

So, the code for 'fruit' is '1'.

Hence, option (b) is correct.

7   *Mathematical Reasoning*

1. Here, the sum of each horizontal, vertical and diagonal lines are equal i.e. 12. For horizontal,

In row I, $5 + 6 + 1 = 12$

In row III, $7 + 2 + 3 = 12$

Similarly, in row II, $\boxed{0} + 4 + 8 = 12$

For vertical, in column II,

$$6 + 4 + 2 = 12$$

In column III, $1 + 8 + 3 = 12$

Similarly, in column I,

$$5 + \boxed{0} + 7 = 12$$

For diagonals, In I, $5 + 4 + 3 = 12$

In II, $7 + 4 + 1 = 12$

Hence, option (a) is correct.

2. In row I, $8 \times 10 + 10 = 90$

In row II, $6 \times 9 + 9 = 63$

Similarly, in row III, $4 \times ? + ? = 40$

[Let $? = x$]. Then, $4 \times x + x = 40$

$\therefore \; 5x = 40 \Rightarrow x = \dfrac{40}{5} = 8$

Therefore, $8 = ?$

So, 8 replaces the (?).

Hence, option (d) is correct.

3. Consider rowwise,

In row I, $P \xrightarrow{-5} K \xrightarrow{-5} F$

In row II, $N \xrightarrow{-5} I \xrightarrow{-5} D$

Similarly in row III, $L \xrightarrow{-5} G \xrightarrow{-5} \boxed{B}$

Now columnwise,

Column I $P \xrightarrow{-2} N \xrightarrow{-2} L$

Column II, $K \xrightarrow{-2} I \xrightarrow{-2} G$

Similarly, column III, $F \xrightarrow{-2} D \xrightarrow{-2} \boxed{B}$

So, letter 'B' will replace the (?).

Hence, option (a) is correct.

4. In, row I,

$$1 \times 5 = 5, \; 5 \times 5 = 25, \; 25 \times 5 = 125$$

In row III,

$$7 \times 2 = 14, \; 14 \times 2 = 28, \; 28 \times 2 = 56$$

Similarly, In row II,

$$3 \times 4 = 12, \; 12 \times 4 = 48, \; 48 \times 4 = 192$$

So, 48 replaces the (?).

Hence, option (c) is correct.

5. Here, we see that, prime numbers are given in the box. So, 67 will replace the (?) as all other numbers are composite.

Hence, option (d) is correct.

6. Here, we see that, even numbers are given in the box. So, 984 will replace the (?).

Hence, option (c) is correct.

7. Here, the given pattern is (Top – Bottom) $\times$ (Left + Right) = Middle

In, figure I,

$$(13 - 7) \times (4 + 6) = 6 \times 10 = 60$$

In figure II,

$$(17 - 9) \times (3 + 2) = 8 \times 5 = 40$$

Similarly, In figure III

$$(11 - 5) \times (4 + 1) = 6 \times 5 = 30$$

So, 30 will replace the (?).

Hence, option (a) is correct.

8. Here, in each case

(Top left $\times$ Top right) – (Bottom left $\times$ Bottom right) = Middle

In figure I,

$$5 \times 6 - 3 \times 4 = 30 - 12 = 18$$

In figure II,
$$7 \times 4 - 8 \times 2 = 28 - 16 = 12$$
Similarly, in figure III,
$$9 \times 4 - 3 \times 7 = 36 - 21 = 15$$
So, 15 will replace the (?).
Hence, option (d) is correct.

9. Here, in figure I,
$$9 + 8 + 7 = 24 \times 2 = 48$$
In figure II, $8 + 6 + 5 = 19 \times 3 = 57$
Similarly, in figure III,
$$7 + 6 + 4 = 17 \times 4 = 68$$
So, 68 will replace the (?).
Hence, option (a) is correct.

10. In figure I,
$$10 + 3 + 6 + 8 + 2 = 29$$
In figure II, $15 + 6 + 9 + 4 + 7 = 41$
Similarly, in figure III,
$$20 + 8 + 6 + 7 + 8 = 49$$
So, 49 will replace the (?).
Hence, option (a) is correct.

11. Here, (Top + Right) − (Bottom
+ Left) = Middle
In figure I, $(62 + 18) - (2 + 18)$
$$= 80 - 20 = 60$$
In figure II, $(52 + 26) - (20 + 18)$
$$= 78 - 38 = 40$$
Similarly, in figure III,
$(62 + 19) - (24 + 23) = 81 - 47 = 34$
So, 34 will replace the (?).
Hence, option (c) is correct.

12. Here, (Top right × Bottom left)
+ (Top left × Bottom right) = middle.
In figure I, $5 \times 6 + 3 \times 3 = 30 + 9 = 39$
In figure II, $7 \times 5 + 4 \times 4 = 35 + 16 = 51$
Similarly, in figure III, $5 \times 5 + 3 \times 4$
$$= 25 + 12 = 37$$
So, 37 will replace the (?).
Hence, option (c) is correct.

13. In, row I, $4 - \dfrac{2}{5} = \dfrac{20 - 2}{5} = \dfrac{18}{5}$

In row II, $7 - \dfrac{5}{3} = \dfrac{21 - 5}{3} = \dfrac{16}{3}$

Similarly, In row III,
$$3 - ? = \dfrac{25}{9} \implies 3 - \dfrac{25}{9}$$
$$\therefore \quad ? = \dfrac{27 - 25}{9} = \dfrac{2}{9}$$
So, $\dfrac{2}{9}$ will replace the (?).

Hence, option (d) is correct.

14. As, $12^2 + 8^2 = 144 + 64 = 208$
Similarly, $14^2 + 9^2 = 196 + 81 = 277$
So, 277 will replace the (?).
Hence, option (b) is correct.

15. Here, in each case the pattern is
(Left × Right) ÷ 3 = Middle
In figure I, $9 \times 5 \div 3 = 45 \div 3 = 15$
In figure II, $8 \times 6 \div 3 = 48 \div 3 = 16$
Similarly, in figure III,
$$9 \times 4 \div 3 = 36 \div 3 = 12$$
So, 12 will replace the (?).
Hence, option (a) is correct.

16. Here, (Top left number × Top right
number) ÷ 3 = Bottom number
In figure I, $\dfrac{39 \times 1}{3} = 13$

In figure II, $\dfrac{4 \times 3}{3} = 4$

Similarly, in figure III, $= \dfrac{8 \times 6}{3} = 16$

Hence, option (a) is correct.

17. In figure I, $\dfrac{27 + 3}{2} = 15$,

In figure II, $\dfrac{6 + 56}{2} = 31$

Similarly, in figure III, $\dfrac{9 + 81}{2} = 45$

Hence, option (a) is correct.

18. In each case, the sum of numbers
in diagonally opposite sectors are
the same.
In figure I, $5 + 4 = 9$ and $1 + 8 = 9$
$6 + 9 = 15$ and $8 + 7 = 15$
In figure II, $19 + 2 = 21$ and
$15 + 6 = 21$
$11 + 7 = 18$ and $9 + 9 = 18$
Similarly, in figure III, $10 + 3 = 13$
and $7 + 6 = 13$
$\implies \quad 14 + 2 = 16$ and $? + 3 = 16$
$\therefore \quad ? = 16 - 3 = 13$
So, 13 will replace the (?).
Hence, option (c) is correct.

19. Here, (Top × Left) + Right = Middle
In figure I, $(5 \times 4) + 10 = 20 + 10 = 30$
In figure II, $(7 \times 5) + 9 = 35 + 9 = 44$
Similarly, in figure III, $(6 \times 6) + ? = 44$
$\implies 36 + ? = 44$
$\therefore \quad ? = 44 - 36 = 8$
So, 8 will replace the (?).
Hence, option (d) is correct.

20. Here, (Top × Left) ÷ (Right × Bottom)
= Middle

In figure I, $(12 \times 4) \div (6 \times 4)$
$$= 48 \div 24 = 2$$
In figure II, $(8 \times 5) \div (5 \times 1)$
$$= 40 \div 5 = 8$$
Similarly, in figure III,
$$(7 \times 8) \div (2 \times 7) = 56 \div 14 = 4$$
So, 4 will replace the (?).
Hence, option (b) is correct.

21. Here, (Top × Bottom) + Left = Right
In figure I, $(3 \times 3) + 2 = 9 + 2 = 11$
In figure II, $(7 \times 8) + 3 = 56 + 3 = 59$
Similarly, in figure III, $(6 \times 5) + 4 =$
$30 + 4 = 34$
So, 34 will replace the (?).
Hence, option (d) is correct.

22. Four number starting from 4 in
clockwise direction are multiplied
by consecutive natural numbers
(starting from 2) to get the opposite
sector number.
As, $4 \times 2 = 8$, $9 \times 3 = 27, 16 \times 4 = 64$
and $25 \times 5 = 125$
So, 125 replace the (?).
Hence, option (b) is correct.

23. Using the correct symbols, we have
Given expression,
$$15 - 3 + 10 \times 5 \div 5$$
$$= 15 \times 3 - 10 \div 5 + 5$$
$$= 45 - 2 + 5 = 50 - 2 = 48$$
So, 48 will replace the (?).
Hence, option (c) is correct.

24. Using the correct symbols, we have
Give expression, 65 P 5 D 3 T 27 M
16 T 2 $= 65 \div 5 \times 3 + 27 - 16 + 2$
$= 13 \times 3 + 27 - 16 + 2$
$= 39 + 29 - 16 = 68 - 16 = 52$
So, 52 will replace the (?).
Hence, option (a) is correct.

25. Using correct symbols, we have
Given statement,
$a - b - c \implies a < b < c$
Option (a) $a - b + c$
$\implies a < b > c \neq a < b < c \neq a < b < c$
(false)
Option (b) $c \times b + a$
$\implies c \not> b > a \implies c \leq b > a$
$\neq a < b < c$ (false)
Option (c) $a \pounds b \pounds c$
$\implies a \neq b \neq c \neq a < b < c$ (false)
Option (d) $c + b + a$
$\implies c > b > a \implies a < b < c$ (true)
Hence, option (d) is correct.

26. Using correct symbols, we have
Given statement,
$a + b - c \Rightarrow a > b < c$
Option (a) $b - c - a$
$\Rightarrow b < c < a \Rightarrow a > c > b$ (false)
Option (b) $c - b + a$
$\Rightarrow c < b > a \neq a > b < c$ (false)
Option (c) $c + b - a$
$\Rightarrow c > b < a = a > b < c$ (true)
Option (d) $c \times b \div a$
$\Rightarrow c \not> b \not< a, c \leq b \geq a$ (false)
Hence, option (c) is correct.

27. Option (a)
If we interchange + and −, then
LHS $= 4 \times 2 - 6 \div 2 + 12$
$= 8 - 3 + 12 = 20 - 3$
$= 17 \neq$ RHS   (false)
Option (b) If we interchange × and +,
then   LHS $= 4 + 2 \times 6 \div 2 - 12$
$= 4 + 2 \times 3 - 12 = 4 + 6 - 12$
$= 10 \neq$ RHS   (false)
Option (c) If we interchange ÷ and ×
, then LHS $= 4 \div 2 + 6 \times 2 - 12$
$= 2 + 12 - 12$
$= 2 =$ RHS   (true)
Hence, option (c) is correct.

28. Given expression,
$27 - 18 + 15 = 30$
From option (a), after interchanging
$15 + 18 - 27 = 33 - 27 = 6 \neq$ RHS
   (false)
From option (b), after interchanging
$\Rightarrow \quad 18 + 27 - 15 \Rightarrow 45 - 15$
$\Rightarrow \quad 30 =$ RHS $\Rightarrow$ LHS = RHS
So, option (b) is correct.

29. Here, after interchanging the digits
and signs, we get option (a),
$4 \times 6 + 2 = 26 \Rightarrow 24 + 2 = 26$
$\Rightarrow \quad 26 = 26 \Rightarrow$ LHS = RHS
Hence, option (a) is correct.

30. Here, the rule is $a \bigstar b = (a + b)^2$
As, $7 \bigstar 2 = (7 + 2)^2 = (9)^2 = 81$
and $9 \bigstar 5 = (9 + 5)^2 = (14)^2 = 196$
Similarly, $8 \bigstar 8 = (8 + 8)^2$
$= (16)^2 = 256$
So, 256 replaces the (?).
Hence, option (b) is correct.

31. Here, as given
$(4 + 5) \ominus (2 + 5)$
$\downarrow \qquad \downarrow$
$9 \qquad\quad 7$
and $(8 + 4) \ominus (3 + 2)$
$\downarrow \qquad \downarrow$
$12 \qquad\quad 5$
Similarly, $(9 + 7) \ominus (3 + 4)$
$\downarrow \qquad \downarrow$
$16 \qquad\quad 7$
So, 167 will replace the (?).
Hence, option (c) is correct.

32. As,
$27 \times 37 \times 42 = 42 \times 27 \times 37$
and
$65 \times 96 \times 23 = 23 \times 65 \times 96$
Similarly,
$56 \times 84 \times 75 = 75 \times 56 \times 84$
So, $75 \times 56 \times 84$ will replace the (?).
Hence, option (d) is correct.

33. As,
$(7 + 2) \quad (4 + 3) \quad (1 + 3)$
$\downarrow \qquad\quad \downarrow \qquad\quad \downarrow$
$9 \qquad\quad 7 \qquad\quad 4$
and
$(2 + 4) \quad (4 + 3) \quad (1 + 2)$
$\downarrow \qquad\quad \downarrow \qquad\quad \downarrow$
$6 \qquad\quad 7 \qquad\quad 3$
Similarly,
$(5 + 2) \quad (2 + 3) \quad (2 + 1)$
$\downarrow \qquad\quad \downarrow \qquad\quad \downarrow$
$7 \qquad\quad 5 \qquad\quad 3$
So, 753 will replace the (?).
Hence, option (b) is correct.

34. Given, $x \# y$
$\Rightarrow \quad x > y$ and $y \$ z$
$\Rightarrow \quad y = z$
It means, $x > y = z$
From option (a), $x \bigstar z$
$\Rightarrow \quad x < z$ (false)
From option (b), $y \bigstar x$
$\Rightarrow \quad y < x$ (true)
From option (c), $z \# x$
$\Rightarrow \quad z > x$ (false)
So, option (b) is true.
Hence, option (b) is correct.

35. Here, using the proper signs, we
get option (a)
$2 \times 5 - 6 + 2 = 6$
LHS $= 2 \times 5 - 6 + 2$
$= 10 - 6 + 2$
$= 12 - 6$
$= 6$
$\therefore$ LHS = RHS
Hence, option (a) is correct.

8 Puzzle Test

1. On the basis of given information,
the position of five different houses
is shown below

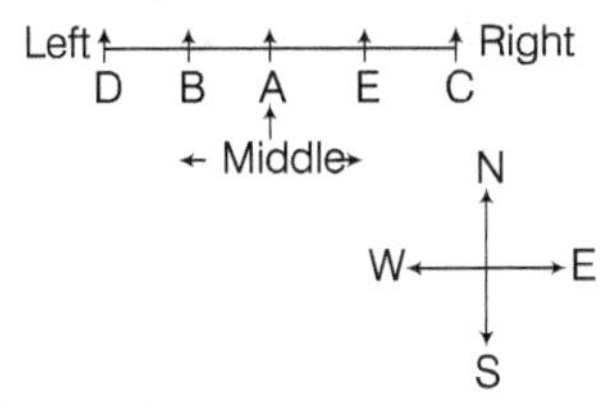

As, we can see in above diagram
that, house 'A' is in the middle.
Hence, option (d) is correct.

2. On the basis of given information,
the sitting arrangement of five girls
in a row is shown below

From the above diagram, it is
clearly shown that, Preeti and Tina
are sitting adjacent to Veena.
Hence, option (d) is correct.

3. On the basis of given information,
the arrangement of five people is
shown below

	Sandwich	Lays	Pizza	Pepsi	Milk Shake	Pastry
Ajay	✓	✗	✗	✗	✓	✗
Pihu	✗	✓	✗	✓	✗	✓
Liya	✓	✓	✗	✓	✓	✗
Gauri	✗	✗	✓	✗	✓	✗
Raj	✗	✗	✗	✓	✓	✗

As, we can see in the above arrangement that, Liya buys the most number of items, i.e. 4.
Hence, option (c) is correct.

Solution (Q. Nos. 4-5) On the basis of given information, the arrangement of three cities is shown below

Cities	P	Q	R
Hill station	✗	✓	✗
Historical places	✗	✗	✓
Industries	✓	✗	✗

4. From the above table, it is clearly shown that, 'Q' is the only city which is neither a historical city nor an industrial city.
Hence, option (c) is correct.

5. From the above table, it is clearly shown that, 'P' is the only industrial city.
Hence, option (b) is correct.

Solution (Q. Nos. 6-7) On the basis of given information, the arrangement of four teachers of a school is shown below

	L	M	P	D
English	✓	✓	✓	✗
Hindi	✗	✗	✓	✗
Maths	✓	✗	✗	✓

6. From the above table, it is clearly shown that, L and P are the only two teachers who teaches two subjects. So, two teachers can teach two subjects.
Hence, option (a) is correct.

7. For 'Hindi' subject there is only one teacher.
Hence, option (c) is correct.

Solution (Q. Nos. 8-10) On the basis of given information, we have the arrangement of the seven singers in a line as below.

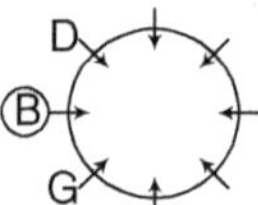

8. From the above diagram, it is clearly shown that, singer 'G' is to the extreme right of the line.
Hence, option (c) is correct.

9. From the above arrangement we can see that, 'D' is standing at the centre in a line on the stage.
Hence, option (b) is correct.

10. Here, if we start counting from the left end in below diagram, 'C' is on number 3rd.

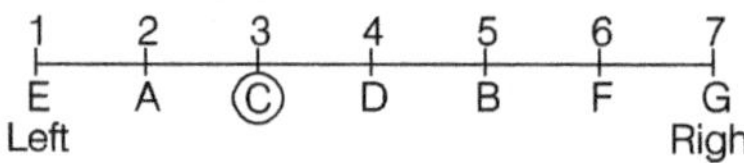

Hence, option (a) is correct.

Solution (Q. Nos. 11.-13) On the basis of given information, the order in which all of them are sitting is as given in below diagram.

11. 'W' is sitting to the right of T.
Hence, option (c) is correct.

12. Here, 'P and Q' are sitting at the extreme ends.
Hence, option (a) is correct.

13. 'W' should change place with 'R' to make its place third from North.
Hence, option (c) is correct.

Solution (Q. Nos. 14-16) On the basis of given information, the sitting arrangement is as shown in the figure.

14. From the given arrangement, it is clear that, B is sitting between D and G.

Hence, option (b) is correct.

15. As, we can see in the diagram that H is sitting directly opposite to G.

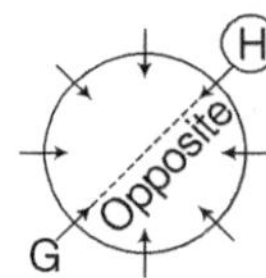

Hence, option (c) is correct.

16. As, we can see in the diagram that, GAC are the three friends sitting immediately to the right of B.

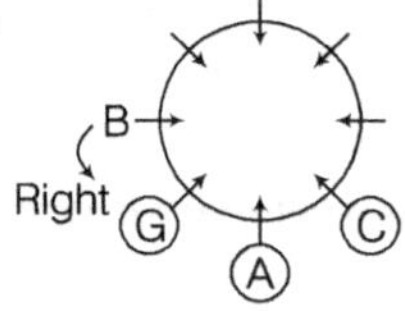

Hence, option (b) is correct.

Solution (Q. Nos. 17-18) On the basis of given information, the arrangement of seven books is shown below

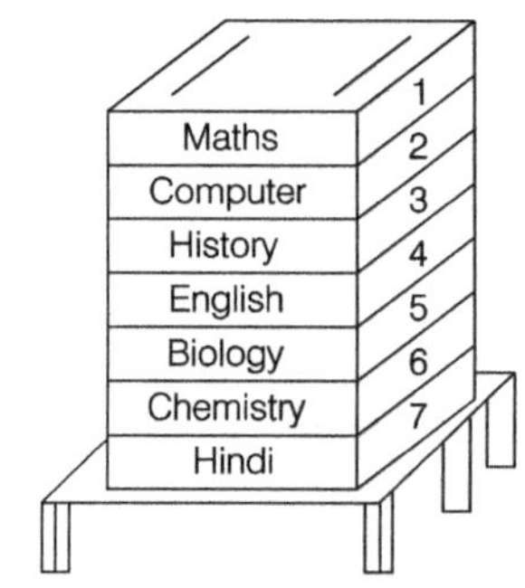

17. 'Biology' is between English and Chemistry.
Hence, option (c) is correct.

18. After interchanging the position of book on the basis of given information, 'Computer' will be between Maths and Hindi as shown below.
History English Maths Computer Hindi Chemistry Biology
Hence, option (b) is correct.

Solution (Q. Nos. 19-22) On the basis of given information, the arrangement of seven students in a class is shown below

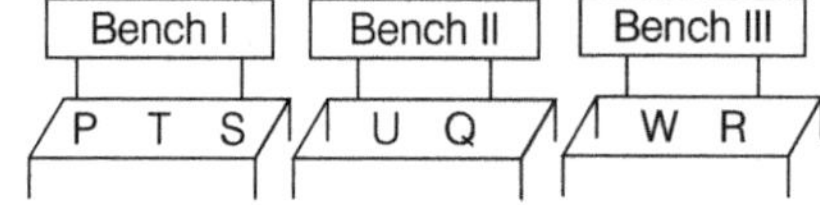

From the given information, Q and R are girls. T, U and W are boys and no information regarding gender of P and S.

19. On bench I, three students are sitting.
Hence, option (a) is correct.

20. From the given information, there are either 3 or 4 boy students in the group of seven students.
Hence, option (d) is correct.

21. From the given information, Q sits with U.
Hence, option (b) is correct.

22. According to the given options, option (c) is correct, because 'TUW' is the group of boys.
Hence, option (c) is correct.

9 *Direction Sense Test*

1. Given, Then,

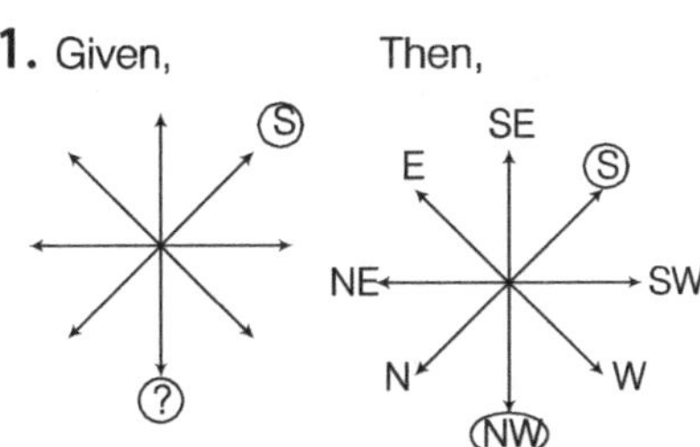

So, NW replaces the (?).
Hence, option (b) is correct.

2. Given, Then,

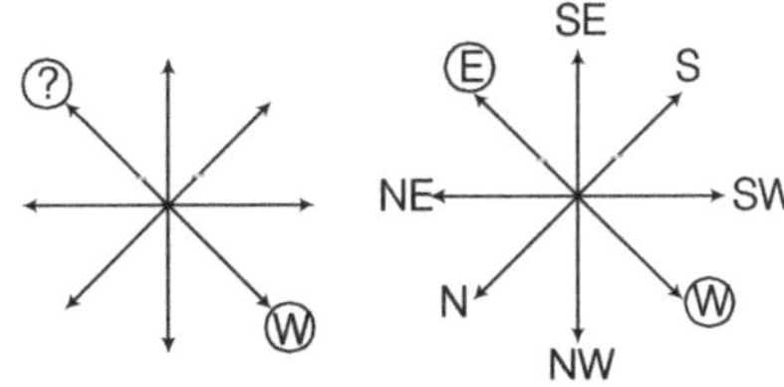

So, E replaces the (?).
Hence, option (c) is correct.

3. Given, Then,

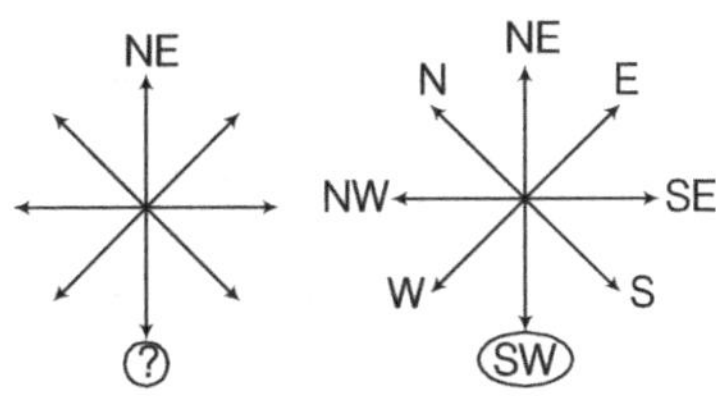

So, 'SW' replaces the (?).
Hence, option (a) is correct.

4. Given, Then,

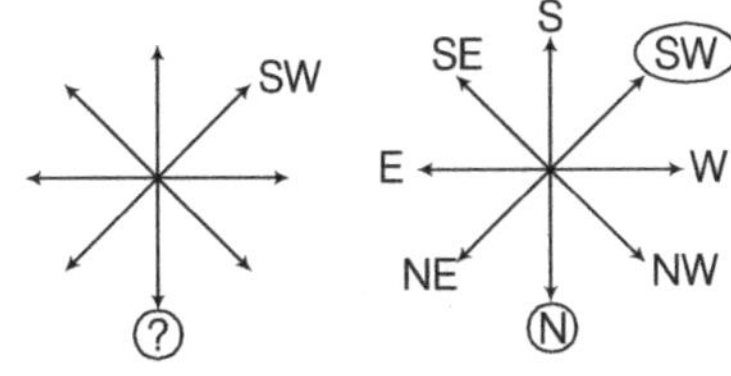

So, 'N' replace the (?).
Hence, option (d) is correct.

5. Given, Then,

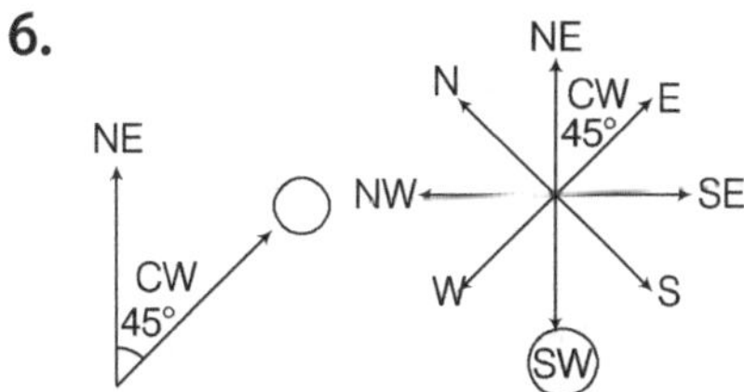

So, 'NE' will come in the circle.
Hence, option (b) is correct.

6.

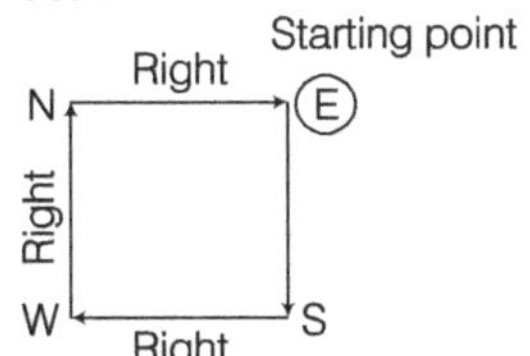

On moving clockwise 45° from North-East direction, we face East direction.
Hence, option (c) is correct.

7. Here, Manish starts towards South direction

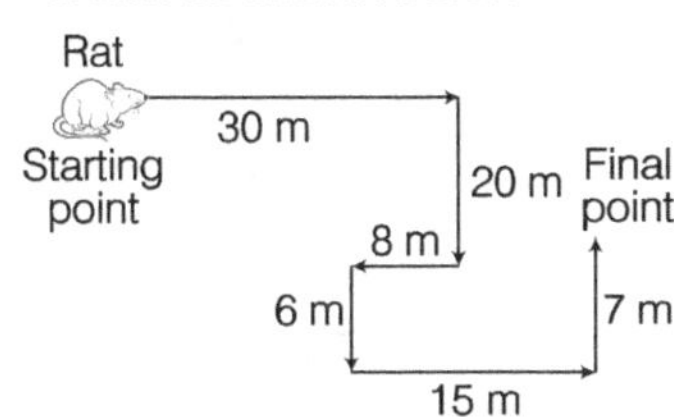

Hence, option (b) is correct.

8. The direction diagram can be drawn as shown below

Rat

Clearly rat is facing North direction.
Hence, option (a) is correct.

9. The directions diagram can be drawn as shown below

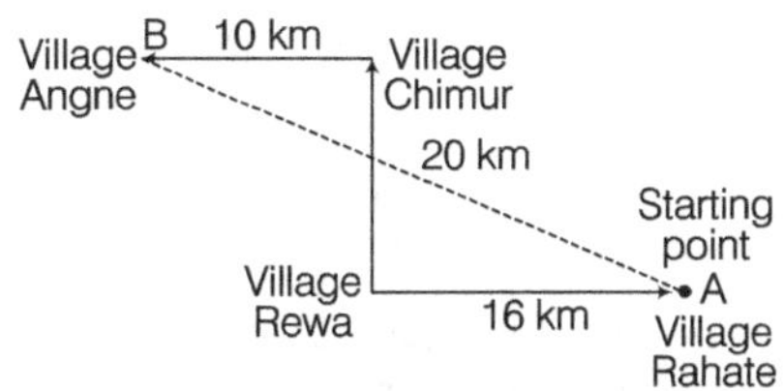

From the above figure, it is clear that A and B denote the starting and finishing points respectively.
So, B is to the North-West of point A.
Hence, option (b) is correct.

10. The direction diagram can be drawn as shown below

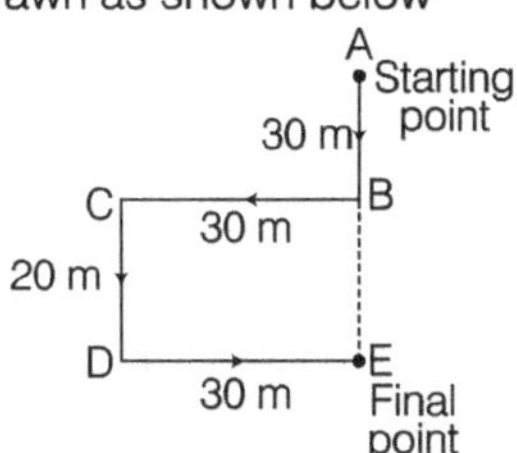

Here, CD = BE = 20 m
and AB = 30 m
∴ Required distance = AB + BE
= 30 + 20
= 50 m
So, he is 50 m far from his starting position.
Hence, option (b) is correct.

11. Here, Kajal facing North and turns 45° anti-clockwise as shown below

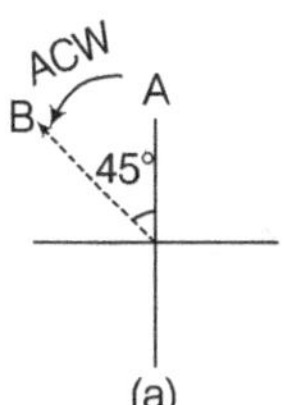

Now, she turns 135° clockwise, then

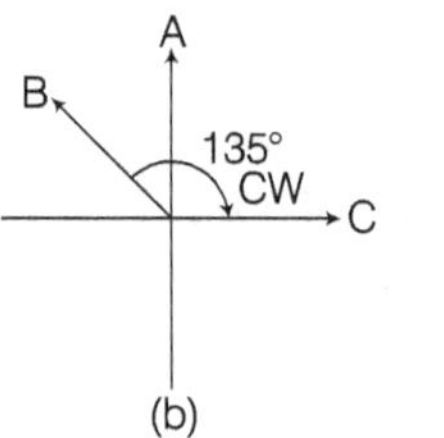

(b)

Again, she turns 90° clockwise, then

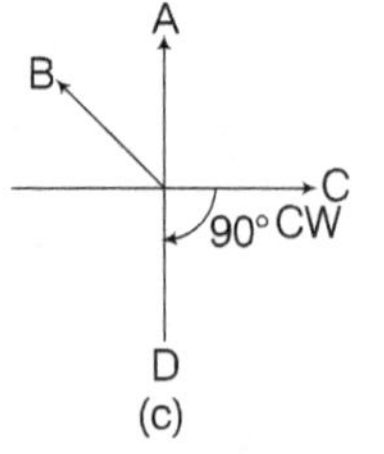

(c)

From the figure (c) she finally faces in the direction South.
Hence, option (c) is correct.

12. Here, Sorabh is facing towards West and turns 90° clockwise as shown below

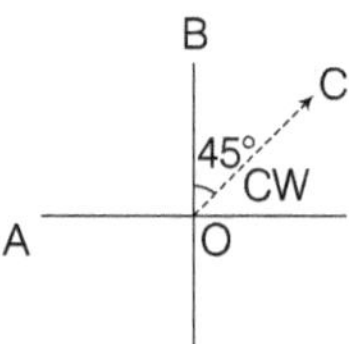

Now, he turns 45° clockwise, then

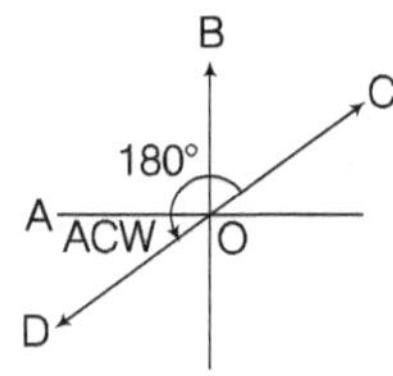

Again, he turns 180° anti-clockwise.
Finally, on moving 180° anti-clockwise, he faces in the South-West direction

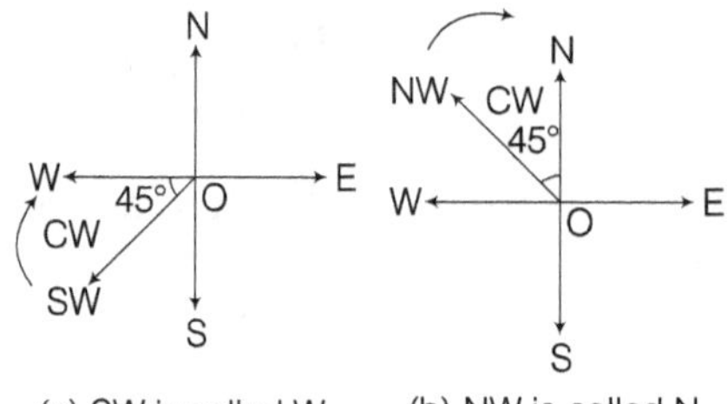

Hence, option (b) is correct.

13. The direction diagram can be drawn as shown below

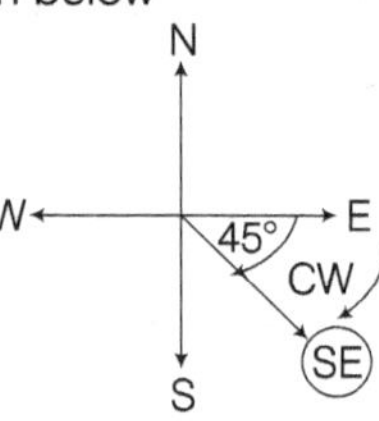

(a) SW is called W   (b) NW is called N

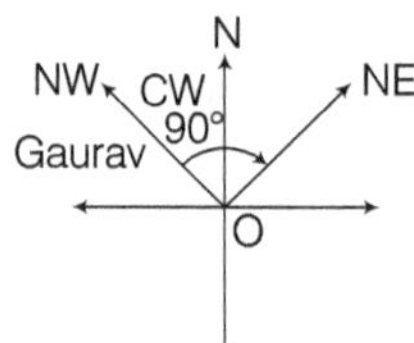

(c) SE is called S

Here, each direction moves 45° in clockwise direction. Thus, East when moved clockwise through 45° will become South-East as shown below

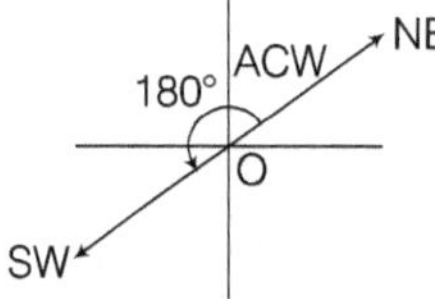

Hence, option (b) is correct.

14. Here, it is given that, Gaurav facing North-West and he turns 90° clockwise, then

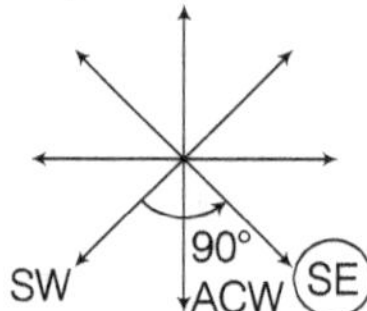

Now, he turns 180° anti-clockwise, then

Again, he turns 90° in same direction, then

It is clearly shown that, Gaurav is facing South-East direction.
Hence, option (a) is correct.

15. Here, it is given that, a ship is sailing towards South-East and captain ordered to turn the ship 135° anti-clockwise, then

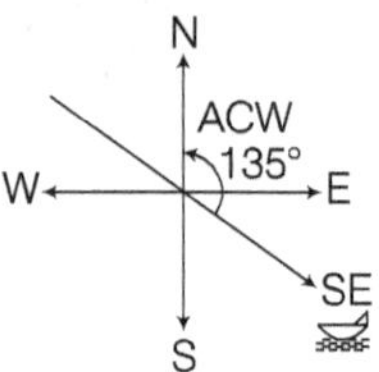

Then ship turned 225° clockwise.

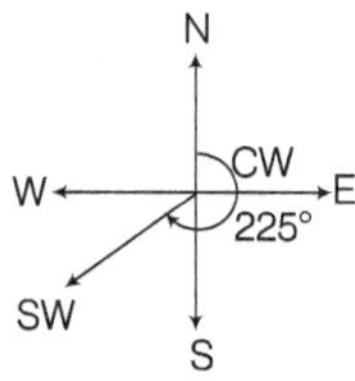

From the above diagram, it is clear that after turning 225° clockwise, ship is sailing South-West.
Hence, option (c) is correct.

16. It is given that, Sandeep was facing the 'DOMINOS' at the beginning and he turned anti-clockwise to face South-East, then

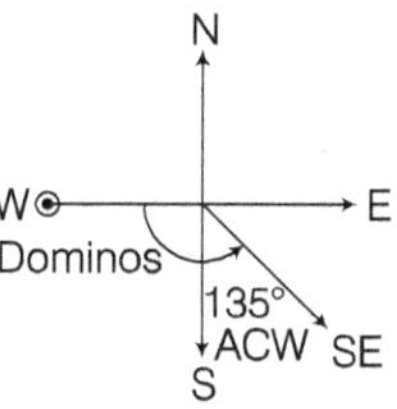

from the above figure, it is clearly shown that the DOMINOS is in WEST and moving anti-clockwise from West to South-East, 135° angle is formed.
Hence, option (c) is correct.

17. The direction diagram can be drawn as shown below

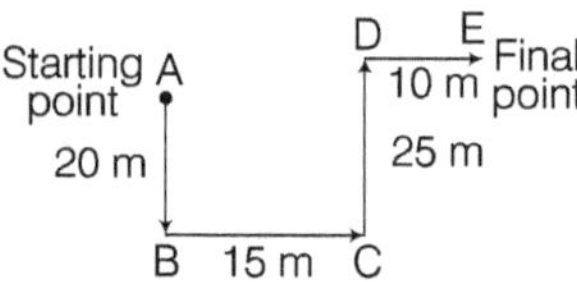

∴ Total distance covered by Harsh
= AB + BC + DC + DE
= 20 + 15 + 25 + 10
= 70 m
Hence, option (d) is correct.

18. Meenu starts from P and walks 6 km East upto Q,

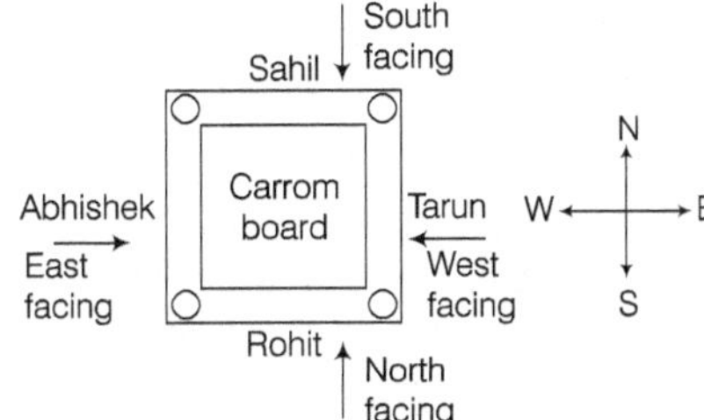

turns Southwards and moves 5 km upto R. At R, she turns to the East and walks 6 km upto S.

Then, she turns Northwards and walks 10 km upto T.

Clearly, QO = RS = 6 km

PO = PQ + QO = 6 + 6 = 12 km

OT = ST − OS

∵   OS = QR = 5 km

⇒ OT = 10 − 5 = 5 km

∴ Meenu's distance from the starting point P,

$PT = \sqrt{PO^2 + OT^2} = \sqrt{12^2 + 5^2}$

$= \sqrt{144 + 25} = \sqrt{169} = 13$ km

So, Meenu is 13 km far from her starting point.

Hence, option (c) is correct.

19. The direction diagram of the minute hand at 9 :15 pm is shown below

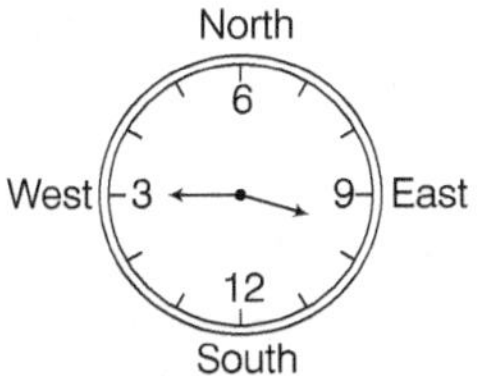

It is clearly shown that, the minute hand is in west direction.

Hence, option (a) is correct.

21. The direction diagram can be drawn as shown below

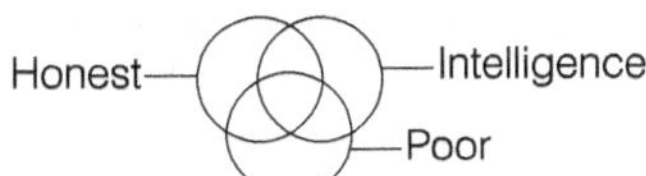

It is given that, Sahil faces South, Abhishek faces East, Tarun faces West, then 'Rohit' faces North.

Hence, option (b) is correct.

20. The direction diagram can be drawn as

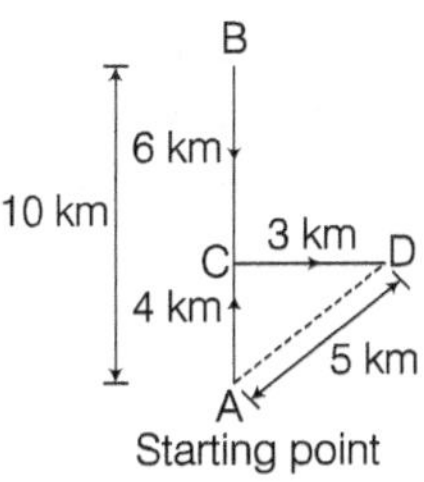

Clearly, D is to the North-East of A.

Here,   AC = AB − BC

      = 10 − 6 = 4 km

∴ Distance from starting point A,

$AD = \sqrt{AC^2 + CD^2}$

$= \sqrt{4^2 + 3^2} = \sqrt{16 + 9}$

$= \sqrt{25} = 5$ km

So, Vijay is 5 km to the North-East of his starting point A.

Hence, option (b) is correct.

22. The direction diagram can be drawn as shown below

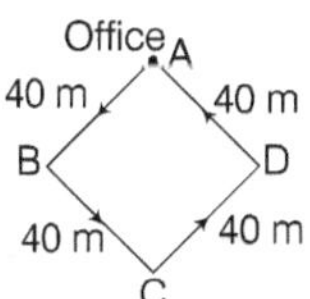

Clearly, she is finally moving in the direction DA i.e. North-West.

Hence, option (d) is correct.

10   *Venn Diagram*

1. Brinjal is a vegetable and hence, included in it. Fruit is not related to both of them. So, the Venn diagram can be drawn as shown below

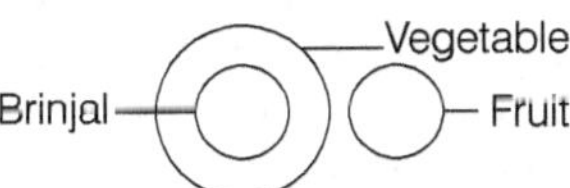

Hence, option (b) is correct.

2. Door and window both are the parts of house, but they are not related to each other. So, the Venn diagram is as shown below

Hence, option (a) is correct.

3. All the three, honest, intelligent and poor are related as some honest can be intelligent, some intelligent can be poor and some poor can be honest. Also, some poor can be honest and intelligent interrelated. So, the Venn diagram is as shown below

Hence, option (d) is correct.

4. All the three are the parts of computer and not related to one another. So, the Venn diagram is as shown below

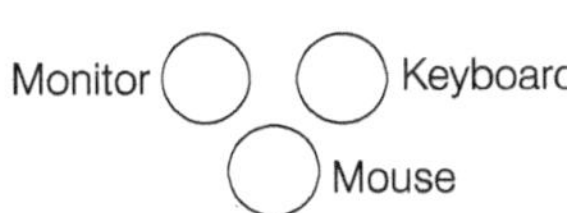

Hence, option (a) is correct.

5. A book has chapters and a chapter has topic. So, the Venn diagram is as shown below

Hence, option (b) is correct.

6. Picture is there in tv and radio is not related to both of them. So, the Venn diagram is as shown below

Hence, option (c) is correct.

7. Cup, plate and spoon all are different. So, the Venn diagram is as shown below

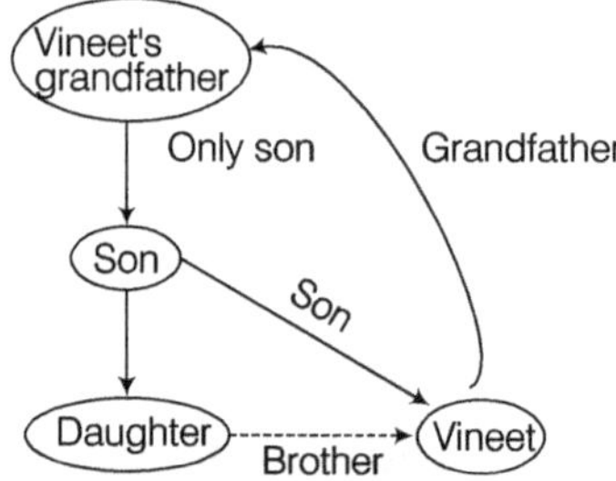

Hence, option (a) is correct.

8. Copy is a part of stationery and car is not related to both of them. So, the Venn diagram is as shown below

Hence, option (c) is correct.

9. Educated people who are employed are represented by the region of triangle and circle which is $2 + 5 = 7$.
Hence, option (b) is correct.

10. People who are educated, but are neither employed nor backward are represented by number which lie inside the triangle only i.e. 9.
Hence, option (a) is correct.

11. Number '2' is represented by trained nurses who are neither married nor in hospital, because it is common region in square only.
Hence, option (b) is correct.

12. Some clothes are bright and some flowers are also bright, but not all bright things are clothes or flowers. Also, clothes and flowers are not related. This can be represented as

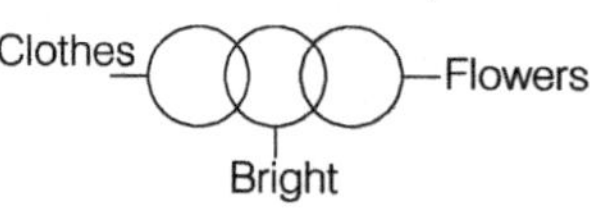

Hence, option (d) is correct.

13. The people who speak all the three languages is represented by 'U', which is common to all the three circles.
Hence, option (b) is correct.

14. The students who likes ice-cream and cake but not dosa is 'F', which is common to the circle and rectangle, but lies outside the triangle.
Hence, option (b) is correct.

11 Blood Relations

1. The only son of Vineet's grandfather is the father of Vineet and daughter of Vineet's father is the sister of Vineet. So, Vineet is the brother of that lady.
This can be represented as

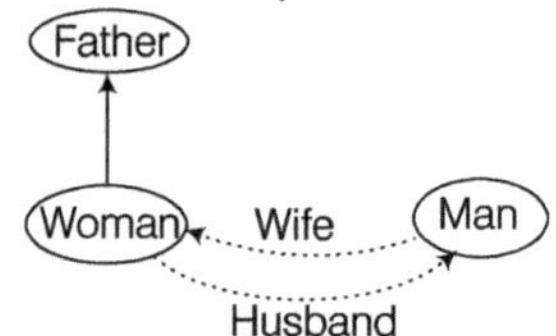

Hence, option (b) is correct.

2. The only daughter of the woman's father is she herself. So, the woman and the man has a wife-husband relationship.
This can be represented as

Hence, option (c) is correct.

3. Son of woman's mother's mother means the brother of mother. And brother of mother is maternal uncle. So, woman is related as niece to that man.
This can be represented as

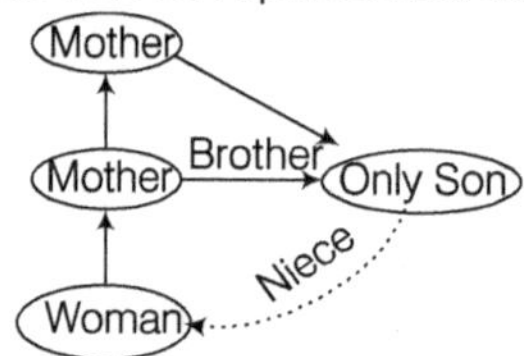

Hence, option (a) is correct.

4. Uncle of Naman's son is the brother of Naman. As given information, the son of man is brother of Naman. Therefore, the man (in the park) is related as father to Naman. This can be represented as

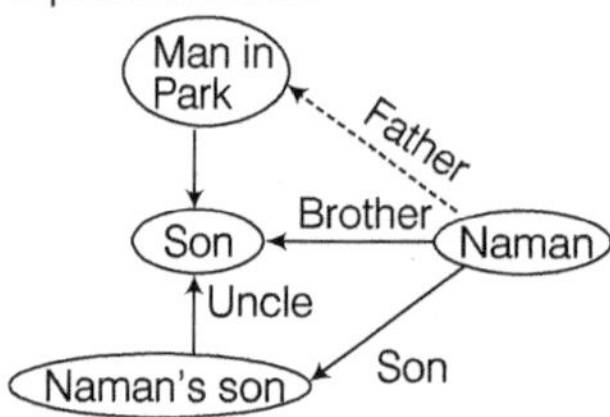

Hence, option (d) is correct.

5. The only daughter of Neeraj's wife is the daughter of Neeraj and the Neeraj's daughter is the wife of that man. So, Neeraj is the father-in-law of that man.
This can be represented as

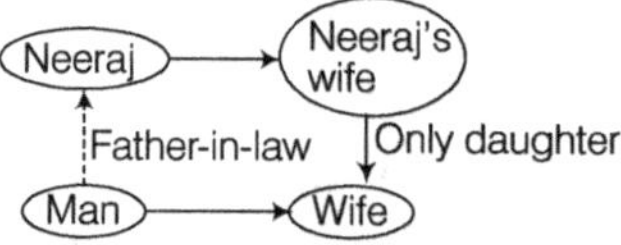

Hence, option (a) is correct.

6. Since, P is the mother of Q. So, Q must be either daughter or son of P. But it is given that Q is not daughter of P.
∴ Q is the son of P.

Hence, option (a) is correct.

7. The relation can be represented as

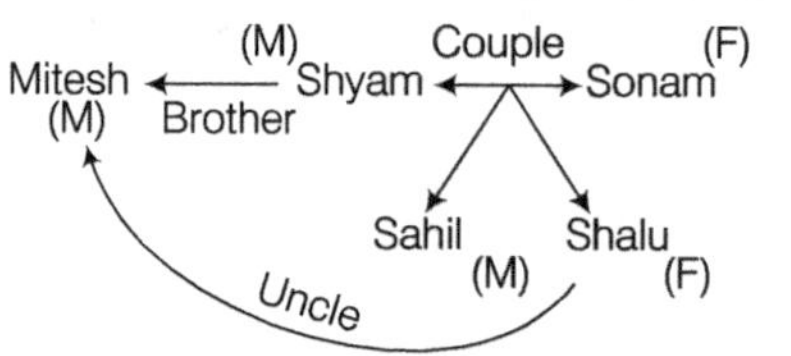

∴ Mitesh is the uncle of Shalu.
Hence, option (d) is correct.

8. Here, given that L and M are children of O, then

Now, from statement I

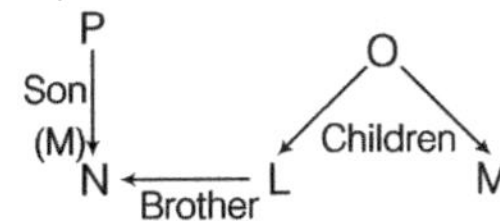

This statement is not necessary because in the question O has only two children. So, this statement is not sufficient.
From statement II,

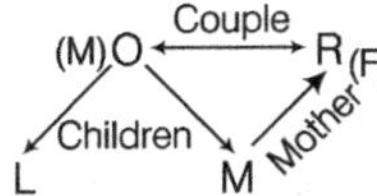

So, it is clear from the statement II that, the father of L is O.
Therefore, only statement II is necessary to answer this question.
Hence, option (b) is correct.

9. From the given information, it is clear that C is the brother of B but B can be brother or sister of C. So, how is B related to C depends on the gender of B. Thus, to establish the relationship between B and C, gender of B should be known. So, only statement II is necessary to answer this question.
Hence, option (b) is correct.

10. The relation can be represented as

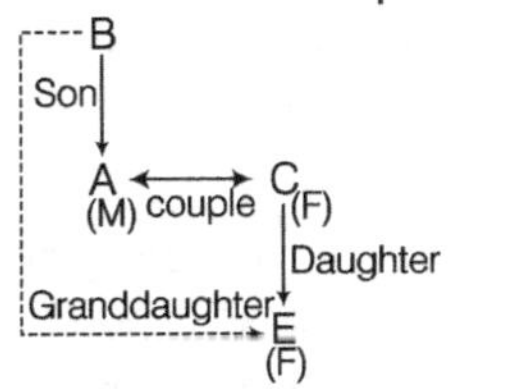

It is clearly shown that, E is granddaughter of B.
Hence, option (a) is correct.

11. The relations can be represented as

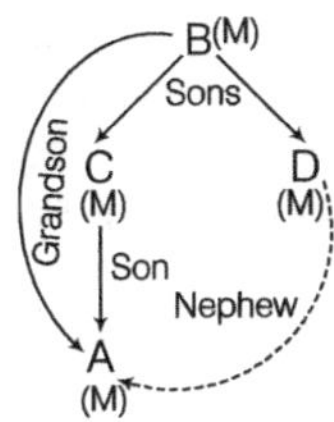

It is clearly shown that, C and D are two sons of B. So, C and D are brother. Therefore, A is nephew of D.
Hence, option (d) is correct.

12. The relations can be represented as

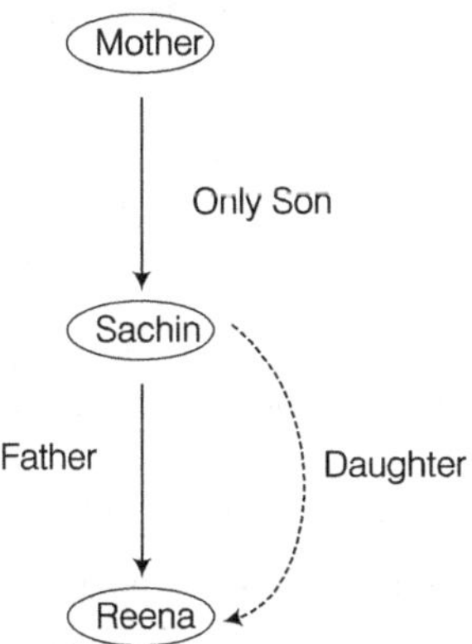

Here, it is given that P is the brother of Q and father of R. Q is the either brother or sister of P. So, R and S are cousins.
Hence, option (a) is correct.

13. The only son of Sachin's mother is Sachin himself. So, Sachin is the father of Reena.
This can be represented as

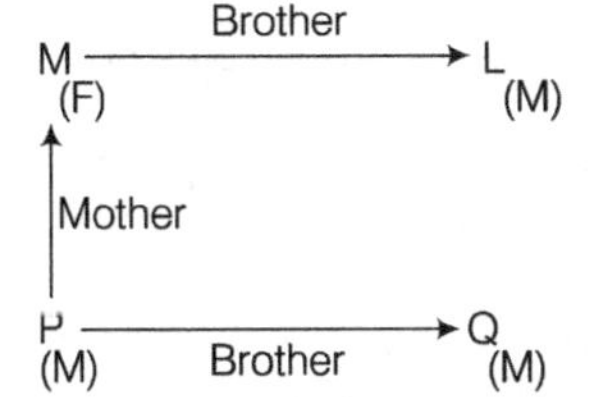

Hence, option (b) is correct.

14. The relation can be represented as

Since, M is the mother of P and P is the brother of Q. So, M is the mother of Q and hence, L is the uncle of Q.
Hence, option (b) is correct.

15. As per question,
C is the sister of A. And A is the brother of B.

∴ C is the sister of B.
Hence, option (a) is correct.

16. Husband and wife = 2
Married sons = 4
Daughter-in-law = 4
Unmarried son = 1
Unmarried daughter = 3
∴ Total members in the family = 2 + 4 + 4 + 1 + 3 = 14
Hence, option (d) is correct.

17. The relation can be represented by

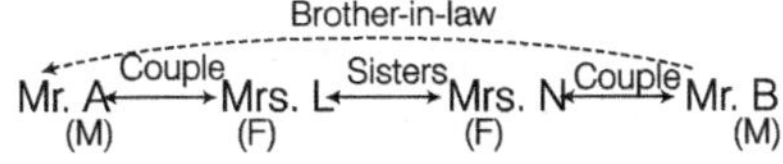

It is clearly shown from the above diagram that Mr. A is brother-in-law of Mr. B.
Hence, option (c) is correct.

18. There are 7 members in Mr. Sharma's family. Mother and father of Mr. Sharma, Mr. and Mrs. Sharma, his son and two daughters.

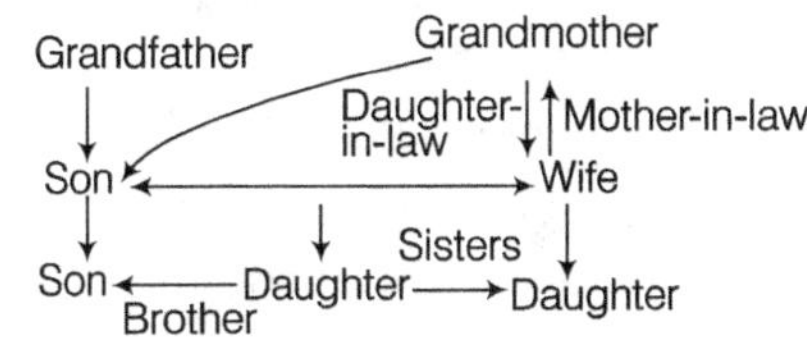

Hence, option (d) is correct.

Solution (Q. Nos. 19-22) On the basis of given information, the relation of five persons, who are sitting around dinning table can be represented as

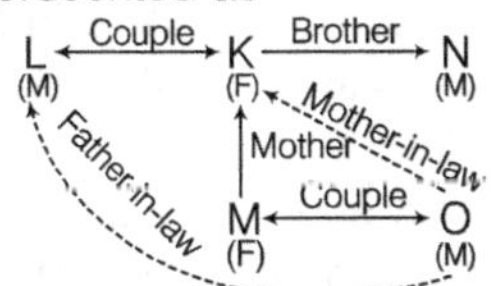

19. From the above diagram, we can see that, L is father-in-law of O.
Hence, option (a) is correct.

20. From the above diagram, it is clear that, K is the mother-in-law of O.
Hence, option (c) is correct.

21. It is clear from the diagram that, N is brother-in-law of L.
Hence, option (b) is correct.

22. It is clear that M is daughter of L.
Hence, option (d) is correct.

Solutions (Q. Nos. 23-24) On the basis of given information, the relation of six family persons can be represented as

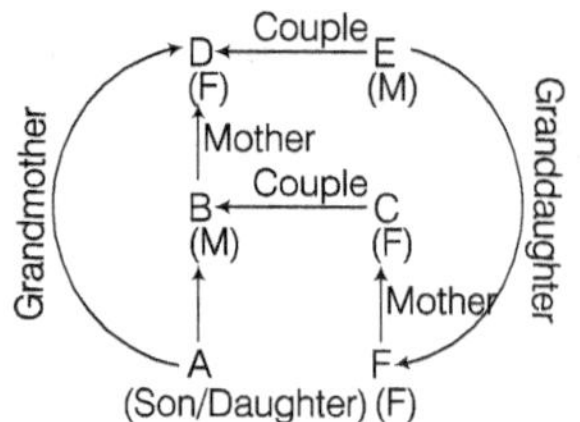

23. It is clearly shown that C is the mother of A.
Hence, option (a) is correct.

24. It is clearly shown in the diagram that, the gender of A is not given, so there should be 3 or 4 female members in the family.
Hence, option (c) is correct.

12 Similar Pairs

1. Hammer is a tool that is used to hit nails into a piece of wood or a wall. Similarly, a screwdriver is a tool that is used for turning screws.
So, option figure (d) will complete the second pair.
Hence, option (d) is correct.

2. As the shape of the ice-cream cone is cone, similarly the shape of the given container is cylindrical.
So, option figure (c) will complete the second pair.
Hence, option (c) is correct.

3. The design in first figure is completed and divided into four equal parts to obtain the second figure.
On following this pattern, option figure (b) will complete the second pair.
Hence, option (b) is correct.

4. The inner shape in first figure is removed to obtain the second figure.
On following this pattern, option figure (d) will complete the second pair.
Hence, option (d) is correct.

5. A line is increased in the first figure to obtain the second figure.
On following this pattern, option figure (a) will complete the second pair.
Hence, option (a) is correct.

6. The first figure gets vertically inverted to obtain the second figure and lining pattern remains the same. On following this pattern, option figure (c) will complete the second pair.
Hence, option (c) is correct.

7. Triangle is made from three lines. Similarly, square is made from four lines. So, option figure (a) will complete the second pair.
Hence, option (a) is correct.

8. The inner design is enlarged and becomes outer design and the outer design is reduced and becomes inner design with shade. On following this pattern, option figure (b) will complete the second pair.
Hence, option (b) is correct.

9. The first figure is laterally inverted to obtain the second figure. On following this pattern, option figure (c) will complete the second pair.
Hence, option (c) is correct.

10. The first figure rotates 90° in clockwise direction to obtain the second figure. On following this pattern, option figure (c) will complete the second pair.
Hence, option (c) is correct.

11. The number of sides of the main figure is increased by one and the number of vertical lines in the figure is decreased by one. On following this pattern, option figure (a) will complete the second pair.
Hence, option (a) is correct.

12. The shapes in the middle of the figure interchange their positions and the elements at RHS and LHS positions interchange their positions. On following this pattern, option figure (d) will complete the second pair.
Hence, option (d) is correct.

13. The whole figure gets laterally inverted and the symbols interchange their respective positions. On following this pattern, option figure (b) will complete the second pair.
Hence, option (b) is correct.

14. The inner shape is enlarged and becomes the middle shape and the middle shape is compressed and becomes the inner shape. On following this pattern, option figure (d) will complete the second pair.
Hence, option (d) is correct.

15. The first figure rotates 180° clockwise direction to obtain the second figure. On following this pattern, option figure (a) will complete the second pair.
Hence, option (a) is correct.

16. The number of sides in the main figure is decreased by one and the circles inside the figure, move outside and a new black dot appears inside the figure.
On following this pattern, option figure (a) will complete the second pair.
Hence, option (a) is correct.

17. The black portion becomes white and white portion becomes black. On following this pattern, option figure (c) will complete the second pair.
Hence, option (c) is correct.

18. The bottom figure and the upper most figure rotates 180° and the upper most figure with line comes inside the figure. On following this pattern, option figure (a) will complete the second pair.
Hence, option (a) is correct.

19. The shaded portion of the first figure is taken forward after rotating it 90° in clockwise direction ⟳ to obtain the second figure. On following this pattern, option figure (b) will complete the second pair.
Hence, option (b) is correct.

20. The first figure is laterally inverted to obtain the second figure.
On following this pattern, option figure (b) will complete the second pair.
Hence, option (b) is correct.

21. The first figure rotates 90° in anti-clockwise direction   to obtain the second figure. On following this pattern, option figure (b) will complete the second pair.
Hence, option (b) is correct.

22. The whole figure rotates 90° clockwise, inner figure becomes outer figure and outer figure becomes inner figure and triangular arrow head changes to spear arrow head. On following this pattern, option figure (c) will complete the second pair.
Hence, option (c) is correct.

23. The figure inside the main figure flips out side and the figure at the top of the main figure flips inside. On following this pattern, option figure (b) will complete the second pair.
Hence, option (b) is correct.

24. The top most and lower most figure interchange their position and the slanting lines appear in the middle figure. On following this pattern, option figure (b) will complete the second pair.
Hence, option (b) is correct.

13 What Comes Next?

1. Here, one side of the rhombus is removed in each step, in clockwise direction.
On following this pattern, option figure (c) will come next.
Hence, option (c) is correct.

2. Here, the number of lines are increased by two in each step.
On following this pattern, option figure (c) will come next.
Hence, option (c) is correct.

3. Here, alternative figures are same. So, fifth figure will be same as third figure.
On following this pattern, option figure (d) will come next.
Hence, option (d) is correct.

4. Here, an arrow and a line is added, alternatively in each step.
On following this pattern, option figure (d) will come next.
Hence, option (d) is correct.

5. Here, the small arrow is rotating 90° and 45° anti-clockwise in each alternate step and the other arrow is rotating 135° clockwise in each step.
On following this pattern, option figure (d) will come next.
Hence, option (d) is correct.

6. Here, each time a bead is removed from right hand side stick.
On following this pattern, option figure (c) will come next.
Hence, option (c) is correct.

7. Here, triangle is moved diagonally and the circle is moving one step in anti-clockwise direction to get the next figure.
On following this pattern, option figure (d) will come next.
Hence, option (d) is correct.

8. In first step, we move 90° clockwise and the dot inside the square disappear.
In second step, when we move 90° clockwise again the dot inside the square appears. This pattern is followed by the following step that comes next.
Hence, option (b) is correct.

9. Here, starting from the extreme right, one part is removed at a time in a set order.
On following this pattern, option figure (d) will come next.
Hence, option (d) is correct.

10. Here, starting from the extreme right, the elements turned upside down one-by-one in each step.
On following this pattern, option figure (d) will come next.
Hence, option (d) is correct.

11. Here, the whole figure is rotating 60° in clockwise direction in each step.
On following this pattern, option figure (c) will come next.
Hence, option (c) is correct.

12. Here, the triangle and rectangle are moving one step in clockwise direction and the dot and square are moving one step in anti- clockwise direction to get the next figure.
On following this pattern, option figure (a) will come next.
Hence, option (a) is correct.

13. Here, each element is moving one step in clockwise direction in each step.
On following this pattern, option figure (c) will come next.
Hence, option (c) is correct.

14. Here, starting from the extreme left, first figure is rotating 90° clockwise, second and third figure remains unchanged and fourth figure is rotating 90° clockwise to get the next term.
On following this pattern, option figure (d) will come next.
Hence, option (d) is correct.

15. Here, the white arrow is rotating 60° anti-clockwise, the line with black dot is rotating 120° anti-clockwise and the line with white circle and the black arrow both are rotating 180° to get the next figure.

On following this pattern, option figure (a) will come next.

Hence, option (a) is correct.

16. Here, white circle is rotating 90° clockwise 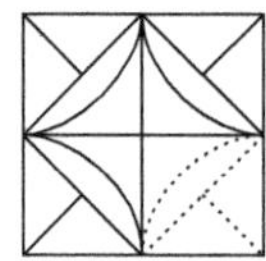, square is rotating 45° clockwise 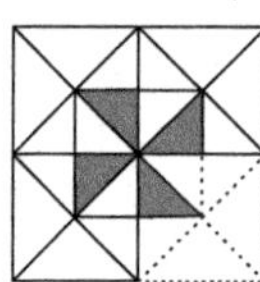, dot is rotating 135° clockwise and arrow is rotating 180°, to get the next term. On the following this pattern option figure (d) will come next.

Hence, option (d) is correct.

17. Here, the alternate figures are same. So, the missing figure will be same as second figure. On following this pattern, option figure (b) will complete the series.

Hence, option (b) is correct.

18. Here, all the elements are laterally inverted and shifted one place downward. The element at the bottom is moved to the top in each step. On following this pattern, option figure (a) will complete the series.

Hence, option (a) is correct.

19. Here, the whole figure is rotating 45° clockwise in each step. On following this pattern, option figure (a) will complete the series.

Hence, option (a) is correct.

20. The series follows the following pattern in each successive step Each element is shifted upward diagonally and the top right element converted into new element and shifted downward and becomes bottom left element.

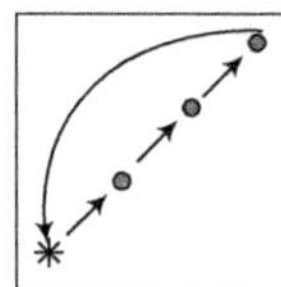

On following this pattern option figure (b) will complete the series.

Hence, option (b) is correct.

21. Here, considering rowwise, the two parts of the first figure are joined along the straight sides and the common side is then removed to form the second figure.

On following this pattern, option figure (b) will complete the matrix.

Hence, option (b) is correct.

22. Here, considering rowwise, the second figure is the part of first figure but in different form. On following this pattern, option figure (c) will complete the matrix.

Hence, option (c) is correct.

23. The pattern is completed as

Hence, option (b) is correct.

24. The pattern is completed as

Hence, option (d) is correct.

25. Here, considering rowwise, the first figure is compressed and inserted into the second figure to get the third figure. On following this pattern, option figure (b) will complete the matrix.

Hence, option (b) is correct.

26. Here, considering rowwise, the first figure is laterally inverted to obtain the third figure.

On following this pattern, option figure (d) will complete the matrix.

Hence, option (d) is correct.

27. Here, looking across and down, only the dots which are at common place in first two squares are carried forward to the third square. On following this pattern, option figure (a) will complete the matrix.

Hence, option (a) is correct.

28. Here, looking across and down, the first and second figures are combined to obtain the third figure. On following this pattern, option figure (c) will complete the matrix.

Hence, option (c) is correct.

29. Here, in the row, the figure is rotating 45° clockwise and in the column, the figure is rotating 135° clockwise in each step. On following this pattern, option figure (c) will complete the matrix.

Hence, option (c) is correct.

30. In first row, the arrow moves 90° in anti-clockwise direction and increases by one arrow. In second step it again moves 90° in anti-clockwise direction and increases by one arrow.

On following this pattern option figure (a) will complete the matrix.

Hence, option (a) is correct.

31. Here, in each row, four circles are added to the outside of the first figure to obtain the third figure. On following this pattern, option figure (b) will complete the matrix.

Hence, option (b) is correct.

32. Here, looking across and down, lines common to the first two squares are removed in third square. On following this pattern, option figure (b) will complete the matrix.

Hence, option (b) is correct.

33. Here, considering columnwise, one side is increased from first figure to second figure and two sides are increased from second figure to third figure. On following this pattern, option figure (d) will complete the matrix.

Hence, option (d) is correct.

34. Here, in each row, the outer figure is removed each time. On following this pattern, option figure (a) will complete the matrix.

Hence, option (a) is correct.

14 Odd One Out

1. Here, all the figures except figure (b), are same when rotated. So, option figure (b) is odd one out. Hence, option (b) is correct.

2. Here, in all the figures except figure (d), the number of lines used to make the inner shape is one less than the number of lines used to make the outer shape. So, option figure (d) is odd one out.
Hence, option (d) is correct.

3. Here, in all the figures except figure (d), the inner and outer figures are same. So, option figure (d) is odd one out.
Hence, option (d) is correct.

4. Here, in all the figures except figure (d), the circles are on the opposite side of the line. But in figure (d) the circles are on the same side. So, option figure (d) is odd one out.
Hence, option (d) is correct.

5. Here, in all the figures except figure (c), the two shapes are made of equal number of lines. So, option figure (c) is odd one out.
Hence, option (c) is correct.

6. Here, all the figures, except figure (d) are same when rotated. So, option figure (d) is odd one out.
Hence, option (d) is correct.

7. Here, in all the figures except figure (a), three different shapes are shown on different faces of the cubes. So, option figure (a) is odd one out.
Hence, option (a) is correct.

8. Here, in all the figures except figure (d), the two shapes are facing each other. So, option figure (d) is odd one out.
Hence, option (d) is correct.

9. Here, in all the figures except figure (d), the subdivided parts are equal in size but in figure (d) the corner parts are not equal in size as the middle part. So, option figure (d) is odd one out.
Hence, option (d) is correct.

10. Here, in all the figures except figure (a), one circle is bisected horizontally and the other vertically. So, option figure (a) is odd one out.
Hence, option (a) is correct.

11. Here, in all the figures except figure (c), the base of the hook is two sided, but in figure (c) it is one-sided. So, option figure (c) is odd one out.
Hence, option (c) is correct.

12. Here, in all the figures except figure (a), the middle circle is not divided into parts. But in option figure (a), the middle circle is also divided. So, option figure (a) is odd one out.
Hence, option (a) is correct.

13. Here, in all the figures except figure (c), the two arrows are pointing towards in same direction. But in figure (c) the arrows are pointing in opposite direction.
So, option figure (c) is odd one out.
Hence, option (c) is correct.

14. Here, in all the figures except figure (c), the circles placed at both the sides of the arrow are arranged in specific pattern i.e. black circle is adjacent to white circle and vice-versa. But in figure (c) two black circles and two white circles are adjacent to each other. So, option figure (c) is odd one out.
Hence, option (c) is correct.

15. Here, in all the figures except figure (b), the number of spikes at the top is equal to the number of lines used to make the shape. So, option figure (b) is odd one out.
Hence, option (b) is correct.

16. Here, in all the figure except figure (d), the two straight lines have identical elements on both ends. So, option figure (d) is odd one out.
Hence, option (d) is correct.

17. Here, all the figures except figure (d), are made of three different lines. But in figure (d) there is a curved line. So, option figure (d) is odd one out.
Hence, option (d) is correct.

18. Here, in all the figures except figure (d), the three shapes are different but in option figure (d) the inner most and the outer most figures are same i.e. triangle. So, option figure (d) is odd one out.
Hence, option (d) is correct.

15 Mirror and Water Images

1. The correct mirror image is

VERBAL | ⅃AƁЯƎⱽ

Hence, option (d) is correct.

2. The correct mirror image is

QUALITY | YTI⅃AUꝖ

Hence, option (c) is correct.

3. The correct mirror image is

24759 | ℑ⅃ᘓⵑ⨭ⵑⵑⵑ

Hence, option (b) is correct.

4. The correct mirror image is

DL3N469F | ꟻ964N3⅃D

Hence, option (b) is correct.

5. The correct mirror image is

disturb | ꓒⱯⱯⱯⱯⱯⱯ

Hence, option (a) is correct.

6. Here, the option (c) represent the same as look in the mirror. Since, mirror image of T, O and H are same as original image. Hence, option (c) is correct.

7. The correct mirror image of the given object is

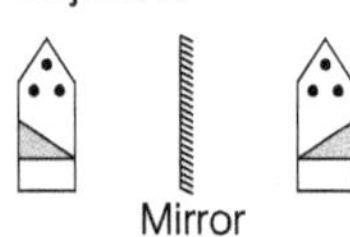

Mirror

Hence, option (d) is correct.

8. The correct mirror image of the given object is

Mirror

Hence, option (d) is correct.

9. The correct mirror image of the given object is

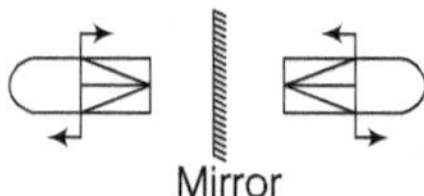

Mirror

Hence, option (b) is correct.

10. The correct mirror image of the given object is

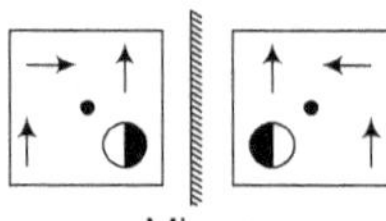

Mirror

Hence, option (b) is correct.

11. The correct mirror image of the given object is

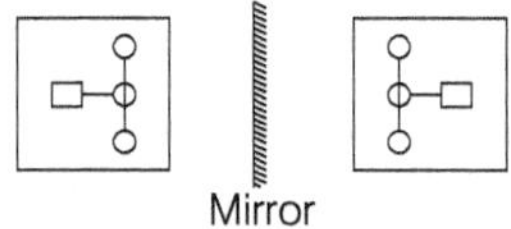

Mirror

Hence, option (d) is correct.

12. The correct mirror image of the given object is

2:05 | 20:5

Mirror

Hence, option (b) is correct.

13. The correct water image is

SURFACE
———————————— Water
SURFACE

Hence, option (d) is correct.

14. The correct water image is

1942
———————————— Water
1942

Hence, option (c) is correct.

15. The correct water image is

rise
———————————— Water
rise

Hence, option (a) is correct.

16. The correct water image is

U 4 P 15 B 7
———————————— Water
U 4 P 15 B 7

Hence, option (c) is correct.

17. The correct water image of the given object is

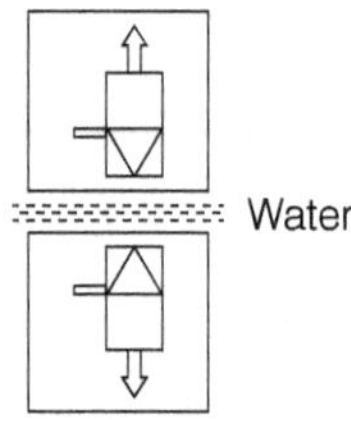

Water

Hence, option (a) is correct.

18. The correct water image of the given object is

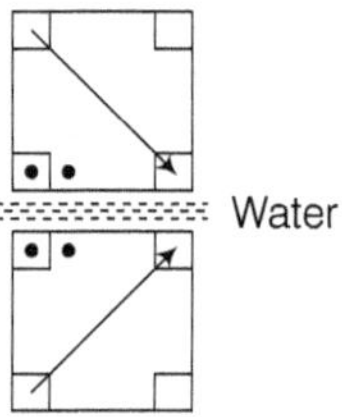

Water

Hence, option (c) is correct.

19. The correct water image of the given object is

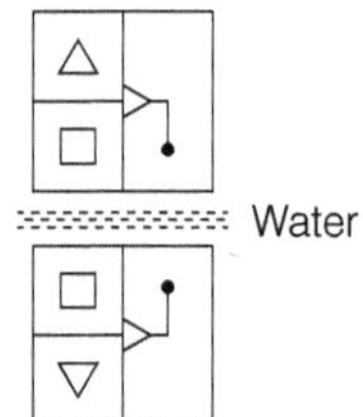

Water

Hence, option (a) is correct.

20. The correct water image of the given object is

Hence, option (c) is correct.

16 Cubes and Dice

1.

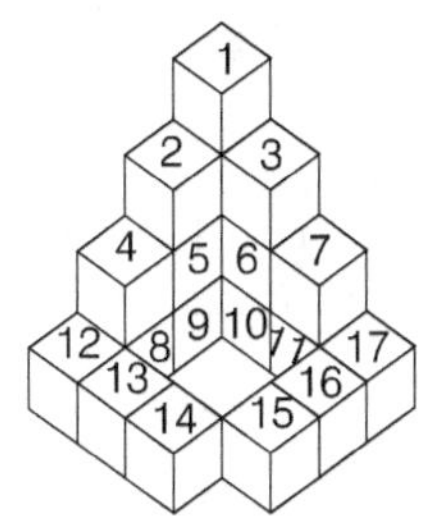

In the given figure, there are 17 visible cubes and 3 hidden cubes below the cube number 1.
So, the total number of cubes
= 17 + 3 = 20
Hence, option (b) is correct.

2.

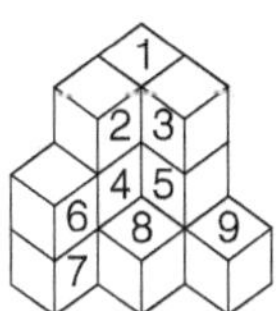

Here, there are 9 visible cubes, 2 hidden cubes below the cube number 1 and 1 hidden cube each below the cubes number 4 and 5.
∴ Total number of cubes
= 9 + 2 + 1 + 1 = 13
Hence, option (d) is correct.

3.

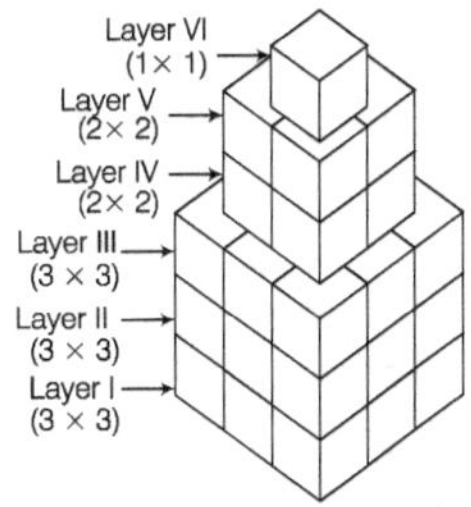

Here, there are 9 cubes each in layers I, II and III, 4 cubes each in layer IV and V and 1 cube in layer VI.
∴ Total number of cubes
= 9 + 9 + 9 + 4 + 4 + 1 = 36
Hence, option (b) is correct.

4.

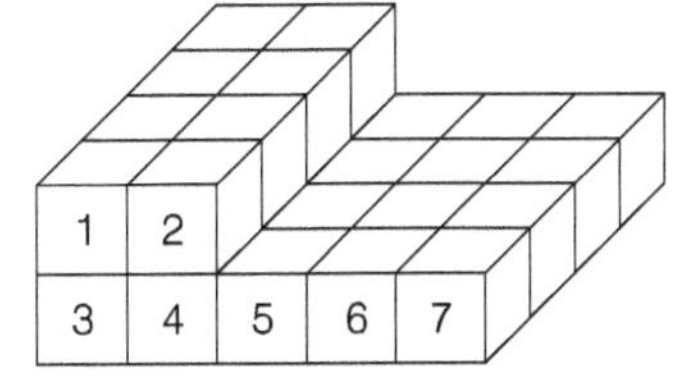

Here, there are 7 layers and each layer contains 4 cubes.
∴ Total number of cubes = 7 × 4 = 28
Hence, option (c) is correct.

5. Pairs of opposite faces are (A and D), (F and B) and (E and C). In option fig. (a), F is shown adjacent to B. In option fig. (c), E is shown adjacent to C and in option fig. (d), D is shown adjacent to A. So, these alternatives are not possible. Only the cube given in option fig. (b) can be formed because F, E and D can be on adjacent faces.
Hence, option (b) is correct.

6. Pairs of opposite faces (5 and 3), (2 and 4) and (1 and 6). In option fig. (a), 6 is shown adjacent to 1. In option fig. (b), 3 is shown adjacent to 5 and in option fig. (c), 2 is shown adjacent to 4. So, these alternatives are not possible. Only the cube given in option fig. (d) can be formed because 1, 3 and 4 can be on adjacent faces.
Hence, option (d) is correct.

7. Pairs of opposite faces are

⬚ ↔ ⬚, ⬚ ↔ ⬚, and ⬚ ↔ ⬚

In option fig. (a), ⬚ is shown adjacent to ⬚. In option fig. (b), ⬚ is shown adjacent to ⬚ and in option fig. (c), ⬚ is shown adjacent to ⬚. So, these alternatives are not possible. Only the cube given in option fig. (d) can be formed because ⬚, ⬚ and ⬚ can be on adjacent faces.
Hence, option (d) is correct.

8. Pairs of opposite faces are (⬚ and ⬚), (⬚ and ⬚) and (⬚ and ⬚). In option fig. (a) and (b), the wrong shaded pattern is given. In option fig. (c), ⬚ is shown adjacent to ⬚. So, these alternatives are not possible. Only the cube given in option (d) can be formed because ⬚, ⬚ and ⬚ can be on adjacent faces.
Hence, option (d) is correct.

9. Pairs of opposite faces are (⬚ and ⬚), (⬚ and ⬚) and (⬚ and ⬚). Here, all the four cubes can be formed from the given net because no opposite faces are shown adjacent to each other in these cubes.
Hence, option (d) is correct.

10. Pairs of opposite faces are

(⬚ and ⬚), (⬚ and ⬛), (⬚ and ⬚). In figures (I) and (II) ⬚ is shown adjacent to ⬚. So, these alternatives are not possible. Cubes shown in figures (III) and (IV) can be formed because the faces of these cubes can be adjacent to each other.
Hence, option (d) is correct.

11. Pairs of opposite faces are (⬚ and ⬚), (⬚ and ⬚) and (⬚ and ⬚) cubes given in figures (I) and (II) can be formed because the faces of these cube can be adjacent to each other. In figures (III) and (IV), ⬚ is shown adjacent to ⬚. So, these alternatives are not possible.
Hence, option (a) is correct.

12. Pairs of opposite faces are (⬚ and ⬚), (⬚ and ⬚) and (⬛ and ⬛). Here, all the four cubes can be formed from the given net because no opposite faces are shown adjacent to each other in these cubes.
Hence, option (d) is correct.

13. Pairs of opposite faces are (A and B), (D and E) and (C and F). Here, 'D' is opposite to E. So, the face having 'E' is at the bottom of the cube.
Hence, option (c) is correct.

14. Given, opposite faces are (⚄ and ⚅), (⚃ and ⚄) and (⚁ and ⚀). In option fig. (a), the opposite faces are (⚄ and ⚃), (⚄ and ⚅) and (⚀ and ⚄) which is not correct according to the above given information.
In option fig. (b), opposite faces are (⚅ and ⚄), (⚄ and ⚃) and (⚃ and ⚀) which is not correct according to the above information. In option fig. (c), opposite faces are (⚅ and ⚄), (⚃ and ⚄), and (⚃ and ⚀) which is correct according to the above given information.
In option fig. (d), opposite faces are (⚃ and ⚅) and (⚃ and ⚄) which is not correct according to the above given information.
Hence, option (c) is correct.

15. Number '6' is common in both positions of the dice. Now, the adjacent faces of '6' are 1, 2, 3 and 4.

So, the remaining number, i.e. '5' will be opposite to number '6'.
Hence, option (d) is correct.

16. Here, 3 and 4 are common digits in both positions. So, the remaining two faces will be opposite to each other as shown below:

Position (i)	3	5	4
Position (ii)	3	2	4
	Common	Opposite	Common

So, it is clear that 5 lies opposite to 2.
Hence, option (a) is correct.

17. The face having number '1' appears in both the positions. Clearly, the face having number 2, 3, 5 and 6 are adjacent to the face having '1'. So, the face having '4' will be just opposite to '1'.
Hence, option (d) is correct.

18. The face having 3 dots is common in both positions. So, moving clockwise starting from 3, we get

Position (i)	3	4	6
Position (ii)	3	5	2
	Common	Opposite	Opposite

So, it is clear that the face having 6 dots will be at the top, when the face having 2 dots is at bottom.
Hence, option (c) is correct.

19. The face having 5 dots appears in both the positions. Clearly, the faces having 4, 3, 1 and 2 dots are adjacent to the face having 5 dots. So, the face having 6 dots will be opposite to the face having 5 dots.
Hence, option (d) is correct.

20. From the given four positions, the face having 3 dots is common in three positions, i.e. (I), (II) and (IV). So, the faces having 4, 6, 1 and 2 dots are adjacent to the face having 3 dots. Clearly, the remaining 5 dots will be on the face opposite to the face having 3 dots.
Hence, option (b) is correct.

17 Counting of Figures

1. On labelling the figure, we get

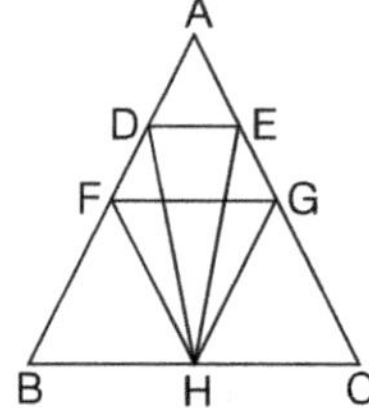

The number of horizontal lines are DE, FG and BC, i.e. 3.
The number of slant lines are AB, FH, DH, EH, GH and AC, i.e. 6.
Thus, the total number of lines
= 3 + 6 = 9
Hence, option (c) is correct.

2. On labelling the figure, we get

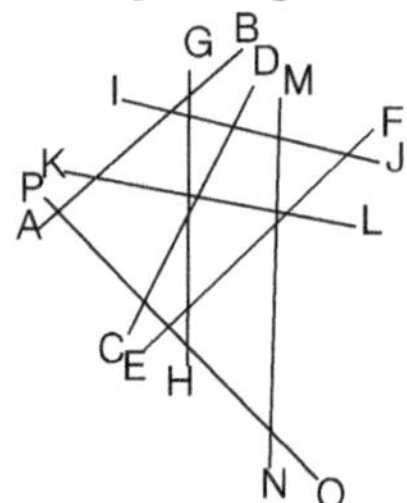

It is clear that, the number of lines are AB, EF, GH, CD, PO, KL, IJ, MN, i.e. 8.
Thus, the total number of lines are
= 8
Hence, option (c) is correct.

3. On labelling the figure, we get

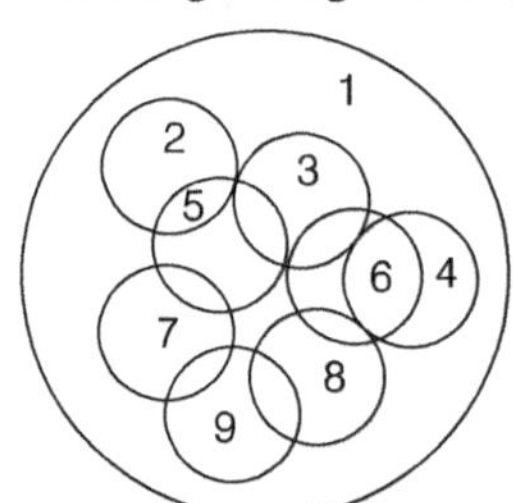

It is clear that, the figure has nine circles.
Hence, option (b) is correct.

4. On labelling the figure, we get

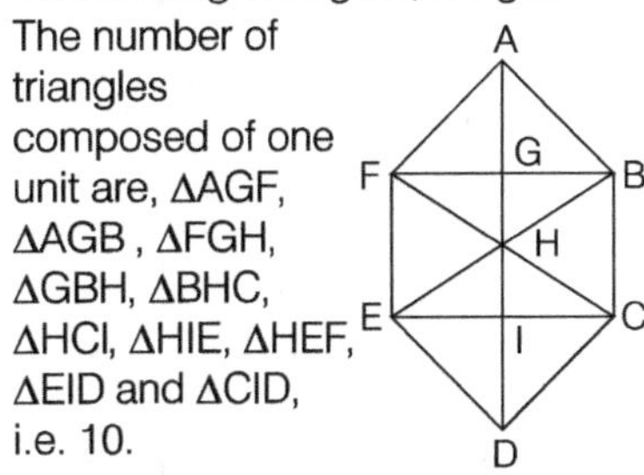

The number of triangles composed of one unit are, ΔAGF, ΔAGB, ΔFGH, ΔGBH, ΔBHC, ΔHCI, ΔHIE, ΔHEF, ΔEID and ΔCID, i.e. 10.

The number of triangles composed of two units are ΔAFB, ΔFBH, ΔEHC, ΔECD, ΔEHD, ΔHCD, ΔABH and ΔAFH, i.e. 8.

The number of triangles composed of three units are ΔFEC, ΔFBC, ΔBEC and ΔBFE, i.e. 4. Thus, the total number of triangles = 10 + 8 + 4 = 22.

Hence, option (a) is correct.

5. On labelling the figure, we get

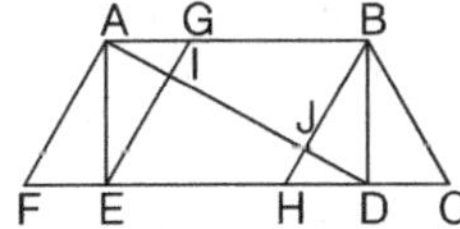

The number of triangles composed of one unit are ΔAEF, ΔAIE, ΔAGI, ΔJHD, ΔJBD and ΔBCD, i.e. 6. The number of triangles composed of two units are ΔAGE, ΔBHD, ΔABJ and ΔIED, i.e. 4. The number of triangles composed of more than two units are ΔADF, ΔBHC, ΔABD and ΔAED, i.e. 4. Thus, the total number of triangles
= 6 + 4 + 4 = 14

Hence, option (a) is correct.

6. On labelling the figure, we get

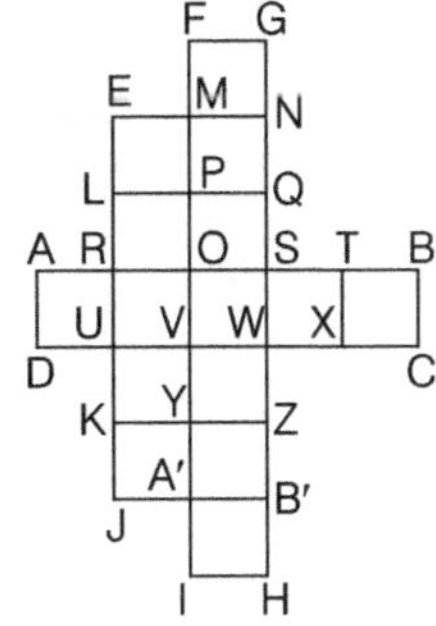

The number of squares composed of one unit are □ARUD, □ROVU, □OSWV, □STXW, □TBCX, □EMPL, □LPOR, □UVYK, □KYA'J, □FGNM, □MNQP,
□PQSO, □ VWZY, □ YZ B'A', □ A'B'HI, i.e. 15.

The number of squares composed of more than one units are, □ENSR, □LQWU, □RSZK, □ UWB'J, i.e. 4.

So, the total number of squares
= 15 + 4 = 19

Hence, option (d) is correct.

7. On labelling the figure, we get

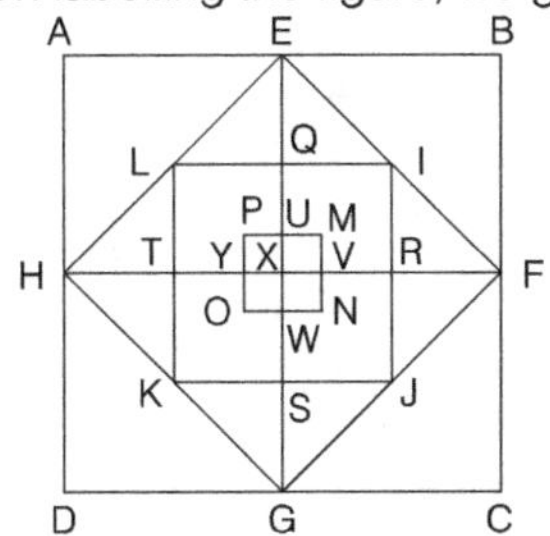

The number of squares composed of one unit are
□ PUXY, □ UMVX, □XVNW, □ YXWO, i.e. 4.

The number of squares composed of two units are □ LQXT, □ QIRX, □XRJS and □TXSK i.e.4.

The number of squares composed of three units are □ EBFX, □ XFCG, □HXGD and □AEXH, i.e. 4.

The number of squares composed of more than three units are □ PMNO, □LIJK, □ EFGH and □ ABCD, i.e. 4.

Thus, the total number of squares
= 4 + 4 + 4 + 4 = 16

Hence, option (c) is correct.

8. On labelling the figure, we get

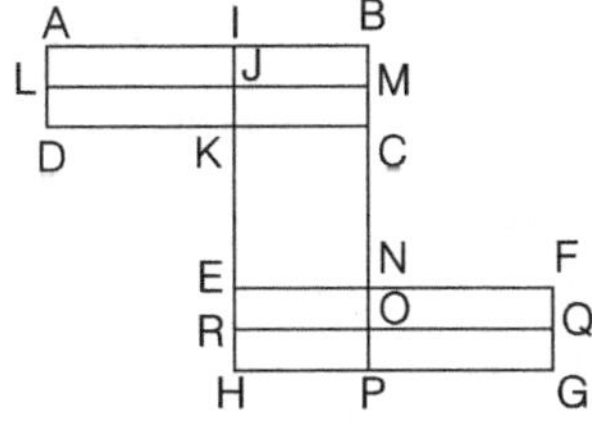

The number of rectangles composed of one unit are
□ AIJL, □IBMJ, □ LJKD, □JMCK, □ KCNE, □ ENOR, □ NFQO, □ OQGP and □ ROPH, i.e. 9.

The number of rectangles composed of two units are
□ABML, □ LMCD, □ AIKD, □IBCK, □ JMNE, □ KCOR,
□ EFQR, □ RQGH, □ ENPH and □ NFGP, i.e. 10.

The number of rectangles composed of more than two units are □ ABCD, □IBNE, □IBOR, □ IBPH, □ JMOR, □ JMPH, □ KCPH and □EFGH, i.e. 8.

Thus, the total number of rectangles = 9 + 10 + 8 = 27

Hence, option (b) is correct.

9. On labelling the figure, we get

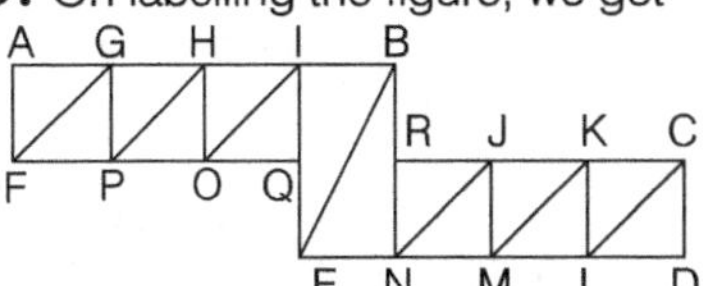

The number of triangles are, ΔAGF, ΔGPF, ΔGHP, ΔHOP, ΔHIO, ΔIQO, ΔIBE, ΔBEN, ΔRJN, ΔJMN, ΔJKM, ΔKLM, ΔKCL and ΔCDL, i.e. 14.

The number of squares are, □AGPF, □ GHOP, □ HIQO, □RJMN, □ JKLM, □ KCDL, i.e. 6. So, the total number of triangles = 14, the total number of squares = 6

Hence, option (c) is correct.

10. On labelling the figure, we get

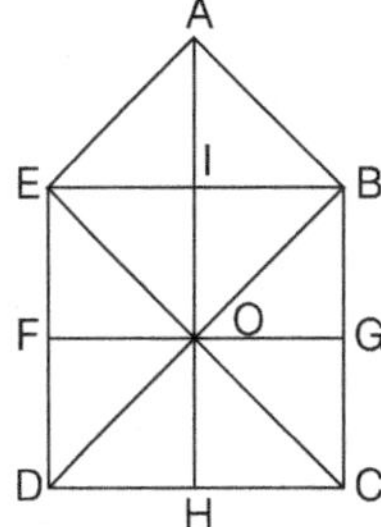

The number of triangles composed of one unit are ΔAIB, ΔAIE , ΔEIO, ΔIBO, ΔEFO, ΔBOG, ΔOGC, ΔOCH, ΔOHD and ΔFOD, i.e. 10.

The number of triangles composed of two units are ΔAEB, ΔAEO, ΔABO, ΔEBO, ΔBOC, ΔOCD and ΔEOD, i.e. 7.

The number of triangles composed of more than two units are ΔECD, ΔBCD, ΔEBD and ΔEBC, i.e. 4.

So, the total number of triangles
= 10 + 7 + 4 = 21

Hence, option (c) is correct.

11. On labelling the figure, we get

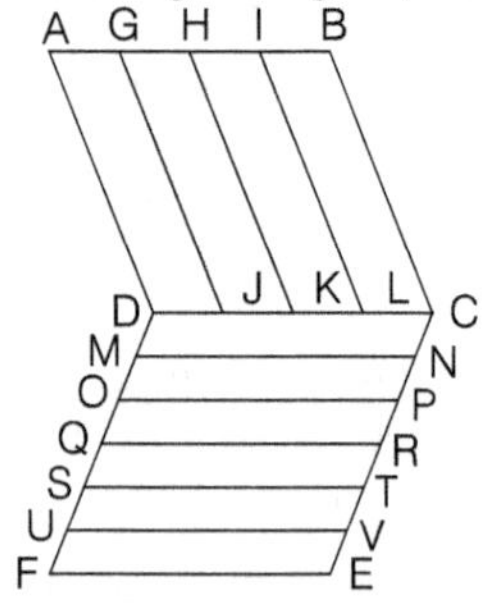

The number of horizontal lines are AB, DC, MN, OP, QR, ST, UV and FE, i.e. 8.

The number of slant lines are AD, GJ, HK, IL, BC, DF and CE, i.e. 7.

Thus, the total number of straight lines = 8 + 7 = 15

Hence, option (a) is correct.

12. On labelling the figure, we get

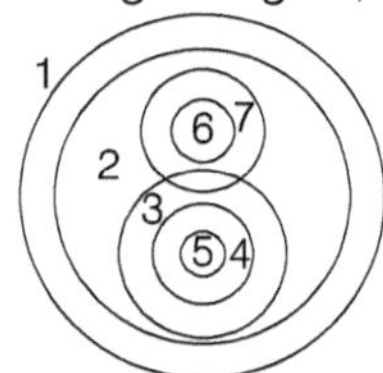

It is clear, that the total number of circles are 7.

Hence option (b) is correct.

13. On labelling the figure, we get

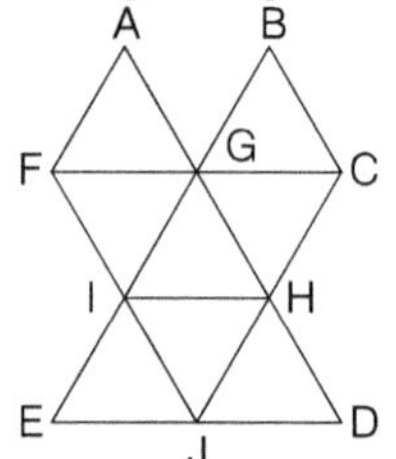

The number of triangles composed of one unit are ΔAGF, ΔBGC, ΔGIH, ΔFGI, ΔGCH, ΔIHJ, ΔIJE and ΔHDJ, i.e. 8.

The number of triangles composed of more than one unit are ΔGED, ΔFCJ, i.e. 2.

Thus, the total number of triangles
= 8 + 2
= 10

Hence, option (a) is correct.

14. On labelling the figure, we get

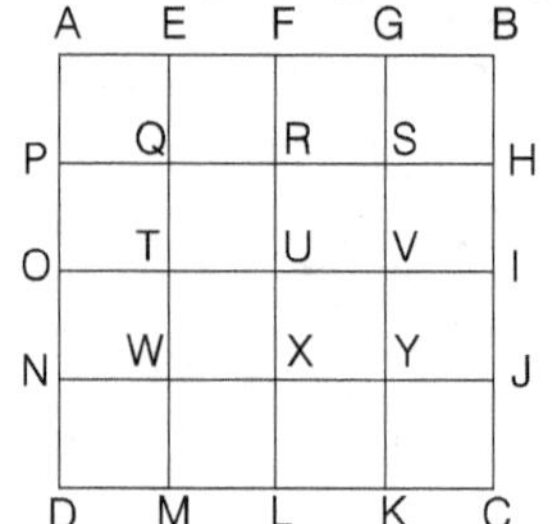

The number of squares composed of one unit are
☐ AEQP, ☐ EFRQ, ☐FGSR, ☐ GBHS, ☐PQTO, ☐QRUT, ☐RSVU, ☐ SHIV, ☐ OTWN, ☐TUXW, ☐UVYX, ☐ VIJY, ☐ NWMD, ☐WXLM, ☐ XYKL, and ☐ YJCK, i.e. 16.

The number of squares composed of four units are
☐ AFUO, ☐EGVT, ☐ FBIU, ☐ PRXN, ☐ QSYW, ☐ RHJX, ☐ OULD, ☐ TVKM, ☐ UICL, i.e 9.

The number of squares composed of more than four units are
☐ AGYN, ☐ EBJW and ☐PSKD, ☐QHCM and ☐ ABCD, i.e. 5.

Thus, the total number of squares
= 16 + 9 + 5 = 30.

Hence, option (b) is correct.

15. On labelling the figure, we get

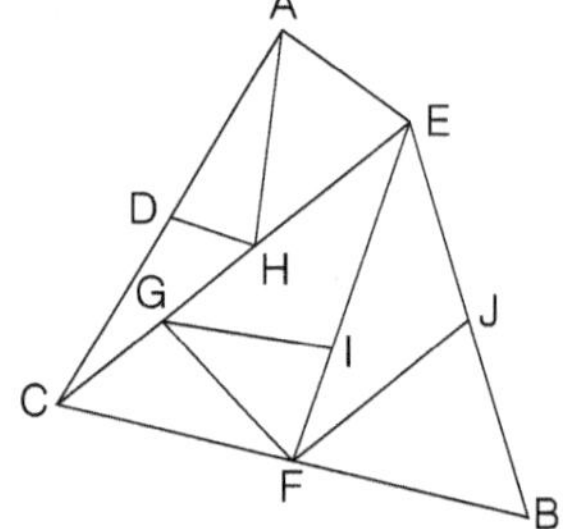

The number of triangles composed of one unit are ΔADH, ΔAEH, ΔCDH, ΔGEI, ΔGIF, ΔCGF, ΔEJF and ΔJBF, i.e. 8.

The number of triangles composed of two units are ΔGEF, ΔEFB and ΔAHC, i.e 3.

The number of triangles composed of more than two units are ΔAEC, ΔECF, ΔECB, i.e. 3.

Thus, the total number of triangles
= 8 + 3 + 3 = 14

Hence, option (c) is correct.

16. On labelling the figure, we get

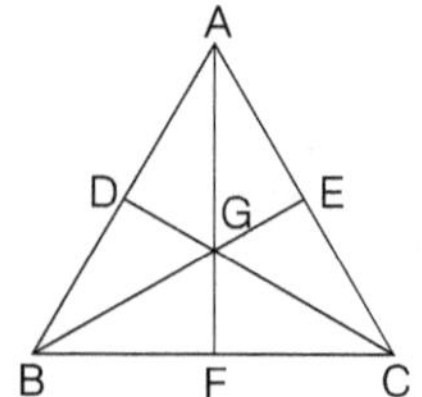

The number of triangles composed of one unit are ΔBGF, ΔGFC, ΔDGB, ΔEGC, ΔADG and ΔAGE, i.e. 6.

The number of triangles composed of two units are ΔBGC, ΔAGB and ΔAGC, i.e. 3.

The number of triangles composed of three units are ΔBEC, ΔBDC, ΔABE, ΔADC, ΔAFC and ΔAFB, i.e. 6.

The number of triangles composed of more than three units is ΔABC, i.e. 1.

Thus, the total number of triangles
= 6 + 3 + 6 + 1 = 16

Hence, option (a) is correct.

17. On labelling the figure, we get

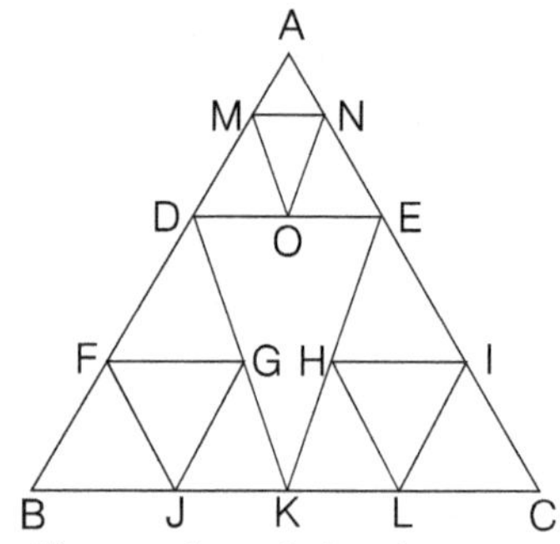

The number of triangles composed of one unit are ΔAMN, ΔMOD, ΔNOE, ΔDGF, ΔEHI, ΔHKL, ΔILC, ΔFBJ, ΔFGJ, ΔGJK, ΔDEK, ΔHIL and ΔMNO, i.e. 13.

The number of triangles composed of four units are ΔADE, ΔDBK and ΔEKC, i.e. 3.

The number of triangles composed of more than four units is ΔABC, i.e. of 1.

Thus, the total number of triangles
= 13 + 3 + 1
= 17

Hence, option (b) is correct.

18. On labelling the figure, we get

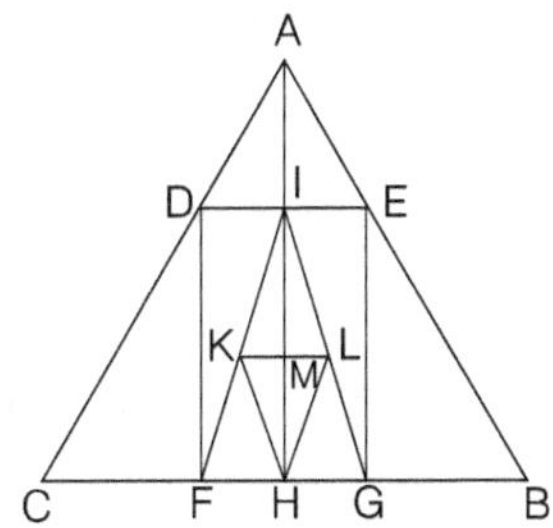

The number of triangles composed of one unit are ΔAID, ΔAIE, ΔDIF, ΔDFC, ΔIEG, ΔEBG, ΔIMK, ΔIML, ΔKMH, ΔMLH, ΔKHF and ΔLHG, i.e. 12.

The number of triangles composed of two units are ΔADE, ΔKLH, ΔIKL, ΔIKH and ΔILH, i.e. 5. The number of triangles composed of more than two units are ΔIFG, ΔIFH, ΔIGH, ΔABC, ΔAHC, ΔAHB, i.e. 6.

Thus, the total number of triangles
$$= 12 + 5 + 6 = 23$$
Hence, option (d) is correct.

19. On labelling the figure, we get

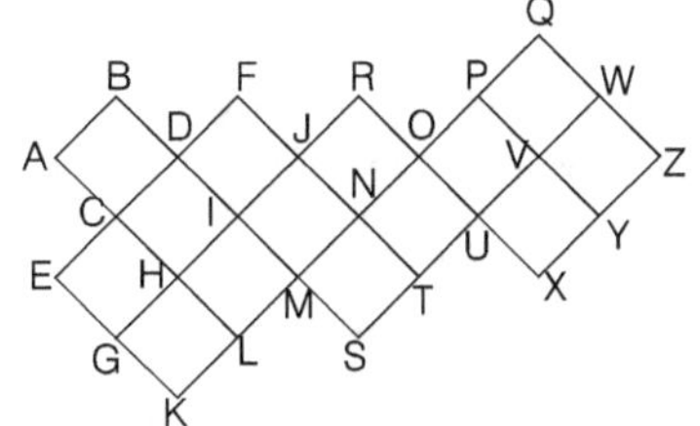

The number of squares composed of one unit are ☐ ABDC, ☐ ECHG, ☐ GHLK, ☐ CDIH, ☐ HIML, ☐ DFJI, ☐ IJNM, ☐ MNTS, ☐ JRON, ☐ NOUT, ☐ OPVU,

☐ UVYX, ☐ PQWV and ☐ VWZY i.e. 14.

The number of squares composed of more than one units are ☐ EDMK, ☐ CFNL, ☐ IRUS and ☐ OQZX i.e. 4.

Thus, the total number of squares
$$= 14 + 4$$
$$= 18$$
Hence, option (b) is correct.

20. On labelling the figure, we get

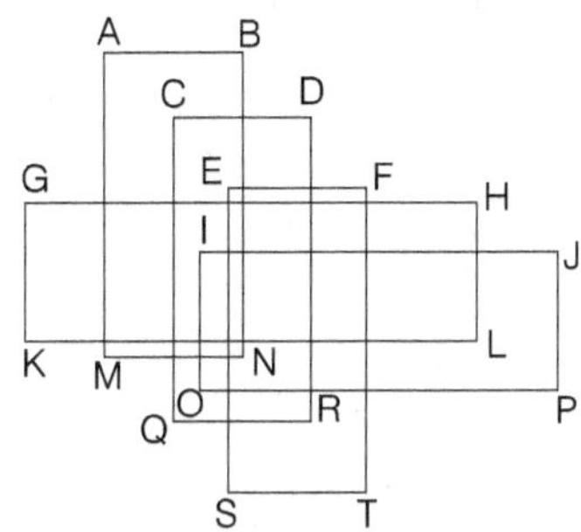

The number of horizontal lines are AB, CD, EF, GH, IJ, KL, MN, OP, QR and ST, i.e. 10.

The number vertical lines are GK, AM, CQ, ES, BN, IO, DR, FT, HL and JP, i.e. 10.

So, the total number of lines
$$= 10 + 10 = 20$$
Hence, option (c) is correct.

21. On labelling the figure, we get

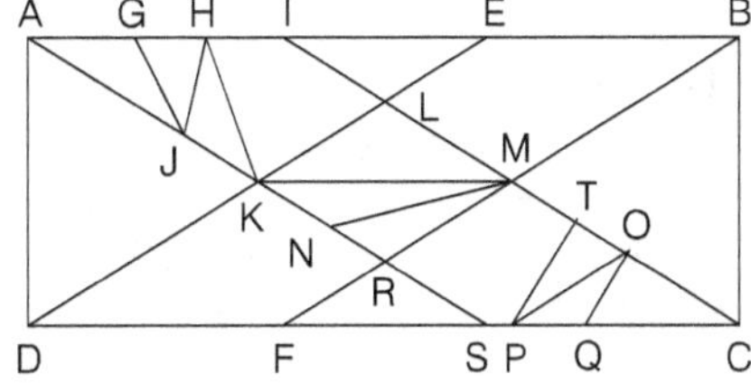

The number of horizontal lines are AB, DC and KM,
i.e. 3.

The number of vertical lines are AD and BC, i.e. 2.

The number of slant lines are AS, IC, DE, BF, GJ, HJ, HK, MN, TP, OP and OQ, i.e. 11.

Thus, the total number of lines
$$= 3 + 2 + 11$$
$$= 16$$
Hence, option (d) is correct.

22. On labelling the figure, we get

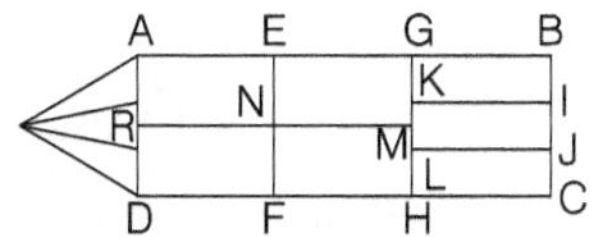

Number of rectangles composed of one unit are ☐ AENR, ☐ RNFD, ☐ EGMN, ☐ NMHF, ☐ GBIK, ☐ KIJL and ☐ LJCH, i.e. 7.

The number of rectangles composed of more than one unit are
☐ AGMR, ☐ RMHD, ☐ AEFD, ☐ EGHF, ☐ GBJL, ☐ KICH, ☐ AGHD, ☐ EBCF, ☐ GBCH and ☐ ABCD,
i.e. 10.

Therefore total number of rectangles
$$= 7 + 10$$
$$= 17$$
Hence, option (d) is correct.

Practice Set (1)

1. As, president is the head of the country, similarly principal is the head of the school.

Hence, option (c) is correct.

2. The letter 'E' will complete all the four words as TIME, EGO, HALE and EARTH.

Hence, option (b) is correct.

3. The words DARK and HORSE together will make a new word DARKHORSE.

So, the correct answer is 2R.

Hence, option (d) is correct.

4. The letter N, when moved from first word leaves a new word, i.e. RAGE and when placed into the letters of the second word makes a new word OWEN.

Hence, option (a) is correct.

5. The series can be represented as

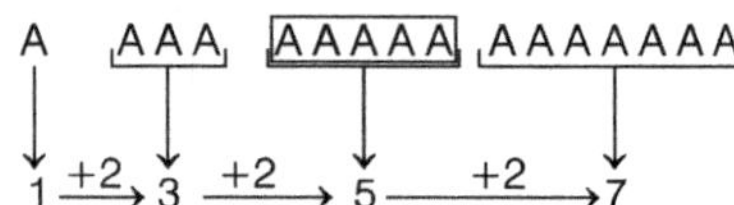

So, AAAAA will complete the series.

Hence, option (b) is correct.

6. On putting the values of the letters in the given expression, we get

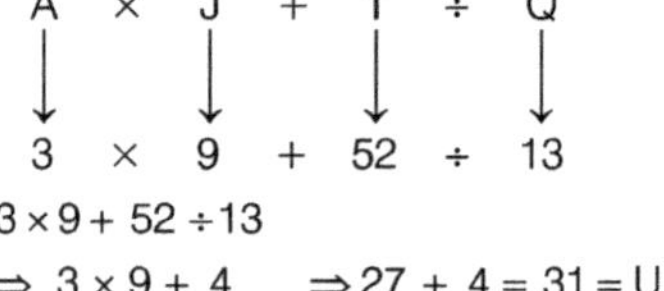

$3 \times 9 + 52 \div 13$

$\Rightarrow 3 \times 9 + 4 \quad \Rightarrow 27 + 4 = 31 = U$

[as given in question]

Hence, option (c) is correct.

7. As, $7 \times 9 = 63$

Similarly, $2 \times 1 = 2$

Hence, option (a) is correct.

8.

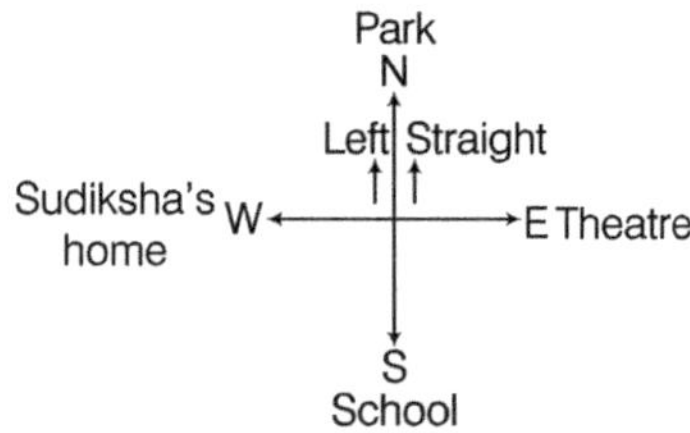

Clearly, the school is towards South.

Hence, option (a) is correct.

9. We know that, the king of jungle is lion but here, lion is called cat.

So, the king of jungle is cat.

Hence, option (d) is correct.

10. The pattern is as follows

(Top + Bottom) × (Left + Right)

= Middle number

In figure I, $(5 + 2) \times (7 + 4)$

$= 7 \times 11 = 77$

In figure II, $(10 + 5) \times (4 + 4)$

$= 15 \times 8 = 120$

Similarly, in figure III, $(7 + 7) \times (1 + 4)$

$= 14 \times 5 = 70$

So, 70 will replace the question mark.

Hence, option (b) is correct.

11. Only son of Yana's grandfather is her father and the son of her father is her brother. This can be represented as

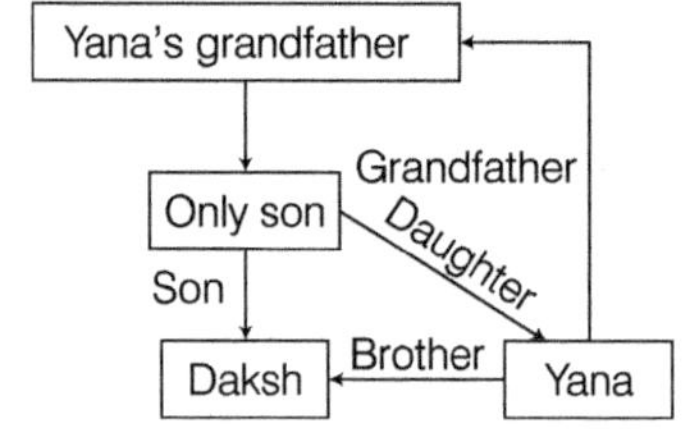

So, Daksh is the brother of Yana.

Hence, option (b) is correct.

Solution (Q. No. 12) The given information can be represented as

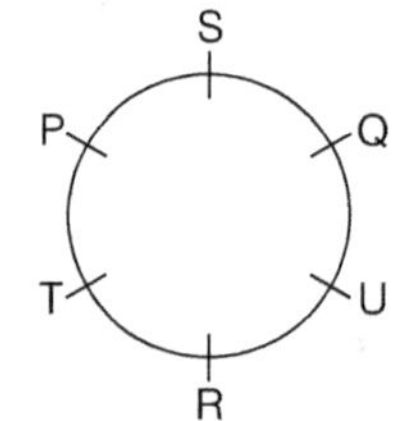

12. Clearly, Q is sitting between S and U.

Hence, option (b) is correct.

13. Pencil is related to stationery and chair is different. The relation can be represented as

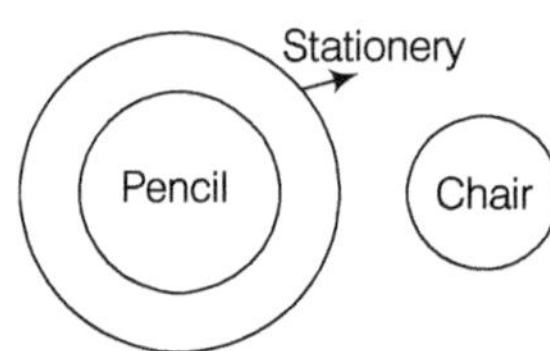

Hence, option (b) is correct.

14. Given, $20 \times 10 \div 6 + 2$

Now, on substituting the signs, we get

$20 + 10 \times 6 \div 2$

$\Rightarrow 20 + 10 \times 3 \Rightarrow 20 + 30 = 50$

Hence, option (d) is correct.

15. Except Asia, all others are country but Asia is a continent.

Hence, option (c) is correct.

16. In first pair, the shaded sector becomes unshaded and *vice-versa*.

On following this pattern, option figure (c) will complete the second pair.

Hence, option (c) is correct.

17. The pattern is as follows

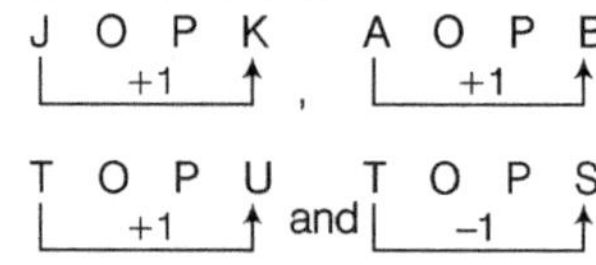

Here, except TOPS, all others follow similar pattern. So, letters' group TOPS is odd one out.

Hence, option (d) is correct.

18. The mirror image can be obtained as

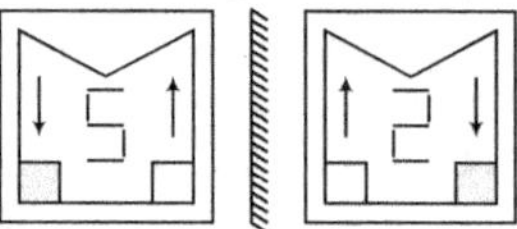

Hence, option (a) is correct.

19. In each successive step, the whole figure rotates 90° anti-clockwise and an arrow with the circle is removed and a square is added. On following this pattern, option figure (d) will complete the series.

Hence, option (d) is correct.

20. In all the figures, except figure (c), the number of leaves is even, where as it is odd in figure (c).

Hence, option (c) is correct.

21. The figure may be labelled as

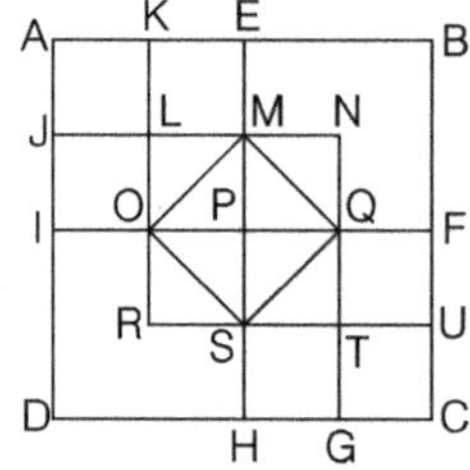

Number of squares formed from single unit are, ☐ AKLJ, ☐ KEML, ☐ JLOI, ☐ LMPO, ☐ MNQP, ☐ OPSR, ☐ PQTS, ☐ QFUT, ☐ STGH, ☐ TUCG

and ☐ MQSO = 11

Number of squares formed from more than one units are ☐ AEPI, ☐ EBFP, ☐ PFCH, ☐ IPHD, ☐ LNTR and ☐ ABCD = 6

Number of squares formed from more than five units are JNGD and BKRU = 2

Therefore, total number of squares = 11 + 6 + 2 = 19

Hence, option (d) is correct.

22. The given Fig. (X) can be completed as

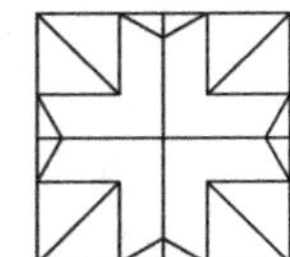

Hence, option (b) is correct.

23. The correct water image is

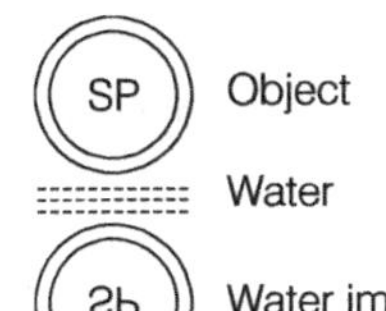

SP — Object

Water

2b — Water image

Hence, option (a) is correct.

24.

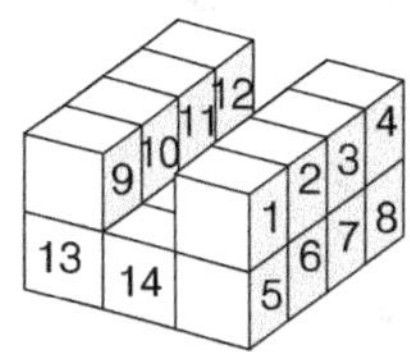

Here, there are 14 visible cubes, 3 hidden cubes below the cubes 10, 11 and 12 and 3 hidden cubes in the row of cube 14. ∴ Total number of cubes

$= 14 + 3 + 3 = 20$

Hence, option (c) is correct.

25. '2' is common in both the positions, so the adjacent faces of 2 are 1, 6, 5 and 3. Thus, the remaining face having 4 will be opposite to 2.

Hence, option (d) is correct.

Practice Set 2

1. The series follow the pattern as shown below

$4 \xrightarrow{\times 2} 8 \xrightarrow{\times 3} 24 \xrightarrow{\times 2}$

$48 \xrightarrow{\times 3} 144 \xrightarrow{\times 2} 288 \xrightarrow{\times 3} \boxed{864}$

Hence, option (b) is correct.

2. As,

B   A   G   Similarly,   T   O   M
+1 +3 +5   +1 +3 +5
C   D   L   U   R   R

Hence, option (a) is correct.

3. The letter 'S', when moved from first word leaves a new word i.e. TOOL and insert into the letters of second word makes a new word i.e. SLOW.

Hence, option (d) is correct.

4. The two words 'HOT' and 'LINE', when joined together will make a new meaningful word i.e. HOTLINE.

So, the correct answer is Q2.

Hence, option (a) is correct.

5. The letter 'M' will complete both the words as shown below

The words are LEMON and MATCH.

Hence, option (b) is correct.

6. Given, $\dfrac{R \times A}{Q} = ?$

On putting the values of the letters, we get

$\dfrac{27 \times 6}{3} = 27 \times 2 = 54$

$= 18 \times 3$

$= O \times Q$

$[\because O = 18 \text{ and } Q = 3]$

Hence, option (a) is correct.

7. Except 200, all others are perfect squares of a number as

$(20)^2 = 400, (10)^2 = 100, (30)^2 = 900$

But 200 is not a perfect square of any number.

So, 200 is different.

Hence, option (d) is correct.

8.

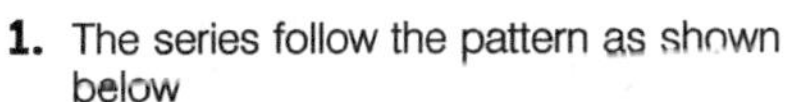

Distance between $AE = AD + ED$

$= 4 + 2$ $[\because AD = CB]$

$= 6$ m

On comparing the above drawn direction graph with standard direction graph we see that, she is in North direction.

Hence, option (a) is correct.

9. Except brother, all others are female relations. So, brother is different from others.

Hence, option (c) is correct.

10. Here, the rule is

(Top left × Bottom right)

+ (Top right × Bottom left)

= Middle number

In figure I, $(8 \times 4) + (12 \times 2)$

$= 32 + 24$

$= 56$

In figure II, $(7 \times 4) + (3 \times 1) = 28 + 3 = 31$

Similarly, in figure III, $(5 \times 2) + 9 \times 4$

$= 10 + 36 = 46$

Hence, option (b) is correct.

11. Given, $4 - 4 \div 24 \times 8 + 2$

Now, on substituting the signs according to the question, we get

$4 \times 4 + 24 \div 8 - 2$

$= 4 \times 4 + 3 - 2$

$= 16 + 3 - 2$

$= 16 + 1 = 17$

Hence, option (c) is correct.

12. The number common in all the three figures represents actors who are both directors and producers. So, there are 7 actors who are both directors and producers.

Hence, option (a) is correct.

13. The relation can be represented as

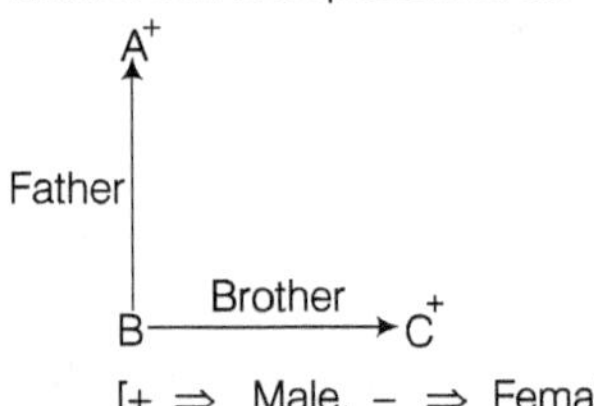

Here, the gender of B is not given, so we cannot determine the relation of B to A. B can be either a son or a daughter of A.

Hence, option (d) is correct.

Solution (Q. No. 14) The given information can be represented as

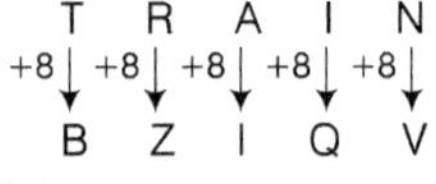

	Football	Hockey	Cricket	Basketball
Abhishek	✓	✓	✓	✓
Parag	✓	✓	✓	
Vaibhav	✓	✓	✓	
Arpit		✓	✓	✓
Shantanu	✓		✓	

14. Cricket is played by all the boys.

Hence, option (d) is correct.

15. As,

$$\begin{array}{ccccc} T & R & A & I & N \\ {+8}\downarrow & {+8}\downarrow & {+8}\downarrow & {+8}\downarrow & {+8}\downarrow \\ B & Z & I & Q & V \end{array}$$

Similarly,

$$\begin{array}{ccccc} A & L & O & N & E \\ {+8}\downarrow & {+8}\downarrow & {+8}\downarrow & {+8}\downarrow & {+8}\downarrow \\ I & T & W & V & M \end{array}$$

Hence, option (b) is correct.

16. Here, in each step the next letter to the previous term is given and is repeated number of times as its positional value in English alphabetical order.

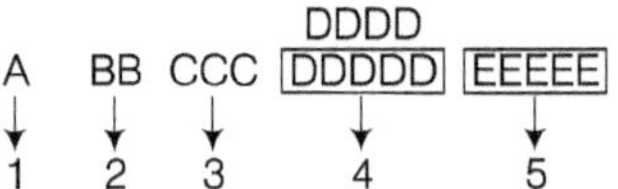

$$\begin{array}{ccccc} A & BB & CCC & \boxed{DDDDD} & \boxed{EEEEE} \\ \downarrow & \downarrow & \downarrow & \downarrow & \downarrow \\ 1 & 2 & 3 & 4 & 5 \end{array}$$

So, DDDDD does not belong to the series.

Hence, option (c) is correct.

17. The figure may be labelled as shown below

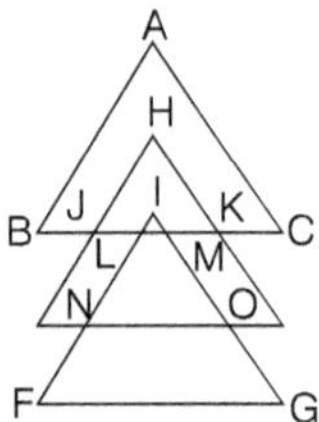

∴ Number of triangles
= ΔABC, ΔHDE, ΔIFG, ΔHJK, ΔILM and ΔINO i.e. 6

Hence, option (b) is correct.

18. The paces of elements on the top are interchanged and the bottom circle becomes shaded. On following this pattern, option figure (a) will complete the second pair.

Hence, option (a) is correct.

19. The correct water image is

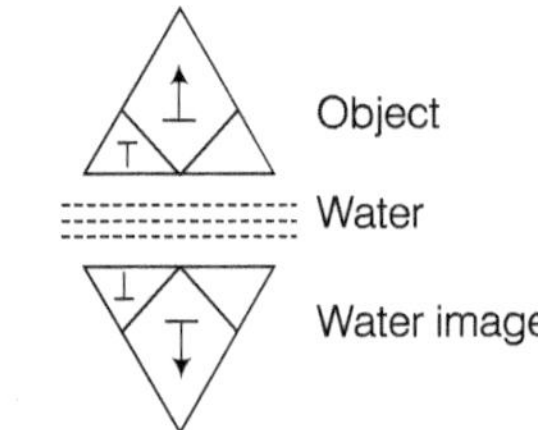

Hence, option (b) is correct.

20. Here in each step, $ is moving 90° in anti-clockwise direction, O is moving 180° and @ is moving 180° and 90°, alternatively in clockwise direction.

On following this pattern, option figure (b) will come next.

Hence, option (b) is correct.

21. In all the figures, except figure(c) the central portion of the figure is shaded but in figure (c) the outer portion is shaded. So, option figure (c) is different from the rest.

Hence, option (c) is correct.

22. A building is extended vertically, similarly a street is extended horizontally.

Hence, option (c) is correct.

23. The correct mirror image is

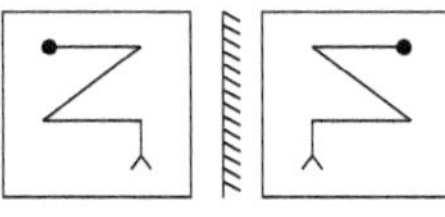

Hence, option (c) is correct.

24. The pairs of opposite face are

In cube (b), (■ and ▣) are shown on adjacent faces, in cube (c) and (d) (▣ and □) are shown on adjacent face.

So, these cubes cannot be formed. Only the cube (a) can be formed because no opposite faces are shown on adjacent to each other.

Hence, option (a) is correct.

25.

There are 12 rows and each row has 2 cubes each.

∴ Total number of cubes

$$= 12 \times 2$$
$$= 24$$

Hence, option (d) is correct.